Women in the Frontier Land:
Mestiza Consciousness
in the Novels of

Tahmima Anam
and
Chimamanda Ngozi Adichie

Women in the Frontier Land:
Mestiza Consciousness in the Novels of

Tahmima Anam and Chimamanda Ngozi Adichie

Gopinath Khutia & Sambit Panigrahi

BLACK EAGLE BOOKS
DUBLIN, USA | BBSR, ODISHA

🦅 Black Eagle Books
USA address:
7464 Wisdom Lane
Dublin, OH 43016

India address:
E/312, Trident Galaxy, Kalinga Nagar,
Bhubaneswar-751003, Odisha, India

E-mail: info@blackeaglebooks.org
Website: www.blackeaglebooks.org

First International Edition Published by
Black Eagle Books, 2023

Women in the Frontier Land: Mestiza Consciousness in the Novels of Tahmima Anam and Chimamanda Ngozi Adichie

By **Gopinath Khutia & Sambit Panigrahi**

Copyright © **Gopinath Khutia & Sambit Panigrahi**

All rights reserved. No part of this publication may be reproduced, stored in a retrieval system, or transmitted, in any form or by any means, electronic, mechanical, photocopying, recording or otherwise without the prior permission of the publisher.

Cover & Interior Design: Ezy's Publication

ISBN- 978-1-64560-351-1 (Paperback)
Library of Congress Control Number: 2023931345

Printed in the United States of America

CONTENTS

Abstract — vii-ix

Chapter I: — 11
Introduction

Chapter II: — 48
War and Women Subjectivity in
A Golden Age and *Half of a Yellow Sun*

Chapter III: — 105
Racism and Beyond: A Study of
Americanah and *The Bones of Grace*

Chapter IV: — 177
Women against Religious Extremism in
The Good Muslim and *Purple Hibiscus*

Chapter V: — 231
Conclusion

Works Cited — 240

ABBREVIATIONS

AGA   *A Golden Age*
BLW   Bangladesh Liberation War
BW   Biafran War
BS   *Beloved Strangers*
HYS   *Half of a Yellow Sun*
OED   *Oxford English Dictionary*
PH   *Purple Hibiscus*
TGM   *The Good Muslim*
TBG   *The Bones of Grace*
WAF   Women Against Fundamentalism

Abstract

Presented in the form of five different chapters including "Introduction" and "Conclusion," this book investigates into women subjectivity vis-à-vis war, racism, and fundamentalism in the three novels – *A Golden Age* (2007), *The Good Muslim* (2011), *The Bones of Grace* (2016) of the British-Bangladeshi writer, Tahmima Anam and three novels – *Purple Hibiscus* (2003), *Half of a Yellow Sun* (2006) and *Americanah* (2013) of the Nigerian writer Chimamanda Ngozi Adichie. By studying these selected books, the book intends to explore women's empathetic reconstruction of the domestic and extra-domestic spaces of the war-devastated societies in Bangladesh and Nigeria respectively and consequently, the difference they make to the world. The work investigates into the complex processes involved in their 'being' and 'becoming' in a war-riven society that is constantly in a state of flux. The book primarily underlines how the complex experience of such disruptive, disintegrative, and divisive forces of war, racism and religious extremism generate in women a new, inclusive, synthetic, and centrifugal consciousness that manifests emphatically through their continually evolving characters and persona. This inclusive consciousness is termed as "mestizo" or "consciousness of the Borderlands" by Gloria E. Anzaldua in her book *Borderlands/La Frontera: The New Mestiza* (1987)—a consciousness that develops in the background of a war-devasted society and a consciousness that is constructive, conciliatory and salvaging in nature.

Based on these precepts, the book is divided into five chapters.

"Chapter One" entitled "Introduction," provides a comprehensive introduction to the two mentioned novelists and their works, does an extensive literature review of the existing critical works on their writings and finally, establishes the stated point of departure.

The Second Chapter "War and Women Subjectivity in *A Golden Age* and *Half of a Yellow Sun*" studies the war-time agency of women in the 1971 Liberation War and the Biafran War respectively. It investigates into the genealogy of the emphatic emergence of women characters from their restrictive domestic spaces in times of national emergency and their eclectic and reconstructivist interventions in the said wars, from the backround.

"Chapter Three" entitled "Racism and Beyond: A Study of *Americanah* and *The Bones of Grace*" studies a black woman's horrid experience of racism, her relentless combat with its detremental ramifications (as seen in *Americanah*), and the contours of identity formation of a Bangladeshi woman (as seen *The Bones of Grace*) who digs deep into the complex roots of her origin to come to terms with her amphibian existence in a civil-war-riven society.

The Fourth Chapter "Women against Religious Extremism in *The Good Muslim* and *Purple Hibiscus*" studies how women deal with the nightmarish evolution of religious extremism in the two mentioned novels. This chapter traces the trajectory of how in the said novels the fundamentalist traits of male characters are purposely pitted against the liberal and emancipatory predispositions of the women characters. The chapter shows how the misuse of religion by the fundamentalists to exert repressive authority on the common masses in a regressive manner is duly confronted by the women characters through their inculcation of an inclusive and pluralistic consciousness.

The concluding chapter highlights the outcome of the book which foregrounds the positivist and reconstitutive roles played by women characters in a war-devastated society, even through their engament in the war is not direct and frontal. The "Conclusion" emphasizes on the significance of women's critical involvement in domestic and extra-domestic spaces of their lives, the emergence of their constructivist subjectivity and their 'philosophy of action' that collectively pave the way for the inculcation of a symbiotic and sustainable outlook on life during the times of war.

Keywords: *Women, subjectivity, consciousness, agency, war, racism, religion.*

Chapter I

Introduction

"It is not our differences that divide us, it is our inability to recognize, accept, and celebrate those differences."

- Audre Lorde

This remark of the African-American civil rights activist Audre Lorde elicits, in a way, the very crux of this dissertation. Difference defines us. We are inherently endowed with multiple differences and variables—genetic, biological, social, political and economic; undeniably, they distinguish us, make us distinct from each other. But these differences do not divide us. We create the divide along so many lines—gendered, racial, and the likes. Because we cannot interlink the differences and fail to comprehend that such differences add to a magnificent variety which is constructively kaleidoscopic. In this book, I intend to explore how women in societies divided by war and racial acrimonies inculcate in them a positivist consciousness that recognise, accept and celebrate such differences—differences that get duly reflected through their philanthropic 'humane agency.' This book intends to explore, emphatically, how women in such societies riven by the divisive and destructive forces of race and war, subsume and exude a novel and pluralistic consciousness that transcends the boundaries created by race and war; these women augur "the tradition of the new" (Carter and McRae 287). Women novelists like Tahmima Anam and Chimamanda Adichie see the 'new' and make the 'new;' they construct 'new' characters and attribute them with 'new' identities that operate with a positivist and constructivist approach in situations of war and racial acrimony.

Let us first ask what is subjectivity? And what is women subjectivity? Simply speaking, subjectivity is a 'construct' formed and shaped by more than one forces—cultural, social, etc. In other words, following Simon de Beauvoir, we can say that one is not born a subject but becomes a subject. According to Sheikh: "Subjectivity is precisely the condition of our being which enables us to recognize ourselves as subjects or persons" (2). Julien Wolfreys, Ruth Robbins, and Kenneth Womack define subjectivity as "the process of attaining and expressing selfhood in and through language or the location of the self-situated and subjectified by cultural, epistemological, ideological and other social discourses and institutions" (Wolfreys et al. 94). In this book, I make an attempt to establish that in the specific context of my chosen texts, women subjectivity is more performative than ideological. Their action and their agency define them and generate a new consciousness in them. Jone Johnson Lewis's take on subjectivity is the most befitting in this context and is worth quoting: "Subjectivity looks at how women saw their activities and roles as contributing (or not) to her identity and meaning. Subjectivity is an attempt to see history from the perspective of the individuals who lived that history, especially including ordinary women" (Lewis 45).

Women subjectivity, being continually involved in

such disruptive phenomena as war, racism, and religious extremism, is subject to a pluralistic existence. Women, being entangled in war, racism, and religious extremism, go through a process of adaptive evolution. Their agency in war, racism, and religious extremism is neither a mere improvement on the previous condition nor emancipation from that. It is a special reaction to the environment threatened by war, racism, and religious extremism. They get immersed in a subjectivity that is dialogic—a subjectivity that elicits presence and expressiveness. Women subjectivity emerges in dialogue with the environment; it operates by subsuming and comprehensively undermining the utterly divisive male/female dualistic tradition. They seriously question rigid essentialism, and the dichotomous/ dualistic thought in various forms. Women's positioning in the mentioned novels is an autopoietic one in the sense that their selves reproduce, maintain, and nurture themselves. They do not eliminate or reduce human qualities drastically; rather, they express a sense of human completeness.

In this book, I have taken up three novels from the Bengal Trilogy—*A Golden Age* (2007), *The Good Muslim* (2011), *The Bones of Grace* (2016)—by the British-Bangladeshi writer Tahmima Anam, and three novels— *Purple Hibiscus* (2003), *Half of a Yellow Sun* (2006) and *Americanah* (2013)—by the Nigerian novelist Chimamanda Ngozi Adichie who, after the publication of her first book *Purple Hibiscus* (2003), is described as "Chinua Achebe's 21st Century daughter". I have taken up these novelists cutting across different national boundaries and frontiers and different sociocultural milieus to substantiate how both the novelists and their women characters "recognize, accept, and celebrate those differences" (Porter n.p.). Tahmima Anam and Chimamanda Adichie highlight "the existence of a subjectivity which is different from masculine subjectivity: a subjectivity in the feminine" (Irigaray vii). My purpose is not to make a comparative analysis between the two, but to critically juxtapose their fictional responses towards the troubled scenarios of their countries during the times of war and racial disturbance. The research method followed is mainly empirical – the analysis of both primary and secondary texts.

Although Adichie and Anam belong to different nationalities, they have a lot in common. Both are female writers writing about women. Their characters are drifted apart by war, racism, and religious radicalism, but are simultaneously anchored to love and humaneness. The complex experience of such disruptive, disintegrating, and divisive forces as war and racism generate in their novelistic world a new, inclusive, synthetic, and centrifugal consciousness. In *Borderlands/La Frontera: The New Mestiza* (1987), Gloria E. Anzaldua calls this consciousness "mestizo" or "consciousness of the Borderlands".

And for embodying and representing women subjectivity and its inclusive consciousness, 'novel' remains the most expedient genre, the most comprehensive of the art forms which offers literary exegeses of the world in which it is firmly rooted. The novel is the representation of nothing but "men and women in action and passion" (Besant and James 12). The first and foremost focus of a novel is on the human as it believes that "the human interest absolutely absorb[s] everything else" (Besant and James 11). The canvas of the novel encompasses the "whole of humanity", moving dynamically among women, men, and manners, lamping and mirroring them:

The novelist studies men and women; he is concerned with their actions and their thoughts, their errors and their follies, their greatness and their meanness; the countless forms of beauty and constantly varying moods to be seen among them; the forces which act upon them; the passions, prejudices, hopes, and fears which pull them this way and that (Besant and James 11).

The novel evokes and arouses sympathy among us and "creates [in us] sentiment which is destined to be a most mighty engine in deepening and widening the civilization of the world" (Besant & James 12). The sympathy that a 'novel' evokes is not merely an identification with the sufferings of others or feeling pity for them. Sympathy connotes "understanding their very souls; it is the reverence… the respect for personality, the recognition of individuality, and the enormous value, the perception of one's relation to another, his[her] duties and responsibilities" (Besant & James 13-14).

Tahmima Anam's novels are local in colour, revolving around the lives of civilians during and after the 1971 Bangladesh Liberation War. She pens how "disruptive events- both private and civic-intrude on the gentle rhythms of life" (Finnerty 43) and brings out how common people especially women respond to such disruptions. Her novels are human stories. They narrate anecdotes of how during a national emergency, the common people emerged from within their lived spheres of mundaneness, how they rose to extraordinary heights in their ordinary lives, how mothers survived with their children, how mothers and sisters prevented the family from falling apart and getting disintegrated due to the devastating socio-economic effects of the war, how they helped soldiers in several ways, how they contributed in several fronts including the social and the economic ones.

Like Jane Austen, Anam's domain is the domestic front; yet, she is not ahistorical and apolitical in her approach towards the delineation of her stories; she does not create stories from a vacuum; rather, her writing is intrinsically embedded in the socio-economic problematic of her immediate surrounding that was in absolute turmoil due to the devastating effects of the war. Her texts are embedded in the immediate context of the war. Due to her unremitting engagement with the problematics of a conflict-ridden society—a society that is riven by civil war— she is able to create a universalist appeal in her writing for almost every society in the world has undergone similar experiences. That is why, in a sense, Anam addresses the general human problematic that includes the issues of race, gender, nationality etc., and this precisely why her writing is amenable to many and it transcends boundaries — boundaries of race, of culture, and nationality. On the universalist approach of her writing, critic Amy Finnerty writes: "By framing epic geopolitics on this human scale, Anam makes them accessible to readers from Chicago to Dublin who might otherwise be intimidated by the political and social intricacies of a foreign setting" (43).

Anam writes her novels from a personal pinch, to connect with the people of her own land, to come to terms with the past, or rather with her nation's history that, of course, is nothing but a reflection of the collective history of its affected individuals. In a sense, Anam intends to inculcate a sense of identity with her motherland and its communities; she tries to develop an emotional, intellectual and an ontological rapport with her Motherland she no longer lives in. As she is far away from her birthplace

Bangladesh, writing fiction on her motherland keeps her rooted to her birthplace, renews her bond with the land, and issues a sense of being in a relationship with Bangladesh. Her first two books i.e. *A Golden Age* and *The Good Muslim* were "an effort to reclaim a piece of [her] history that [she] thought had been lost to [her]. [She] didn't inherit those markers of identity in the way [her] contemporaries had, the ones who had grown up in Bangladesh. So, it was an act of trying to belong" (Kuruvilla 12).

Moreover, Anam in her conversation with Elizabeth Kuruvilla declares that "novel writing is a political act" and most importantly, it is an art form, a democratic medium, a haven and a meeting point for all the opposites and deviants, a book and a critique of life in which one must understand, harmoniously feel with and feel into the other:

> In a novel, the idea must be embedded within....And I think that is a very important political act as well because I might have a certain opinion about the role of people like Sohail, the religious leader in *The Good Muslim*, but in a novel, it is important for the reader to feel empathy for him, to try to understand that everything that he did came from a real place (Kuruvilla 25).

In the interview with Farhana Shaikh, Tahmima Anam states categorically that she would be happy to be equated with writers like Monica Ali or Zadie Smith who write along similar lines and address similar issues and concerns. She also states that she would be happier and it would be more appropriate if she is equated with and placed alongside writers "who write about their own countries too, like Chimamanda Ngozi Adichie who writes about Nigeria" (Shaikh 2009).

Finnerty specifically admires Anam's profound reading and comprehension of her nation's complex and civil-war-riven history; she particularly admires Anam who despite not having firsthand experience of the defining events in the history of the Liberation War in Bangladesh, has been able to masterfully fictionalized it. Finnerty opines:

> Remarkably for one born after these consequential events, she is able, through her fiction, to bring them to life and even make them contemporary. Despite the vast contours of her subject matter, her storytelling is paradoxically intimate, zooming in close on her idiosyncratic characters- each one utterly defiant of stereotypes (Finnerty 43).

Chimamanda Ngozi Adichie, along with Unoma Azuah known for *Everything Good Will Come* (2005), Sade Adeniran known for *Imagine This* (2007) and Sefi Atta famous for *A Bit of Difference* (2012) and others belong to the Third-Generation Nigerian female writers who have achieved global distinction for their writings. In their novels, one can mark a clear shift from the writings of the first and second-generation Nigerian women novelists like Flora Nwapa and Buchi Emecheta in whose novels identity of women is "constrained by nationalist priorities that privileged masculinity" (Bryce 49). But on the contrary, in the novels of the third-generation Nigerian women novelists, a radically different kind of discourse emerges. In their novels, it is observed that "the feminine is neither essentialized and mythologized nor marginalized, but unapologetically central to the realist representation of a recognizable social world" (Bryce 49).

Adichie's difference from her male and female

literary predecessors is pointed out by Heather Hewett in her review entitled *Finding Her Voice:*

> Gone is the optimistic hope of the country's first generation of English- language writers. In its place is a more complex assessment of urban, post-independence Nigeria, an attempt to reflect the country's changes in their writing, and a rejection of the qualities many readers associate with the mostly male-authored canonical texts of Nigerian literature-the proverbial inflections of Chinua Achebe, the mythic ritualism of Wole Soyinka, the magical realism of Ben Okri. (Hewett 9)

Adichie firmly believes that the idea of gender or gender roles does delimit women's subjectivity and draw a dividing line between dos and don'ts. In Adichie's paradigm, it is implied that the preexisting gender stereotype is waived off not only from the realm of writing but also from every sphere of human activity and we stop asking and expecting from women certain things which we have historically believed to be typical of them. She explains

> The problem with gender is that it prescribes how we should be rather than recognizing how we are. Imagine how much happier we would be, how much freer to be our true individual selves, if we didn't have the weight of gender expectations (14).

She is of the firm conviction that in days to follow, her hopes and anticipations shall bear fruit and we shall be able to create a world that would be bereft of all inequalities—the inequalities of race, of gender, of class. Adichie says: "And I would like today to ask that we begin to dream about and plan for a different world. A fairer world. A world of happier men and happier women who are truer to themselves" (12).

Although her writings have an African mooring and they are rooted in African experience, they are about human experiences, and human agency, about tropes like love, loss at war, religion, its exploitation by fanatics, about migration, and othering of human beings based on skin colour, and racial and gender differences. Olanna in *Half of a Yellow Sun*, Ifemelu in *Americanah* and Kambili in *Purple Hibiscus* are some such representational characters that undergo similar exploitation on the basis of colour, race and gender.

Ernest N Emenyonu in the Introduction to the book *A Companion to Chimamanda Ngozi Adichie* makes an apposite observation:

> With *Half of a Yellow Sun* (2007) and *The Thing Around Your Neck* (2009), she established herself as Africa's pre-eminent storyteller who uses her tales to give meaning to the totality of the world as she perceives it, producing in effect, narratives that seek to shape a new world of understanding as they give expression to realities people know and human commitments and awareness they need to know (1).

Born in the 1970s, both Tahmima Anam and Chimamanda Ngozi Adichie are contemporaries. Their fictional world records testing times when people are "divided by war and united by love" (Adichie 2016). The contexts of their texts are different. Anam talks about the 1971 Bangladesh Liberation War between East Pakistan and West Pakistan that occurred due to the exertion of hegemony, especially linguistic one of the West over the East, and due to the formation of the new nation Bangladesh and of course, due to the rise of Islamist fundamentalism. Adichie talks about the Nigerian Civil War that took place due to the post-colonial ethnic tension, the tyrannical reign of the coloniser's religion, and the experience of racism outside Africa. Rehana of *A Golden Age* and Olanna of *Half of a Yellow Sun* have different footings and different settings. The experience of Ifemelu's traumatic experiences in *Americanah* and Zubaida's troubled emotional encounters and experiences *The Bones of Grace* go in opposite directions. Maya's journey and experience in *The Good Muslim* are different from those of Kambili in *Purple Hibiscus*. The phenomena their characters encounter are indeed different from one another. Both Anam and Adichie are "miniaturists, painting on a square of ivory" (Forster 53) i.e their collective narrative locus is narrow, centered on "two or three families" which allegorise the national scenario.

And both of them wrote on events like war, post-war experiences, formation of a new nation, rise of issues consequent to them, and women's instrumental involvement in those events. And they correctly portray the gestures and vibes that emerge from the "hidden life" (Forster 35) of the affected women, from their "dreams, joys, sorrows and self-communings" (Forster 36).

In their works, Anam and Adichie accurately capture nation-forming moments, the emergence of national conflicts, their aftereffects and side effects and the involvement of the "second sex" in those conflicts and the ductile and plastic concerns oozing out of them. They also delineate how their characters have been individuated by a rubbery concern and consciousness. The existence of an individual rests on a web of relations of interconnectedness.

We have a bond; we exist by depending on each other: "No [woman or] man is an island... [She or] he is part of this continent.... Any [woman or] man's death diminishes [her or] him because [she or] he is involved in mankind" (Donne 98). Women characters in their novels have lived and acted on this very belief.

War is a leitmotif in the novels of Tahmima Anam and Chimamanda Adichie. War, in a limited understanding of the word, denotes an "armed hostile conflict between states or nations" ("War" 11) and in a broader understanding of the term, it refers to "a state of struggle, conflict, or antagonism" ("War" 13). The former may be singular, but the latter is plural. For example, apart from the traditional war that is fought on the frontiers of bloodied battlefronts, there is class-war, caste-war, political-war, religious-war, etc. at the background and such connotations become extremely crucial to the understanding of the meaning of the word 'war'; they form a recurrent pattern in the novels of Anam and Adichie. Women characters in their novels are warriors as they run into conflicts; they struggle and cope with the situation in their own fashion. Women in *A Golden Age* deal with the Bangladesh Liberation War and women *Half of a Yellow Sun* deal with Nigerian Civil War i.e. they deal with war in the sense that it is an "armed hostile conflict between states or nations" ("War"). But women in *Americanah, The Bones of Grace, The Good Muslim* and *Purple Hibiscus* have to deal with colour-war or race-war, war with the self, and war against religious extremism i.e. they deal with war in the sense that it is "a state of struggle, conflict, or antagonism" ("War").

Anam and Adichie are indeed different in their handling of different fictional ingredients. The telling is different. Anam's telling is effortless and unembellished, tempting, and ordinary. In Adichie, the narration of the nitty-gritty is sometimes blunt and to the point, always imagistic and logical, arresting, and charming. They have mixed first-person points of view mingled with occasional third-person omniscient points of view; their characters and their states of affairs are examined from both outside and inside.

In Anam and Adichie's presentation of the subjectivity of women, the male characters function as a mirror. For women in the mentioned novels, the process of attaining a comprehensive consciousness becomes possible because of the limited, incomplete, and one-sided performance, and narrow agency of the male characters. Women subjectivity gets well reflected and well mirrored when their tour de force is placed by the side of their male counterparts. Rehana is placed by her dead husband, the wounded Major, and the father figure of the nation Sheikh Mujibur Rahman; Olanna and Kainene are placed by Odenigbo, Richard, and Ugwu; Ifemelu is placed by racist men; Zubaida is placed by Elijah, Anwar, and Rashid; Aunty Ifeoma, Kambili and her mother Beatrice are placed by the fundamentalist Eugene. Maya is placed by Sohail. It is the very presence of their deranged and deviated male counterparts by their sides that orient women towards attaining wholeness.

For Anam and Adichie, an emergency is tantamount to and conducive to the emergence of the new women. Emergency in the sense of crisis indeed offers women to emerge. Both Rehana (*A Golden Age*) and Olanna (*Half of A Yellow Sun*) face the effects of the national crisis within their families; Ifemelu (*Americanah*) faces the effects of the racial crisis in her life; Zubaida (*The Bones of Grace*) faces an identity crisis for herself; Maya (*The Good Muslim*) and Kambili

(*Purple Hibiscus*) face the crisis of religious fundamentalism in their lives. These emergencies have "brought different families of the human race together – to blows at first, but afterward to truce...." (Emerson 2). Fascinatingly however, for these women, these crisis-ridden phenomena have provided the opportunity to have "the instinct of self-help, perpetual struggle to be, to resist opposition, to attain to freedom, and to attain to the mastery and security of a permanent, self-defended being" (Emerson 2).

Based on the above discussions, the book is divided into **five** chapters.

Chapter I

The **first** chapter is the "Introduction" in which Anam and Adichie's fictional world and the art of their fiction is outlined, the design of the book is set down and their points of meeting and points of departure from the other representative fictional responses on war, racism, and religion are set forth. In the "Literature Review" section, the existing body of criticism on the mentioned works is analysed individually to help situate these points of difference in the detour of the novels. In the "Theoretical Framework" section, Gloria E. Anzaldua's notion of "mestizo" or "consciousness of the Borderlands" is explicatively deliberated.

Chapter II

The second chapter is entitled **"War and Women Subjectivity in *A Golden Age, Half of A Yellow Sun*"**. There are two sections in this chapter. In the first section, the focus is on Tahmima Anam's *A Golden Age,* and in the second section, the focus is on Chimamanda Ngozi Adichie's *Half of a Yellow Sun.*

The first part of this chapter shows how with a retrospective gaze at the brave feats of ordinary women,

Tahmima Anam's *A Golden Age* fictionalises the 1971 Bangladesh Liberation War. The chapter shows how the novel remains a conscious distillation of history by bringing to focus the agency of women in the Liberation War. The novelist does so through the depiction of the character of the "hero" Rehana Haque, her struggles and sacrifices as a mother, as a civilian, and as a middle-class Bangladeshi woman. The chapter shows how Rehana's life gets caught in a whirlwind of crises–the loss of her husband, then the loss of her guardianship over her children, and then all of a sudden, the inroad of the war. The chapter highlights how despite confronting overwhelming crises, Rehana does not allow things to disintegrate and how she negotiates the crises with a comprehensive consciousness. Rehana does not fight in the war-front; she remains backstage and within the domestic space. Yet, her contribution to the war is no less: she allows her children to participate in the war for a greater cause; she allows her own house to be used as a base of the "mukti jodhhas"; she shelters a Major and rescues a soldier; she makes food for the soldiers and she continues to remain a constant source of courage to her neighbours. The chapter shows how through the depiction of her character, Anam rediscovers the role of women who remain in the homefront and yet exhibit remarkable agency during the Liberation War.

The second part of this chapter discusses Chimamanda Ngozi Adichie's *Half of a Yellow Sun* that represents in its novelistic world the struggles of women and men during the rise of the 'yellow sun,' i.e., the Biafran War or the Nigerian Civil War. The chapter particularly examines how in this novel, the novelist gazes more at the other side of the war than on the usual side i.e the physical War. Adichie shows how during the war the Igbo women

– Olanna, Kainene, Mrs. Muokelu outstep their societal boundary and come forward to leave their mark through their war-time exploits. Despite having a foreign degree and an aristocratic and politically powerful background, Olanna's foot is firmly planted on the ground. During the war, her life and her life struggles are just like an ordinary Igbo woman. Her Igbo is better than her English. She does not mind helping the boy servant with the domestic chores. When the war breaks out, she engages herself with a democratic, open and inclusive temperament in multiple affairs. She adopts the girl of a helpless woman her lover once slept with, continues teaching poor children amid war, instills a sense of patriotism in them. She does not mind standing in queue for war-time rationed food, helps the war victim Alice by sharing food with her, resques the boy servant Ugwu with all the money she has, stands by Odenigbo and keeps alive in him the dream of free Biafra. Apart from Olanna, we see other women in war-time action. Kainene dispenses vital service by harboring victims of war and by arranging food and shelter for the evacuees and displaced persons. Mrs. Mukelu makes soaps, tries homegrown food and medicine for self-sustainment. The novel not only depicts women's instrumentality in the war, but also exposes its brutal onslaught on them through the depiction of their victimization, e.g. the horrible murder of Aunty Ifeka and the rape of Alice and Anulika.

On the whole, the chapter shows how *A Golden Age* and *Half of a Yellow Sun* have disrupted the fictional glorification of only men's part in the war. By focusing on women's version of war history, the novels rewrite history, acknowledge the role of women in the war, empower them and reveal "the pity of war, the pity war distilled" (Owen 81).

Chapter III

The third chapter entitled **"Racism and Beyond: A Study of *Americanah* and *The Bones of Grace"*** consists of two parts. In the first part, Ifemelu's stay in America for academic purposes, her experience of racism there find a sensitive and stimulating expression. This part of the chapter shows how Ifemelu observes more than one form of racism in America; sometimes she faces overt racism and sometimes a covert one. Ifemelu's discerning eye records how people are divided along colour lines and the consequent dynamics of power. Ifemelu's reaction to racism is mainly expressed through her blog in which is found her observations, reflections on racism, her dialectic engagement with it and with different approaches to racism. In the novel, Ifemelu does not play the blame game. Rather, she tries to understand issues of race from both sides, from both perspectives- the white and the black. When a white woman is surprised at her obsession with hair, Ifemelu does not fume: "How else will she know what hair like mine feels like? She probably doesn't know any black people" (*Americanah* 309). The uniqueness of *Americanah* lies in its understanding of racism holistically; it 'defamiliarises' and 'de-exotifies' racism, and presents it with less emphasis on racial slurs and physical abuses—the corporeal manifestation of racism.

In the second part, *The Bones of Grace* is discussed. The novel is about life-journeys, love, loss, the quest for identity, and certain choices made by women at the backdrop of a country trying to better itself and thrive after the Liberation War. Zubaida, the palaeontologist seems to be in control of her life, but does not know what life has kept for her. Life takes her to strange routes that she has not thought of and the novel indites how she tries to juggle and maneuver resiliently through a series of disturbing events and tries to put her life back on track. Zubaida suffers from insecurities and for her, her origin is important. Though Zubaida relentlessly struggles with the issues of belongingness, she does not create 'imaginary homelands' for herself. Remaining within the disturbed spaces of her country, she acquires self-knowledge not by showing disregard to her troubled past, but by sharpening and refining of her 'self-knowledge' through an inquisitive and assimilative digging of her past along with its thorough and probing investigation.

Chapter IV

The **fourth** chapter **"Women Against Religious Extremism in** *The Good Muslim* **and** *Purple Hibiscus"* is divided into two portions. The first portion is directed at the discussion of Tahmima Anam's *The Good Muslim* in which the emergence of the post-war by-product, i.e., religious dogmatism, is shown in the person of Sohail, a willing fundamentalist and a soldier in the Liberation War. He is confronted with her sister Maya who resists and interrogates her brother's fundamentalist ways which are at odds with hers. *The Good Muslim* is unique in dealing with the issue of fundamentalism. The novel problematizes the idea of being 'a good Muslim' and most important of all, shows us the best way to tackle with religious fanaticism and dogmatism and the female character Maya embodies the defiance of religious fundamentalism and the providence of an alternate, secular way of life. The novel exemplifies, through the character of Maya, a pluralistic consciousness that can "ineluctably subsume the other's otherness" and celebrates through her an empathy that remains "a conciliatory bridge across polarizing differences" (Lal 1).

In the second portion, the focus is shifted to a study of

religious fundamentalism in Chimamanda Adichie's *Purple Hibiscus* where the setting shifts to post-colonial Nigeria. Eugene Achike takes upon himself the burden to bear the legacy of the British colonisers by blindly and dogmatically following and patronizing the religion of the colonisers with a complete disregard to his native religion and culture. He forces his belief on his wife Beatrice and their children Jaja and Kambili who obey him to a certain extent and then rebel against him, in due course. Contrary to Eugene, we see his sister Ifeoma, a university professor, who is a liberal, is able to maintain a balance between the colonial and the native culture and for whom religion is not just a bunch of rules but a means to living a good life. In the novel, we also meet Eugene's daughter Kambili—the novel's protagonist and narrator—who is initially tyrannised and victimised by her father who blindly "drags god into everything" (*PH* 244). In due course of time, Kambili comes under the influence of her aunt and Father Amadi and finally develops a consciousness that is capable of subsuming the extremist and fundamentalist beliefs and ideologies. When religious extremism tends to become instrumental in gender oppression, she takes a liberal, inclusive, and secular path so far as her comprehension of the religion is concerned. On the whole the chapter intends to establish how in this novel, Adichie's take is "secular" in the sense that for her, religion is never an imposition or injunction, but a matter of personal choice which is premised on the liberal views of tolerance.

Chapter V

The concluding chapter entitled "Conclusion" highlights the outcome of the book which foregrounds the positivist and reconstitutive roles played by women characters in a war-devastated society, even though their engagement in the war is not direct and frontal. The "Conclusion" emphasizes on the significance of women's critical involvement in domestic and extra-domestic spaces of their lives, the emergence of their constructivist subjectivity and their 'philosophy of action' that collectively pave the way for the inculcation of a symbiotic and sustainable outlook on life during the times of war.

Literature Review

In this part of the book, the existing body of representative and relevant critical works done on the fictional works of both Adichie and Anam will be critically appreciated to show the research gap and to show wherein the book criss-crosses the road of the others and where it diverges. One novel after another will be dealt with following the order as they have been discussed in different chapters of the book.

On *A Golden Age*

Tazrin Hossain in his book entitled *One is Not Born, But Rather Becomes A Woman: Becoming Woman in Tahmima Anam's Works* has applied feminist and postcolonial theories on the texts of Anam and has focused on the social, cultural, and religious subjugation of women. Hossain's work brings out "the struggle of women as well as the accomplishments of women by analysing Anam's works and will show no one is born a woman but rather becomes a woman by her sacrifices, heroism, deeds, and victory in any situation" (3).

Mandira Sen in her review of *A Golden Age* points out that the question of identity is the most vital aspect of the novel. Rehana the protagonist of the novel oscillates between two identities—Urdu speaking identity and Bengali speaking identity. She speaks Urdu, the language of West Pakistan but lives in East Pakistan as the narrator describes: "Once the war breaks out Rehana becomes conscious of her ambivalent feelings about her adopted country" [East Pakistan i.e. Bangladesh] (Sen 6). As the Liberation War makes its way forward, the image of Rehana changes. After her husband's death, her sisters living in West Pakistan think that she is a traitor and to those in East Pakistan, she is an outsider. She is on neither side and tries hard to keep the balance on either side as the narrator observes: "Rehana maintains relationships with both the living and the dead" (Sen 6). Rehana does not leave East Pakistan, neither does she lose touch with Faiz, her husband's brother who is in West Pakistan.

Christine Pyle's essay, "Symbolism in *A Golden Age*: Rehana as Bangladesh" adduces Rehana as a mother embodying the new-born nation, Bangladesh. She becomes "the mother not only of Sohail and Maya but of all the young revolutionaries who would form the new Bangladesh" (4) and the trials and tribulations in her life "parallels the tumultuous story of the Bengali people from before Partition to the formation of a distinct nation" (Pyle 1).

Sanjib Kr Biswas and Priyanka Tripathi in their article "Relocating Women's Role in War: Rereading Tahmima Anam's *A Golden Age*" show how Anam's novel is a shift from the usual presentation of women in war history as passive and one-dimensional characters to that of active and multi-dimensional ones. Anam's characters are "New Women" who deconstruct the myth of women being sacrificial lambs on the altar of national freedom. With her liberalism, dutifulness to the family, and to the nation "she emerges as the universal mother free from the womanly weakness" (Biswas 528).

In summary, these critical responses to *A Golden Age* carefully analyse the gendered roles played by different characters in the novel; Mandira Sen's review focuses on

Rehana's swing from one identity to another; Christine Pyle's essay presents the allegorical and symbolic function of Rehana and the other characters while Sanjib Kr Biswas and Priyanka Tripathi's article refers to women characters as "new women" and focuses on the new roles women assume during the war. Though Rehana is referred to as a "universal mother" (Biswas 528), what is conspicuously absent is the inclusive consciousness Rehana embodies.

On *Half of a Yellow Sun*

Janice Spleth in "The Biafran War & the Evolution of Domestic Space in *Half of a Yellow Sun*" points out Adichie's focus on the domestic space which has been purposefully posited in the actual battlefield to show the impact of war in the private lives of the Nigerian people. The household of Olanna has become the narrative centre and her domestic space becomes "an essential theatre for the unfolding of events" (Emenyonu and Spleth 130). The focus on the domestic space which is the dominant space of women "produces a gendered view of the Biafran conflict" (130).

In the article "Contrasting Gender Roles in Male-Crafted Fiction with *Half of a Yellow Sun*", the character Carol Ijeoma Njoku is examined as a symbolic figuration of how Adichie's *Half of a Yellow Sun* is an "intervention into Nigerian war narratives- a rediscovery of the Nigeria-Biafra female heroine" (Emenyonu and Njoku 154). The article enunciates how the novel proclaims and reasserts the positive contribution of Igbo women, their resolution, fortitude, and courage in the Biafran war.

In her article "Tales of War for the 'Third Generation': Chimamanda Ngozi Adichie's Half of a Yellow Sun," Serena Guarracino explains that the novel exudes the reaction to the Biafran war from the perspective of the third generation. The article shows that Adichie's presentation woman is neither from a nationalistic and ethnic standpoint. In this article, Guarracino asserts that "the way Adichie's fiction deals with the subject of war offers new insights into the role of woman in a postcolonial and global context" (Guarracino 55).

Lauren Rackley in his book entitled *Gender Performance, Trauma, and Orality in Adichie's Half of a Yellow Sun and Purple Hibiscus* investigates into two novels of Adichie: *Half of a Yellow Sun* and *Purple Hibiscus* and shows how different waves of the trauma of Biafran war enters into the domestic sphere and trouble women. The traumatic experience of women in the domestic sphere allegorises the trauma of the Biafran war. Rackley "interrogates women's experiences within the domestic sphere, ultimately reflecting a larger national trauma that Biafra and later Nigeria undergo as a result of colonial occupation...and concludes with an exploration of the culturally specific practice of orality and storytelling that occurs within both novels that ultimately initiates the healing process for the individual, as well as the nation" (Rackley iv).

In the article, "Rethinking Female Sexuality in Adichie's *Half of a Yellow Sun,*" Sandra Nwokocha surveys how the novel *Half of a Yellow Sun* reveals diverse African identities and diverse gender behaviours during the war. The article also takes into account the fortitude, the hardship, and humanness of women during the war. The argument is put forward "for the ways in which Adichie emphasizes the humanity of her female characters through their claims to sexual freedom, even in the context of overwhelming civil unrest" (Nwokocha 2019). Adichie is looked at as a dynamic feminist novelist who champions a new worldview that authenticates sexual behaviors that have so far been seen as "un-African." According to

Nwokocha, "*Half of a Yellow Sun* forms a counter-narrative to critical approaches that view the female sexual agency as something inherently Western" (Nwokocha 8).

In her book *A Different Story of War: Women Writers Countering Stereotypes and Writing Agency into the Story of Conflict,* Veerle H. van Lieshout shows how in *Half of a Yellow Sun* Chimamanda Ngozi Adichie deconstructs gender stereotypes by studying different kinds of involvements of women in the national and ethnic conflict. Lieshout "argues that postcolonial literary works can offer an important contribution to Conflict Studies by imagining new perspectives on conflict" (2).

In summary, Janice Spleth's article is on how domestic space becomes the epicentre of war-narrative thereby showing the prominence of women in that space; Carol Ijeoma Njoku has made a comparative study of the representation of women's role in the war by male novelists and the representation of women's role in the war by female novelists; Serena Guarracino analyses how the Biafran war is looked at by the third generation; Lauren Rackley focuses on the trauma of war on both the individual and the nation and how oral storytelling heals the trauma. Though the body of critical approaches takes into account the impact of war comprehensively from various perspectives, no one has taken into account the same from a psychological perspective.

On *Americanah*

Niyi Akingbe & Emmanuel Adeniyi in their article "'Reconfiguring *Others*': Negotiating Identity in Chimamanda Ngozi Adichie's *Americanah*" reveal how though Adichie in *Americanah* commits to harmonising the racial and cultural differences of her characters, she has not succeeded in her trial with transculturalism. They argue that "transculturalism in *Americanah* ostensibly failed due to the obtrusive racial intolerance exhibited by the varied characters who appear to have determined to cling to the divisive racial sentiments identified in their attitude" (37). Niyi Akingbe & Emmanuel Adeniyi reveal how Adichie's projection of transculturalism in America has miserably failed because of racism.

Eleanor Anneh Dasi in "The Intersection of Race, Beauty, and Identity: The Migrant Experience in Chimamanda Ngozi Adichie's *Americanah*" discusses how the intersection of migration, racial prejudice, cultural favoritism are factors and determinants in the negotiation of identity and how they break stereotypes, shape and forge the 'self' and form new identities. According to Dasi, the Africans have to meet the western yardstick of beauty with "the diverse definitions of beauty from different cultural perspectives" (140). The novelist brings to our cognizance the "issues of racial stereotypes and cultural prejudices," and thereby sets into motion the "process of demystification of the myth of racial superiority begins, signalling also the start of the African's journey towards a new conceptualisation of self" (Eleanor 140).

Rose A. Sackeyfio in the article "Revisiting Double Consciousness & Relocating the Self in *Americanah*" explores how in *Americanah* the identities of African diasporic subjects get fragmented in the hostile host-land and how their identities get damaged due to the diasporic encounters. For this, Sackeyfio has drawn on the notion of "double consciousness" illustrated in W.E.B. Dubois' *The Souls of Black Folk* (1903) and Paul Gilroy's *The Black Atlantic: Modernity and Double Consciousness* (1993). In the alien culture of the host-land, the culture of their own land gets manifested. In "the clash of cultures," Ifemelu, the central character who came to the USA from Nigeria accepts and embraces her black identity: "Ifemelu comes full circle, longs for *home* and eventually returns, not as a splintered immigrant but a fully realized Nigerian woman" (226).

In *Americanah*, Ifemulu's migration from Nigeria to America helps her grow and develop. The "deterritorialisation", "alienation" and "exile" advance her growth. Ifemelu's migrant experience exposes her to racism, makes her realize her blackness, "what she is" and "what she is not". This reading is provided by Mary Jane Androne in the article, "Adichie's *Americanah:* A Migrant Bildungsroman." Finally, Ifemelu returns to her roots, to Nigeria as a "new person." Mary Jane Androne argues that "Adichie's bildungsroman does not end with identity achieved, but rather identity building as an ongoing process" (241).

Americanah is "a novel about love, about race, and about hair" (Cruz-Gutierrez 257). Christina Cruz-Gutierrez in "'Hairitage' Matters Transitioning & the Third Wave Hair Movement in 'Hair', 'Imitation' & *Americanah*" has shown how Adichie's works are informed by the politics of hair. Cruz-Gutierrez focuses on how hair becomes a vital aspect of body politics, and a marker of one's ethnic and cultural identity. In the USA, Ifemelu holds on to her "natural hair", "natural self". This evinces that she is "in control of her own identity formation from that moment onwards, free from patriarchal epistemological discourses on gender and race" (258).

In summary, Niyi Akingbe & Emmanuel Adeniyi reveal how Adichie's projection of transculturalism in America has miserably failed because of racism; Eleanor Dasi tries to figure out how as a result of migration, racially prejudiced selves are affected and new identities are created; Rose A. Sackeyfio focuses on the fragmentation of identity of the diasporic subjects in the hostland through Ifemelu; Mary Jane Androne considers the novel to be a bildungsroman and opines that Ifemelu's exposure to the experience of racism is behind the continuous process of identity formation of Ifemelu; Christina Cruz-Gutierrez discusses the body politics/hair politics and shows how hair becomes the determiner of one's identity. The articles referred to are on Ifemelu's experience of racism, her growing up, her identity formation, and different discourses on race. Though it is hinted that new identity of Ifemelu is formed, it is not made clear whether the new identity subsumes the previous ones or whether the new identity helps her resolve all her clashes and conflicts.

On *The Bones of Grace*

Umme Salma in the Seventh Chapter entitled "Ambivalence, Autonomous Agency and Transculturation in Tahmima Anam's *The Bones of Grace* of her" in her book *A representation of Transculturation and Agency in Bangladeshi Diaspora Novels in English* looks at the novel as a diasporic work and according to Salma, the central character Zubaida has shown "a transgressive love for transnationalism, as she finds herself situated between a pretentious, progressive home and an indifferent, detached host-land" (163).

Salma is right in pointing out the ambivalence of Zubaida but Salma's argument that Zubauda transcends her entrapment in the homeland/ host-land binary though her "trangressive love for transculturalism" seems inadequate. The novel in the manner of forensic digging helps Zubaida relocate herself in 'love' and imaginatively reconstruct and fill the gaps of her life relying on love and companionship of Elijah, the mainland in the ship of her life.

On *Purple Hibiscus*

Home instead of becoming a haven for the overall growth of children becomes a place of abuse and torture in the hand of fanatics like Eugene. This is illustrated in Edgar Fred Nabutanyi's article "Ritualised Abuse in *Purple Hibiscus*". The novel is a personal account of child abuse in the domestic sphere. In this sphere, religious ritual, or rather, Catholic rituals—to be more particular— are outraged to the point of misuse to an extent that it punishes children for the infringement of parental order and causes them pain. Nabutanyi writes: "*Purple Hibiscus* unmasks Eugene's ritualized abuse of his family in instances where he feels they have deviated from his (distorted) version of religious piety and its attendant rituals" (73).

Oluwole Coker looks at *Purple Hibiscus* from psychoanalytic and gender perpectives. The child in the novel is seen as the medium through whom "the post-independence angst" of Nigeria comes out. The assumed innocence of the child is an advantage to look at domestic and social change: "The child narration technique deployed in Adichie's *Purple Hibiscus* is a device used to engage with post-independence disenchantment in the universe of the novel" (110). The child narrative brings to the fore the subjugated and silenced voices of that time.

Iniobong I. Uko in "Reconstructing Motherhood: A Mutative Reality in *Purple Hibiscus*" reads Adichie's novel as a deconstruction and dismantlemnt of the ideal of motherhood prevalent in African societies. A mother is a sacred and revered figure who is supposed to be "producer", "provider". But in *Purple Hibiscus* the mother takes out life in cold blood, with her eyes wide open. Beatrice poisons her tyrannical husband who is an absolute oppressor, bully to death. Uko "examines the factors that reverse the course of nature, and make a mother, the bearer and nurturer of life, to be the one that terminates life. This twist in the role of the mother is the mutation, the alteration that opens up a vista of issues..." (57).

Janet Ndula in "Deconstructing Binary Oppositions of Gender in *Purple Hibiscus:* Superiority & Silence" also looks at the novel through the gender lens. Women are posited in the dynamics of power and are subject to different paradigms that subjugate and silence them. This paper reveals how "Our self-conceptualization in terms of gender and binary oppositions have been internalized ... and how they are influenced by the human tendency to define each other in inclusionary/exclusionary terms" (Ndula 31).

In summary, Edgar Fred Nabutanyi's focus is on child abuse employing religion; Oluwole Coker's focus is also on how through the point of view of a child the postcolonial anxiety of Nigerian people is brought out and it helps in giving a voice to those silenced so far; Iniobong I. Uko reconsiders the idea of motherhood. Beatrice's cruelty in poisoning her husband is atypical of mothers in African society; Janet Ndula focuses on the subjectivity of women, their victimization and silence, and the dynamics of power. With the death of Eugene, the structures of power fall, and power starts shifting to women. But in all these articles, there is less focus on the dogmatism and tyranny of her father, traditionalism of her grandfather, the liberalism of Aunt Ifemelu which merges and blooms in Kambili's inclusive consciousness.

On *The Good Muslim*

Mandira Sen in the review of *The Good Muslim* points out at the juxtaposition and clash of binaries, the emergence of the good and the bad due to this clash and at the aftermath of the Bangladesh Liberation War. The novel is a record of the post-war scenario. The trauma of war left heavy impressions on the psyche of both Maya and Sohail. Maya developed an aversion towards institutional religion and got detached from it. Sohail got interested and took shelter in religion.

Abdul Majid and Dinnur Jalaluddin deal with the binary presence of the secular (Maya) and the religious (Sohail). During its birth as a nation, Bangladesh grew along these two lines. Maya and Sohail are seen to be embodying the two sides. The paper explores the complex relationship between the two poles. It is suggested that "the skirmish between the siblings is a metaphorical representation of a conflict between the secular and the religious in the efforts towards nation-building" (Majid and Jalaluddin 28).

Saumya Lal has interpreted empathy as 'intrusive'. He thinks that "Maya and Sohail's negotiation of their irreconcilable differences over religion illustrates how their inability to accept gaps in empathy prompts them to adopt conflict-eschewing silences that lead to the complete breakdown of empathy" (Lal 1). While it applies to Sohail's empathy for the war victims, it is not so in the case of Maya. Maya's empathetic response to some extent indeed creates a disturbance in Sohail's life and his son Zaid's, but her intervention is a necessary one and is no intrusion at all.

According to Farzana Akhter, Anam in *The Good Muslim* has demoted Maya. Women like Maya are always on the periphery. Though during the war Maya had an active agency, she is relegated to the passive position after the war. She ends as a mother. At the end of the novel, her former identity during Liberation War is overshadowed by her latter identity once the war is over. This transformation hints at the secondary place women have in the history of war and the "grand narrative of the Liberation War" is negligent of their sacrifice. Akhtar notes: "Maya's reversal of roles from an active participant to a reproductive agent...reiterate that female and male participation in nation-building is regulated by socially constructed ideas of masculinity and femininity" (93).

In summary, Mandira Sen, Abdul Majid, and Dinnur Jalaluddin show the emergence and divergence of the two roads—the secular and the religious in Bangladesh in the post-Liberation War scenario. Saumya Lal points out how there is no empathy at all between Maya and Sohail. It is their desperate effort to accept each other which is instrumental for the failure of an empathetic understanding between them. In this sense, empathy has caused more harm than good; According to Farzana Akhter, the novel does not celebrate the woman's cause; rather, it presents women in a negative light. Maya began as an independent woman, devoted to the cause of the nation but ended as a mother which delimits and underrates women's contribution to the war. But what is not discussed is that Maya successfully comes out of the binary hinge i.e. secular/religious, male/female/, masculine/feminine and a new consciousness dawns on her which like a sponge osmoses all contraries and conflicts.

Theoretical Framework

The radical theory of subjectivity of Gloria E. Anzaldua i.e. "mestizo" or "consciousness of the Borderlands" is employed in the book to analyse the mentioned works. The concept of 'mestiza' can be comprehended as a non-binary, alloying, and connective approach to thinking and thus, is used as a critical tool to study and analyse the mentioned works. In the pioneering book *Borderlands La Frontera: The New Mestiza*, Gloria Anzaldua formulates an influential and vitalizing construct called 'mestiza consciousness' to deconstruct the hegemony of binary paradigms which dictates a set cultural pattern on individuals. Anzaldua takes the oppressive binary paradigms for her own use and proposes both to liberate the subjects stuck in the hinge of binary-hierarchy and to offer resistance to it. Anzaldua undertakes a polemical method to rise above the imposed imaginary and notional borderline that has pushed woman into the periphery. To quote from section 7 of *Borderlands* where Anzaldua categorically states her position and purpose which is defined and oriented by the notion of 'mestiza':

> The work of 'mestiza consciousness' is to break down the subject- object duality that keeps her a prisoner and to show in the flesh and through the images in her work how duality is transcended. The answer to the problem between the white race and the colored, between males and females, lies in healing the split that originates in the very foundation of our lives, our culture, our languages, our thoughts. A massive uprooting of dualistic thinking in the individual and collective consciousness is the beginning of a long struggle, but one that could, in our best hopes, bring us to the end of rape, of violence, of war. (80)

Being a 'mestiza' herself, Anzaldua puts forward a "new consciousness", "a new value system" that will dismantle the schism between "white and colored," between "male and female" and between "us" and "them." In this way, this concept dismantles the hegemony of culturally constructed and dichotomous categorization of social groups into "us" and "them."

To have a better understanding of the Anzalduan approach, we need to look at the nature of binary oppositions and for this, we shall look at the approach of W. E. B. Du Bois and bell hooks. W. E. B. Du Bois in *The Souls of Black Folk* talks of 'double consciousness' in which binaries exist – African/American, Black/White, positive view /negative view. The Negroes in America have this consciousness in which they see themselves through the eyes of others and which deprives them of their true self-consciousness. Du Bois says:

> It is a peculiar sensation, this double consciousness, this sense of always looking at one's self through the eyes of others, of measuring one's soul by the tape of a world that looks on in amused contempt and pity. One ever feels his two-ness,—an American, a Negro; two souls, two thoughts, two unreconciled strivings; two warring ideals in one dark body, whose dogged strength alone keeps it from being torn asunder. (8)

But the deprivation has its benefits; it is an endowment too as this deprivation helps them deeply realize the American situation:

> Work, culture, liberty,—all these we need, not singly but together, not successively but together, each growing and aiding each, and all striving toward that vaster ideal that swims before the Negro people, the ideal of human brotherhood, gained through the unifying ideal of Race; the ideal of fostering and developing the traits and talents of the Negro, not in opposition to or contempt for other races, but rather in large conformity to

the greater ideals of the American Republic,
in order that some day on American soil two
world-races may give each to each those
characteristics both so sadly lack. (Du Bois
50)

If the binaries that partitioned the two races do collapse, there will be togetherness and equality between them and each African will bring into completion the inadequacies or lacks the Americans and vice versa. The duality will be there but the equality will be more equalled, homologous, and be two peas in a pod. Though Du Bois winds up with the breakdown of the binary, it does not articulate the genesis of the third.

In the Preface to *From Margin to Center* (2000), hooks while talking about black Americans opines that the marginalized women subjects are blessed with double consciousness. Both sides of the coin are revealed to them. They can look from both outside and inside. Hooks says:

Living as we did—on the edge—we
developed a particular way of seeing reality.
We looked from both the outside in and the
inside out. We focused our attention on the
center as well as the margin. We understood
both. This mode of seeing reminded us of
the existence of a whole universe, a main
body made up of both margin and center.
(xvi)

Gloria E. Anzaldua goes beyond Du Bois and hooks. She talks about creating a third space, a new self in which the binaries- margin and center, oppressor and oppressed are subject to malleability. One should not 'cradle in' or 'sandwich between' cultures, but must 'straddle' cultures. To stand on the opposite river bank, shouting questions, challenging patriarchal, white conventions is not enough: "A counter stance locks one into a duel of oppressor and oppressed; locked in mortal combat, like the cop and the criminal, both are reduced to a common denominator of violence" (Anzaldúa 78). Hence, a pluralistic, an esemplastic, a many-in-one consciousness is needed.

In her interview with Kakie Urch, Michael L Dorn et al after the "Women Writers' Conference" at the University of Kentucky held in 1993 Gloria Anzaldúa said that 'borderland' with uppercase B transcends socio-spatiality i.e. 'Borderland' is solely about a particular individual, society or space. The landscape of 'Borderland' is all-encompassing. Anzaldúa says:

>...when I capitalize Borderlands, it means that it's not the actual Southwest or Canada-U.S. border, but that it's an emotional Borderlands which can be found anywhere where there are different kinds of people coming together and occupying the same space or where there are spaces that are sort of hemmed in by these larger groups of people. (77)

'Borderland' is a metaphor. The emotional and physical life of the 'mestizos' becomes a 'borderland' neither inhabiting the white nor the black: "Two spaces overlap, one that is neither black nor white but black superimposed on white, a shaded area. People who are in that marginalized space get looked at as being different, as being in some way outcasts because they don't belong to the rigidly defined categories of white or black" (Urch, Dorn, & Abraham 77).

One of the main images in *Borderlands* is 'la nepantla' which helps develop her theory of borderlands- the 'process', 'liminality', and the inherent 'changes'. It takes place in the transitional points of life. In Nahuatl or Aztec language 'nepantla' means "in-between space" and "For Anzaldua, nepantla represents temporal, spatial, psychic, and/or intellectual point(s) of crisis." (Anzaldúa & Keating 322). It is "a long tube or birth canal one moves through in a liminal, post identitarian state where identities are multiplied, fragmented and finally shaken off like a snake's skin" (Urch, Dorn, & Abraham 77).

Anzaldúa's use of the mythical and mental image of Coatlicue fits well in the exploration of the role of women. "Coatlicue is the mountain, the Earth Mother who conceived all celestial beings out of her cavernous womb (Anzaldua 46). Coatlique, Mother Goddess of the Aztecs appears to be the symmetry of binaries - life and death, light and dark, male and female. According to Anzaldua, Coatlique stands for "duality in life, a synbook of duality, and a third perspective something more than mere duality or synbook or duality" (46). Anzaldua further explains: "Coatlicue depicts the contradictory. In her figure, all the symbols...are integrated. Like Medusa, the Gorgon, she is a symbol of the fusion of opposites: the eagle and the serpent, heaven and the underworld, life and death, mobility and immobility, beauty, and horror" (47). When one enters the Coatlicue state, one disrupts the monotonous and stereotypical flow of everyday: "Coatlicue is a rupture in our everyday world" (Anzaldua 46).

Following Anzaldua, we can say that the self of women becomes the womb, the creative space where things are "born, produced and reproduced" (Hartley, 41). War discourse, race discourse and religious discourse manipulate and exploit this womb differently. War discourse excludes the productivity of this womb by excluding and not recognising women's contribution to war, racial discourse by othering it, religious discourse using domination and control.

Anam and Adichie have made sincere efforts to instil the new consciousness into their characters. "La metiza" dwells in the borderlands and takes wing from one culture to another, and is present in all cultures synchronously. It is relevant in the cultural, racial, and feminist deliberation in the post-modern era. In *La Raza (The Cosmic Race)* Jose Vasconcelos first marks out this new 'borderlands-cultural-group.'

Anzaldúa's "mestiza consciousness" overlays with the actions of the women in dealing with/coping with war, racism, and religious extremism and Anzaldúa's concept of mestiza consciousness becomes the exact lens of looking at and doing justice to the exertions of women against the divisive forces.

"Mestiza consciousness" has a wider application and can be used to understand the situation of women all over the world who struggle and negotiate with social, political, religious and other hostilities. The term "mestiza"/ "mestizo"/ "mestizaje" is used in the book not in a narrow sense but in a broad sense. The term is not confined to refer to women of "mixed" race but is extended to include those women who straddle the binary and an array of contradictions.

Chapter II

War and Women Subjectivity in *A Golden Age* and *Half of a Yellow Sun*

Wars have become "an epidemic insanity, breaking out here and there like the cholera or influenza" (Emerson 1), vitiating human civilisation. At the same time, wars put to test our mental, physical, and moral strength. Our fortitude, perseverance, and tenacity not only get bruised and eroded but also get reared, developed, and improved: "War educates the senses, calls the will into action, perfects the physical constitution, and brings [wo] men into such swift and close collision in critical moments that [wo] man measures [wo]man" (Emerson 1). During wars, our humanity or the lack of it, our strength or the lack of it, our worth or the lack of it become prominent.

We the human beings have a tendency to deal in polarities and binaries. Even when dealing with war and its representation, we do not deviate from that tendency. We continue to locate ourselves within the stereotypical binaries of war narrative: men will fight; women will weep and sometimes be agents of peace. We have developed certain tropes of social identities in which we locate men and women – men are combatants or warriors whereas women are non-combatants; men are violent and women are nonviolent. These paradigms do not reveal what roles men and women play during war.

Historiography in general has privileged responses to male writers of War along with its male participants whereas its responses to female writers of the War along with its female participants have been pathetically downgrading. Chimamanda Adichie and Tahmima Anam have shown, in their writings, a shift of paradigm by counting on the activities of women and their experiences during the war, thus shedding light on the hitherto neglected aspect of war history. They have proven that women have a lion's share in the Bangladesh Liberation War and the Nigeria-Biafra War.

This chapter will be divided into two sections. In the first section, the focus will be on Tahmima Anam's *A Golden Age* while the second one will focus on Chimamanda Adichie's *Half of a Yellow Sun*. In each section, the focus will be on the victimisation of women and their agency during the war. They become the objects of violence and yet, they do not claim an eye-for-an-eye or a tooth-for-a-tooth tactic. They become "motherists" enriched with double consciousness and are blessed with "mestiza consciousness".

Rehana in Tahmima Anam's *A Golden Age* and Olanna in Chimamanda Adichie's *Half of a Yellow Sun* are faced with the trauma of war. They struggled to live multiple realities and became very adept in adjusting to it. They experience and belong to multiple situations and multiple worldviews which are at loggerheads with each other and develop a new consciousness capable of manoeuvring the clashing ideas and situations. Moreover, the new consciousness empowers them to negotiate with social, political and other hostilities, and set them free from the personal, social, political and other conflicts and contradictions.

A Golden Age and the Emergence of the Middleclass during War

Tahmima Anam, the "daughter of a Golden Age" was born in 1975, four years after the 1971 Bangladesh Liberation War, to Shaheen Anam and Mahfuz Anam, editor of *Daily Star*, a diplomat, a freedom fighter in the Liberation War. At Harvard, Anam wrote her Ph.D. dissertation on Bangladesh people's memories of war entitled "Fixing the Past: War, Violence, and Habitations of Memory in Post-Independence Bangladesh" and for this, she had to interview many people in Bangladesh about their experiences in the war. It provided her with the material for *A Golden Age*. In an interview with Terry Hong, Anam states that she did lots of research for her first book which was spontaneously carried over to the second. Instead of using books, she preferred to ask people who were there during the War, and what were their experiences, and then she tried to forget the research so that the readers do not ever feel like she has just given them a history lesson.

Srinath Raghavan in the book *1971: A Global History of the Creation of Bangladesh* argues that "The war of 1971 was the most significant geopolitical event in the subcontinent since its partition in 1947" (4). According to Raghavan, the history of the emergence of Bangladesh, then, is no more than the chronicle of a birth foretold (6). The impossibility of unity of the two wings is corroborated by Salman Rushdie's scathing image of undivided Pakistan in *Shame* as a "country divided into two Wings a thousand miles apart, that fantastic bird of a place, two Wings without a body, sundered by the land-mass of its greatest foe, joined by nothing but God ..." (307). The seed of the partition of West Pakistan lies in linguistic and economic reasons: "There were substantial differences in the social, cultural, and political life and traditions . . . differences in the economic conditions of the two parts and the imbalance in the structure of power" (Raghavan 6). There was a wide geographical gap between the two wings – West and East Pakistan and in addition to it, there was tension regarding language. From the very beginning, the administrative authority of the undivided Pakistan insisted that Urdu will exclusively be the official language in East Pakistan. This insistence cum whip provoked protests from the Bengali-dominated East Wing "who feared that this policy would undermine their career prospects and demanded that Bengali be recognized as an official language" (Raghavan 6). There was also economic exploitation of East Pakistan by West Pakistan. The economic benefits earned from the export of Jutes grown by East Pakistan was enjoyed by West Pakistan. The economic assistance from foreign countries also invested in the development of West Pakistan.

Moreover, West Pakistani Muslims considered themselves pure in terms of their religion and considered the East Pakistanis including the Hindus impure. So, 1971 provided the former with the scope to maneuver, not only to purge East Pakistanis along with their Hindu elements, but also to uproot and eradicate them. As Saikia quite aptly points out: "Muslim Pakistani men assumed that the sacrifice of the 'Hindu women were necessary to undo the national malaise" (61). It is also fascinating to observe that the East Pakistanis were categorized as Hindu or Pro-Hindu irrespective of their amalgamated religious existence. They were reduced to the status of inferiority compared to the dominant superior West Pakistani Muslim men and women, and were considered to be non-human, in a sense. In a way, they were "marginalized and excluded from the rank of humanity" (Saikia 61).

Anam grew up outside Bangladesh and was a non-resident. Hers is therefore the outsider's perspective. Moreover, she belongs to "the post-1971 generation" and her such belongingness provides her with" a unique perspective to look at both the country and the war" (Sadique 29). Anam's growing up in such cosmopolitan places as Paris, New York, and Bangkok, and her pursuit of liberal arts at Mount Holyoke College in Massachusetts, "allows her the advantage of both global and local perspectives on the story of Bangladesh" (Basu 33).

Lynn Neary writes about the gap between diasporic identity and the sense of native history in the article in the *Morning Edition:*

> The child of a diplomat, Tahmima Anam grew up far away from her native Bangladesh. But all her life, she heard about that country's war for independence — which took place before she was born — from her Bengali parents and their friends. And when she decided to write a novel about Bangladesh, Anam says, she couldn't imagine writing about anything else except the war (Neary 18).

Yasmin Saikia has added a different dimension to the 1971 Liberation War by referring to several wars which are the bifurcations of the centerpiece, the Liberation War; in a sense, there was war between two states, two countries, two ethnic groups, two linguistic groups, and two gendered groups. And quite unfortunately, there are ample studies and representations of all kinds of wars except the gendered ones:

From March 25 until December 16, 1971, thus several wars broke out in East Pakistan. One was a civil war between East and West Pakistan, the second was an international war between India and Pakistan, and the third was an ethnic war between the Bengalis and the Biharis. There was still another war that broke out- a gender war of men against women in which all groups indulged in terrifying and brutalizing enemy women to create fear and humiliate the other. The war against women is by far the least studied and actively silenced within the 1971 violence (50).

Be it Liberation War or any other war it is a grievous mistake to give it a one-dimensional take. War does not involve a sect. Such war as BLW involves the outside and inside of an entire populace; but in historiography, only the physical aspects of war are recorded and only those who fought on the battlefront are glorified. But they are not the only ones who are heroes. The fact is that there are the sung heroes and there are also the unsung heroes. Women are the unsung heroes of the war. As Aasha Mehreen Amin, Lavina Ambreen Ahmed & Shamim Ahsan in their article, "The women in our Liberation War: Tales of Endurance and Courage" published in *The Daily Star*, the English daily in Bangladesh, opine:

> War heroes include those women who have supported the valiant freedom fighters with food, shelter, funds; who have nursed the wounded and hid weapons risking their own lives. They also include those who have willingly given their sons to war, who have lost their loved ones and even worse, been

subjected to sexual abuse and still survived to tell their stories (Amin 87).

Tahmima Anam's debut novel, *A Golden Age* (2007) captures a defining historical period in Bangladesh through the saga of survival of the ordinary people. The novel is mostly set in Dhaka, and closely spans over "the war-torn months of 1971, with each chapter corresponding to a month or several months of that year in the lives of its characters, tells the story of Bangladesh, its people and the terrible year of its birth from the inside" (Islam 2008). The novel links the domestic sphere inhabited by women to the national sphere where women are subject to violence reinforcing the victimization and exploitation of women during the war. The "whole nation [came] together in a just war of liberation and secession" (Anam 101).

The participation of women, their sacrifice, and the violence they underwent in the Bangladesh Liberation War have been the subject matter of many well-known texts – Nilima Ibrahim's *Birangona Speaking*, Selina Hossein's *Liberation War Stories*, Jahanara Imam's *Ekatturer Dinguli*, and the likes. But none of these novelists have emphasised the agency of women in the War and the humane take of women during the same to an extent that is accomplished by Anam. Nilima Ibrahim's *Birangona Speaking* is an objective rendering of the Bangladesh Liberation War while Tahmima Anam's *A Golden Age* is the subjective rendering of the same. Anam narrates "agency, resistance, and survival, alongside the social processes of healing and recovery" (Ranasingha 115). Ranasingha further explains: "*A Golden Age*... shows how war opened up possibilities of agency for women who could not join the armed resistance and who must find a way to live in the limbo world of a city in curfew" (115).

Anam explores into the prolonged nine-month span in Bangladesh Liberation War in ten chapters of *A Golden Age*: "Prologue in March 1959", "Shona with her back to the sun in March 1971," "Operation Searchlight on 25 March 1971", "Radio Free Bangladesh in April", "Tikka Khan, the Butcher of Bengal! in May", "I loves you, Porgy June", "The red-tipped bird" in July, "Salt Lake in August, September, October", "Take my affliction' in November" and "16 December 1971", covering almost ten years (March 1959-16 December 1971) in the life of the nation and the life of the Haque family as well.

A Golden Age is about a widowed woman Rehana Haque who at the outset of the novel has lost possession of her children, Sohail and Maya to Faiz, the Pakistani brother of her deceased husband. In course of time and in course of the novel, Rehana gets back the possession of her children, brings them back but very soon the 1971 Liberation War breaks into their life. The novel is a testimony to the fight and odyssey of Rehana who is modelled on Tahmima Anam's grandmother in times of the Liberation War. The novel thus translates in its canvas the being and becoming of Rehana, the development of a new consciousness in her which is informed by and during the Bangladesh Liberation War.

Anam has intended to write on Rehana's children, who have participated in the War and therefore have direct experience of the War, but Rehana who represents the hoi polloi assumes control of the story and it ends up being "a novel about a family and not so much about the details of the war. You only see of the war what she sees of the war" (Wagner). Had Anam focused more on Rehana's children, the novel would have become a hardcore war novel with grim realities of war. As the novel centres around Rehana—a middle-class, middle-aged widow—and her world, it ensures that the family remains the locus and women subjectivity is the prism through which Anam has projected the Liberation War.

In the novel, Rehana is found to be a character who is self-actualizing, protective of others around her and loyal to her humanitarian values. The world she inhabits is a paradise soon to be lost, an ideal world, a golden age of freedom soon to be poisoned by the venom of war. The land is ravaged by swarms of invaders. The violence that engulfs Bangladesh crashes down onto it in successive waves, as if from a convalescing sea. But Rehana puts on a brave face trying to prevent from getting buffeted by the incessant and ravaging currents and torrents of events.

Rehana is "a mestizaje" in the sense that she lives in a state of uncertainty during the Liberation War and straddles different selves and states: she is a widow; she is an ordinary woman; she is an "outsider" to the Bengali speaking people of East Pakistan; she is torn between Urdu and Bengali; she finds it hard to live in the "adopted" country. But all these selves evolve and integrate into a mother figure through which she catalyses the divisive binarism. The subaltern position as a helpless widow and mother, an ordinary housewife, Urdu-speaking Other in East Pakistan is turned into something better, engendering a "third space" capable of fusing disparateness, subsuming binarism, and sustaining contradiction. Though Sanjib Kr. Biswas and Priyanka Tripathi refer to the "universal motherhood" in Rehana out of which "she emerges as a saviour for the other sons and daughters apart from her own"– Maya and Sohail (526), what is amiss in their discussion is the rise and flowering of a universal consciousness i.e. "mestiza consciousness" which impels Rehana to dispel the binary of our /their.

The British –Pakistani writer and critic Kamila Shamsie in her review of *A Golden Age* in *The Guardian* lauds the novel because the telling has been done from the vantage point of women:

> One of the novel's great strengths is its decision to show the war from the perspective of the women who cannot join the armed resistance and must instead find a way to live in the limbo world of a city in curfew, where daily life must continue its deceptive normality even while there are guns buried beside the rose-bushes, and visits to the Urdu-speaking butcher are fraught with political tension… (Shamsie 47).

As a "mestiza", Rehana lives this "limbo world", buttresses the existing war discourse, appropriates it through her action and personal experience, and thereby postulates a different parameter of women subjectivity in the context of Bangladesh Liberation War.

In *A Golden Age*, Anam juxtaposes the 'private' / 'personal' and the 'political', and shows how individual, microscale actions are moulded by large-scale incidents and the vice-versa. While narrating the personal feats of Rehana, her struggle for the unity of the family, we are simultaneously and steadily presented with the presence and effect of the Liberation War. Kamila Shamsie observes:

> Throughout the novel, Anam deftly balances the story of a nation against that of family... There is never a moment when we lose sight of the upheaval of Dhaka in 1971, but Anam adroitly weaves these stories into the personal lives of her characters" (Shamsie 66).

And the focus on the struggle of a middle-class woman vis-à-vis the Liberation War makes Anam's novel distinct from her crony writers: "The very subject matter of her novel sets Tahmima Anam apart from other English-language writers of Bangladeshi origin such as Adib Khan or Monica Ali" (Islam 25).

When the novel opens, Rehana is a widow, and she is going to lose the possession of her children to Faiz, the brother of her dead husband. In the courtroom, it is finally proved that Rehana cannot afford a congenial atmosphere for the upbringing of her children. One of her "sins" is that she has taken them to the movie, *Cleopatra*. What happens at home and within the walls of the courtroom allegorically reflects what happens in the world. The devastating division i.e. the separation of the children from the mothers and their shift to Lahore foreshadow the division of East Pakistan and West Pakistan. The novel thus becomes a "moving story of war and brutality in a tale of motherhood" (Burton-Hill's Rev. of *A Golden Age*).

The absence of the Father from the very beginning of the novel is perhaps a deliberate ploy on the novelist's part. The absence of the Father is conveyed to us metonymically i.e., through the grave. He lives mainly in Rehana's memory and continues to be in the discourse of the recent happenings in the family and the nation, having a "liminal" existence between then and now; he is the mysterious and symbolic 'absent-present' who is continually referred to, yet whose presence is relentlessly deferred. Nonetheless, his presence in the form of an unforgettable memory initiates and drives the actions of the characters in the novel. Most importantly, it pushes Rehana to action, attributing her with agency. In the sequel to this novel, *The Good Muslim* it is the absence of the father figure and not just the gruesomeness of the

Liberation War that remains responsible for the radical transformation of the son, Sohail.

Rehana's destiny and that of Bangladesh sways like a frond between East and West Pakistan; she is attached to both yet rooted in none. The tides of death and conflict invade into the Haque family and it presages the entry of War into the national life of Bangladesh. The narrative of Rehana's life moves mildly through tractable toil, unrecompensed love, and endless commitments as Bangladesh moves to War and then deceptively gravitates towards independence. For most of the time, we continue to exist and locomote within the consciousness of Rehana which twirls around her children, the domestic loss, and the civil war: "… the omniscient narrative voice remains entangled with Rehana's consciousness and her politicisation throughout" (Ranasinha 97). The third-person omniscient narrative is also used to intimate "the suffering of a collective group of people connected in grief, all embroiled in the maelstrom that overwhelms the city under siege" (Ranasinha 105).

A Golden Age is not meant for Bengali readers but English readers in Bangladesh and abroad. The novel represents in English a stereotypical image of the Bangladesh Liberation War; but at the same time, it represents an a-stereotypical image of women involved in war. Through the novel, Anam renews her bond with Bangladesh and strengthens her sense of belonging. The novel is centred on the struggles of a mother, Rehana. She is a mother with a difference:

> You are a mother. How many times had she repeated this very phrase to herself? I'm a mother. Above all things, a mother. Not a widow, certainly not a wife. Not a thief. A mother. But now she was something else – a

mother, yes, but not just of children. Mother of a different sort. (*AGA* 162)

Rehana is not merely a mother figure in the private/familial space, but also in the public space. Chaiti Ghosh points out: "Motherhood has been a dominant memorial site where Bangladeshi nationalism has been constructed" (294).

A Golden Age narrows down the narrative focus on a familiar space, and then, defamiliarises it. The familiar, familial space has been deconstructed and reconstructed by stretching the idea of home and by making it pivotal to the national crisis and making it a dialogic and productive space. Ruvani Ranasinha's observation is pretty pertinent here:

> The novel reconceptualises the domestic space as a site of political struggle, in contrast with the emphasis of previous writers (notably Anita Desai) on home as a place of confinement for women. Basing Rehana on her own maternal grandmother, a widow who allowed arms to be buried in her garden, Anam is concerned to examine and recover from a postcolonial feminist historical perspective the role of such women in the war of liberation. Rehana is a very active 'mother' of the nation, in contrast to the metaphoric roles women are conventionally assigned in relation to the nation". (99)

Kamila Shamsie quite appropriately comments that *A Golden Age* "provides windows on a mother's war" (Shamsie 2007). Anam is interested in 'women as heroes' and in the 'unexpected ways that women are heroic'. Rehana is an 'unintentional hero'. During the war, she stumbles into it to save her and her children. In the interview with Terry Hong Anam says:

> I am definitely interested in women as heroes, in the unexpected ways that women are heroic. Rehana is an unintentional hero. The war is going on, but she's just in it to protect her children. That's just what women do, all over the world: they do what it takes to protect their children. That's the kind of heroism I'm interested in. (Hong 49)

As the mother figure of the nation, she has also sacrificed a lot for Bangladesh. Her life is anchored to her children. Her son Sohail has joined the Resistance and her daughter Maya has joined the Communist Party. When war is afoot with the enemy soldiers approaching, and when she smells danger for her children, she gets worried, but does not lose her nerve. She asks Mrs. Rahman to take a position, to offer resistance. The verbal exchange between them is worth quoting:

> 'I tell you, we should all stay here and take a stand.' 'What sort of a stand, exactly?' Mrs. Akram asked. 'We should do something. I'm not giving up so easily.' 'Don't be foolish. You're just a housewife. What on earth could you possibly do?' 'You wait and see. I'm not just good for gin-rummy, I'll have you know'. (*AGA* 86)

It is not mere bravado. She considered the enemy soldiers as "little boys" (96), younger than her children. She does take a stand and feels that it is her country and instead of escaping during an emergency, she must contribute towards the crumbling nation's fortification and make necessary sacrifices. So, she starts the Project Rooftop, making blankets for the refugees.

The Liberation War has divided the "country in two halves" (*AGA* 33). Subsequent to the divide, we see many others divisions and binarism emerge. Sabine Lauret-Taft in the article "You'Re Just a Housewife. What on Earth Could You Possibly Do?" refers to the pervading dichotomies in the novel: "West/East, Lahore/Dhaka, Us vs. Them, daughter/son and father/mother" (5) and the antibook between "the paternalistic description of Sheik Mujib …and motherhood, embodied by Rehana and Mother Bengal" (Lauret-Taft 5).

The way Rehana manages to put different shreds of her identity and of her life together and appropriates differences is foregrounded through her morning activity in the garden:

> She dipped her fingers into the rosebush, heavy with dew and plucked a flower. She held it in her hand as she wandered through the rest of the garden, ducking between the wall-hugging jasmine and the hibiscus, crossing the tiny vegetable patch that was giving them the last of the season's cauliflower, zigzagging past the mango tree, the lemon tree, the shouting-green banana tree. (*AGA* 15–16)

We perceive amid the lush, life-giving and hebetic nature the germination of an inclusiveness, as from the garden, Rehana looks at Shona, a haven in microcosom for all of them. The winter of war "lingers on the leaves and in the wisps of fog that rolls over the delta and hangs low over the bungalow" (*AGA* 15). Though the dismalness of the war is conveyed through pathetic fallacy, hope and a comprehensive consciousness grow in Rehana in a vegetative way.

Rehana has to take a lot of pain to rebuild Shona and to make her join her family here a scenario where the house Shona in which the family reunites metonymically stands for this happy reunion. Shona becomes more than a physical space, a haven and bedrock of solace, security, high moral values, and unified national consciousness. The house stands for a breeding place of an alternative space and the source of positive vibes and moral strength to ward off evil.

When Sohail tells Rehana that he wants Shona to set up Dhaka as the headquarters of the guerrilla operations, she cannot but give consent: "Shona with her back to the sun. Shona that had given her children. Proud, vacant Shona of the many dreams. The house is Yours, Sohail" (117).

She treats Shona as her own dear child, symbolic of the nascent nation, Bangladesh, the treasure house of all her memories, the source of her identity. The thought of leaving it in difficult times unsettles her: "'It's my home, and the home of my children. I would not give it up for anything. Believe me, I've been tested'" (142).

The house Shona is the "melting pot" embodying pluralism and diversity, a site of conciliating differences. It becomes one of the projections of Rehana's "Mestiza consciousness" by functioning as an "image consciousness" (Kurg 1). Shona is not only the hiding place of the Mukhti Bahini. Rehana also shelters in Shona a refugee enemy soldier (Major). Rehana also allows the Hindus, for example, the Senguptas as tenant. Besides being a projection of Rehana's "Mestiza consciousness," Shona thus becomes a symbol of "national integrity and religious integrity" (*AGA* 179).

Anam presents the narrative of the war through the

depiction of the personal accounts of Rehana's life. War is the subtext and its aftermath; familial conflicts constitute the text which reflects the national conflict waged by war whereas the commonplace activities devoid of glamour occupy the centerstage. Through the whole of the novel, we find a loveable, motherly Rehana Haque who is always attached and bound to her children and to the greater cause of the country. By focusing on the falling apart of a family and its ensuing reintegration, and by narrating a story in which a family survives through the mother's imperative and binding presence, Anam showcases such universals as love and and "the milk of human kindness"—values that were put to test in course of the war.

Rehana wades into the heaps of damage and piles of pain engendered by the appalling events, and emerges with enormous grace. The small-scale miracle of her exploits is that rarely does she give in to the disheveling madness felt by the majority of East Bengalees: the ache for rancor. She is bold and untamed in the execution of her resolution. Her bravery soothes those who have gone under that inferno and those who have sacrificed themselves while trying to get them out of that shock. Anam through Rehana takes the hat off to their courage and passes out the hat to those who wring hands for them.

Rehana does her utmost to get back the possession of her children. Yet the same Rehana does not dillydally when Sohail gets ready for the war. She, with motherly care and affection, armors her son for the war not with weapons but with ordinary things that one needs in day-to-day life. She is not a veteran soldier like Shaw's Bluntschli, but she shares his disregard for the romantic notion of war and for the traditional idea of bravery; she also shares his stark pragmatism and common sense that make chocolates more important than bullets on the battlefield. Rehana "counted a few shirts. A lungi. She felt the plastic of his toothbrush. It was like combing her hands through his hair. Satisfied, she left for the kitchen" (Anam 96). The day before Sohail leaves for war, she prepares for him a feast and cooks all her favourite dishes: "malai curry, Polao, Chicken roast, Shami kabab, Dal, extra-thick as it is her duty to send her son to war with a full stomach" (Anam 96).

What adds power to her effort is the gusto with which she wants to do her part. She lies to Faiz, deceitfully and tactfully nods in the support of Pakistan during the dinner with Faiz and Parveen. She also purposely suppresses the fact that Sohail has joined "muktibahini" and Shona has turned into the fortress and the safe haven for the "muktibahini" fighters. She fools Faiz and Parveen through her timely and manufactured pretensions. She feels victorious. It is about 'war' and 'love', and everything is fair in love and war. She has done it so that Sohail can get back the attention of Silvi. To get the consent of Faiz for the release of Sabeer is a kind of victory for her in the familial battlefield where she had lost years ago.

Allegorically, Faiz represents West Pakistan and Rehana represents the East. It is, as if, the blow of the East to the West. When she is reminded that it will not be safe on her part to go with Faiz to the release of Sabeer, she casts it aside and tells the Major as well as to herself: "'No,' she said, angry now, 'I'm not doing enough. I want to do my part. Maybe it's not for my son – maybe it's something else. What, you don't think I can love something other than my children? I can. I can love other things'" (*AGA* 211).

Rehana has got too much horse sense. To achieve her goal she employs charm, bribery, and shows that common sense constitutes the better part of courage. She is not only a victim of war but also an apparatus of the war. In the hurly-burly of war, Rehana's sense of right and wrong has also got reversed. It is not the best time rather the worst times. To save Shona, she has tried for a loan in vain. But finally, he steals the jewelry of the dead wife of a blind man T. Ali. It is not her purpose to fish in troubled waters. Her moral sense is sacrificed at the altar of motherly love. In the Chapter, "The red-tipped bird" set in July, Sohail requests his mother to rescue Sabeer, the husband of Silvi of whom Sohail is enamoured. For this, Rehana has to beg the favour of Faiz who once dispossessed her of her children and with whom Rehana has a standoffish relation. After shrugging her shoulder a bit, she agrees to take the bad with the good.

At first, it seems to her to be the "most distasteful, gruesome task" but she discerns in it an occasion to atone for the moral compromises she has done: "Her son was giving her another chance to atone. The years of slavish devotion, the mothering, the theft – she had always known they would not be enough. She could not help welcoming the prospect of some new sacrifice" (Anam 194). Coupled with this is her ability to go beyond personal gains. She has not completely thrown herself into the protection of her family. The thought of the others, and the question of their security still concern her. When Sohail beseeches Rehana about the saving of Sabeer's neck so that he can impress Silvi, Rehana answers sharply and crossly: "This is the only thing? What about the war, the country, the refugees, all of that? Suddenly none of it matters?" (195). Rehana is sympathetic and empathetic to her blood relations, to her society, her country, and is equitably and evenly considerate of all. The same Rehana steals the jewelry of the dead wife of a blind man T. Ali when she fails to gather money for rebuilding Shona. Chaity Ghosh has rightly remarked:

> Anam refuses Rehana a morally cosy space, though one feels that the author is keen to cast her as an alternative hero. In the pure and sacralised story of liberation we have a compassionate, courageous, lying and wily ...woman who steals, deceives, and makes love to a man whom she sends to his death for the sake of a greater love.... (297)

And "Rehana's reluctance to belong to a narrative that exalts her pain is offered to the reader as a heroic narrative, thus constituting a significant intervention to the genre" (Ghosh 297).

Each war influences the shift in gender roles. Rehana was an ordinary housewife before the war. Her husband died. But she does not take the gun in her hand with a feeling of hotblooded vengeance; rather, she makes some moral and ethical compromises. Through the intriguing portrayal of her character, Anam describes the process through which an ordinary housewife becomes a party to the war and elevates her role and significance as an invisible worrier in the background. If it is not for the war, if it is not for her children, if it is not for her country, women like Rehana would never have expressed themselves to the fullest. For Rehana, her personal life is her filial, familial, national, and political lives blended into one.

While Rehana is present at the release of Sabeer bravely facing the officers, her womanliness does not come to the fore; she never thinks that she is a woman; she is soft and gentle by nature. There is only one thought marked by her singleness of purpose, to secure and release those close to her.

Women need respect and quite unfortunately, they have to prove themselves and reach to the masculine standard to get respect. Women like Rehana have done this and such effort attests to their plasticity and elasticity and their width of human capacities both good and bad, undoing the assumption that women are susceptible and are the soft targets of War.

Women are noncombatants, but they are not non-actants. They offer their resistance in their own tactical and effective ways. They send their children to fight for the country, and in sync with that, they also assist the guerrilla fighters with clothing, digs, hideouts, food, etc. An important function of many noncombatant women during the times of war has been to provide supportive services and act as aide-de-camp to the muktijodhhas. They have prepared and supplied food, have sewed sheets, knit sweaters, and have given first aid to fighters. They would often do the spadework - supply food, sew sheets, stick sweaters, and aid the fighters. Female non-actants also have acted as aide-de-camps by providing shelter to the fighters hiding weapons in their houses and gardens. Furthermore, some women did not hesitate to send their family members to fight while they, apart from other reinforcements, provided emotional and moral stanchion to the latter. Rehana talks to her friend regarding their contribution in the war:

> 'Don't you know? We're at war... I have to do something. To prove I belong here. So I'm doing something.' Rehana felt a tear crawling out of her eye; she tilted her head, sent it back. 'I'm doing something. Making blankets for the refugees.' She felt her lip curling back on to her teeth. (Anam 107)

Another part some women have played is to help their society. Apart from performing their roles as mothers, sisters, and daughters, they published tracts, magazines, which chronicled the activities of the East and West Pakistanis, particularly highlighting the unforeseen difficulties people confronted during the war. Though Clemency Burton-Hill has categorically objected to the fact that Maya represents the tossed and turned condition of those "politically active women who find themselves without a role when wars between men break out" (   ), in my estimation, she does find a role for herself in the war-riven society and executes it with much know-how and effectiveness. The novel is primarily about the trials and tribulations of Rehana and Bangladesh. And Maya is deliberately given a small role and little space to make Rehana the focal point. Maya works as an adjutant, a girl Friday for a newspaper, writing about the "muktibahini" and the brutality of the West Pakistani army. Maya and Sohail become the cornerstone of the story in the second novel, *The Good Muslim*, which is a sequel to *A Golden Age*.

Rehana, repining the absence of her son Sohail, puts a quilt for the fighters for Bangladesh, makes pickles for them. The novel shows the experiences of women who, in the testing and pressing period in the history of the nation, reinvent and delimit their roles and responsibilities during times of difficulty and national emergency.

Rehana is the "unheroic hero", the mediocre hero, the common woman. She is the middle-of-the-road kind who allies feverishly with neither of the contending camps in the crisis period in her life. At first, she does not understand the situation of war. When she sees Joy putting on Sohail's shirt, she cannot understand it—an understanding that is perhaps limited by her motherly concerns. When Joy comes with the news of Aref's death, she asks him foolishly: "Why are you wearing Sohail's shirt?" (Anam 133). But later on, the same Rehana quite bravely saves Sabeer's life.

Is Rehana moved by heroic nerves or is she forced by pure necessity? One way or the other, her move/gesture is devoid of moral quality. It is not cowardice but down-to-earth realism. As others ensconce out of fear and make it appear that the war is non-existent, Rehana comes forward and does what she can though her primary objective is to save her children and she is an "an involuntary revolutionary" (Shamsie 11). She begins by sewing blankets made from her silk saris. She denies any simplistic approach to be imposed on her darling wives, adored daughters, and respected mothers. Torn between the contrary pulls of keeping her and her family's survival afloat and her love and dedication towards her country intact, she suffers from terror and remorse.

For Rehana, all are one. She is the 'mother courage' on the face of the hardships of war and in unfavourable situations; she extends her empathy and favour towards those affected directly and indirectly by War. By allowing her children to participate in the war, she has not at all endangered them. She is not an embodiment of the cruelties of war, and she does not have the hunger for power. By her decision and action, she inspires and instills revolutionary and humanitarian ideals in her children and thereby makes the readers critique war.

Rehana has divided loyalty. She lives in and fights for Bangladesh, yet fluently and fondly speaks Urdu, the language of Pakistan. She is a kind of outsider and speaking "the language of the enemy" (Sen 6) and her sister considers this to be treachery. Rehana realises this gradually. Ruvani Ranasinha in "War, Violence and Memory: Gendered National Imaginaries in Tahmima Anam, Sorayya Khan and Contemporary Sri Lankan Women Writers" enounces Rehana's ambivalence in the following words:

Rehana straddles India, Pakistan and the newly created Bangladesh. She has an 'ambiguous' relationship 'with the country she adopted' and its language, Bengali. Although 'Dhaka is [her] home and the home of [her] children', Rehana is not a native of Dhaka. She was born in Calcutta; her sisters live in Karachi, and there 'wasn't a day that went by that Rehana didn't think of them, out therein the sprawling parched western wing of their country' (105).

In course of the war, and in the course of the novel, Rehana comes to terms with her ambivalences. It is the national emergency, i.e. the Liberation War that helps her overcome her ambivalence. It is through her rupture, the domestic fracture, schism in the family that the partition of Bangladesh from West Pakistan is narrated: "The novel offers a dialectical (rather than synchronic) understanding of how these relational (in terms of both reconciliation and conflict) histories shift over time through the metaphor of mutable familial dynamics" (Ranasinha 100).

Rehana who is always aware of the fragility of human beings becomes sound, strong, and solid by her optimistic and actively eclectic agency which "ignites a mood of hope in the midst of despair, freedom in entrapment" (Sethi 25). While the country falls apart, Rehana makes a steady effort to collect, connect, and meld. Anita Sethi has aptly put:

> This is a novel about how one copes with pain. Rehana carries her grief with grace.... Rather than disintegrating, Rehana creates; she builds a house whose back faces the sun and calls it "Shona", gold, representing everything most precious to her, and the

price she must pay to preserve it. Anam tests the limits of altruism and selfishness as her characters must decide what they most love in the world. (25)

To get rid of differences and dichotomies and to try to resolve all contradictions and ambivalences was the need of that hour and Rehana tried to do that with the best of her abilities. We see the constant rise not only of a comprehensive consciousness but the reflection of an emerging national consciousness in Rehana. It is time for the birth of a nation and a nation is:

...imagined as a community, because, regardless of the actual inequality and exploitation that may prevail in each, the nation is always conceived as a deep, horizontal comradeship. Ultimately it is this fraternity that makes it possible, over the past two centuries, for so many millions of people, not so much to kill, as willingly to die for such limited imaginings (Anderson 7).

Since Anam narrates the struggles of Bangladesh through Rehana, we can read Rehana's new consciousness to be an allegory of the growing national consciousness in Bangladesh. That one consciousness impinges on the other is made clear when hearing from the crowd the nationalistic chanting "Joy Bangla, Joy Bangla, Joy Bangla", she joins them with the thrilling chant: "Rehana suddenly felt young, plunged into a world of limitless possibility" (Anam 49).

In her dialogue with her dead husband Iqbal, the merging of duality takes place. She shares everything at his grave which becomes a kind of melting pot for her, a trustworthy friend, and a kind of confession box for her. The novel begins with her invocation "Dear Husband, I lost our children today" (Anam 3), inviting our attention to her present condition, allegorically the condition of Bangladesh; her losses are both personal and national and inescapably to an inclusive mindset. We get updated about the happenings in her life and the life of the nation. In long monologues, Rehana reports not only the loss of her children but also their return. The novel is the story of her war and about how she has lived: "[It is] the story of our war and how we have lived" (Anam 273). Rehana asks for the forgiveness of her husband for the moral compromises she has made, and for the man she has secretly loved. She tells him all. It helps her to make peace and get peace and harmony.

The novel ends with an optimistic letter:

> The sky is pale and iridescent and today the war has ended, and today I will clutch my flag, hold my breath and wait for our son.
> I know what I have done.
> This war that has taken so many sons has spared mine. This age that has burned so many daughters has not burned mine (Anam 315).

Anam focuses on an unhappily happy conclusion. The war is over. It is the time of change. Change is in the air and in the colour of the sky. Many civilians have died. The death toll remains testimony to the collateral damage that is the unfortunate and irrevocable consequence of every war. But Rehana's son and daughter have made it. They have survived the heartrending catastrophe. Rehana is fully and painstakingly cognizant of the compromises that she has made for the sake of salvaging his family from amidst the general atmosphere of utter and thoroughgoing annihilation in a war-devastated society. She knows the people and their sacrifices.

But an overall analysis of her character and a particular consideration of her ineluctable embeddedness in the prevailing precarity of the circumstances would establish that she is not a selfish, self-seeking, ill-natured mother; rather, she is good-natured and kind whose love for her family and country is sincere and pukka. She does not differentiate between her son and their sons, her daughter, and their daughters. All are her sons; all are her daughters. She is perennially sad for those sons that the war had taken away from her motherland and those daughters who were sacrificed in the war. At the same time, she is contended with whatever her nation and her family could salvage from amidst the debris of the war. Rehana inculcates a sympathetic and empathetic kinship with others who have lost their near and dear ones and takes a firm stand full of integrity: "I have not let it" (Anam 315). She might be critically termed as a flawed character from a stringently ethical and moral standpoint; but she can never be condemned as a heartless and harsh character; rather, she is the one with whom we can feel on the same wavelength and whose slate we can wipe clean.

The novel begins with a bitter conflict – the conflict with Faiz, brother to her deceased husband—over the ownership of her children; but in the end, Rehana fruitfully reconciles with the conflict with zero bitterness with Faiz. For her, Sohail is her son; his friends Aref and Joy are also considered by her as her sons too. She sacrifices her abode Shona for Sohail and when occasion demands, she does not hesitate to risk her life for the sake of a greater cause. And she endeavours her best for the rescue of her neighbour Mrs. Chowdhury's son-in-law Sabeer captured and brutally tortured by Pakistani soldiers.

Another significant facet of her evolving character

and persona is that she inculcates in her a secular and non-partisan disposition; she rises above the narrow confines of religious sectarianism and does not really distinguish between Hindus and Muslims. Her neighbour Supriya Sengupta, a war-victim belonging to the Hindu minority community, denies return to Dhaka after the war. But Rehana requests her: "Come home with me...it's your home too" (Anam 237). She is not merely the symbolic iconograph of the nation whose only saga is the saga of exploitation; rather, she creates her own space in the evolving nation and also a space for others—irrespective of class, caste and religious identity— in which all can harmoniously cohabit. To imagine Bangladesh only in gendered terms (the male war-heroes and the female-sufferers, for instance) and to map the nation with feminine traits and to imagine Bangladesh as a perennially suffering motherland and Rehana as a helpless and non-committal mother-figure would be a nothing but a stereotypical practice, to reduce her to the inferior 'other' as per the superior male narratives.

Rehana fruitfully gets over the idiosyncratic process of 'othering' and all its attendant conflicts including the oscillation between Urdu/Pakistan and Bengali/Bangladesh; she embodies 'mestiza consciousness'. Rehana forgives Faiz, fights for those with whom she does not have blood relations and most importantly, she does not consider anybody as an 'other.' Rather, she forgives all, accepts all, and it is in her forgiveness and acceptance that she becomes the embodiment of an inclusive consciousness: "*A Golden Age* predominantly represents the forging of Bangladeshi national identity defined against the Pakistani oppressor, in terms of an imperative to a unified, holistic subjectivity with a whole nation coming together in a just war of liberation and secession" (Ranasinha 101-102).

Rehana is such an outstandingly admirable character in this novel who can without any inhibition and scruple clasp anyone in her arms. By and large, Rehana finds a way to bridle her grief, her hardship, and her youth and finds a way to embrace and love all. She believes and makes others believe. In the spirit of a true "mestiza", Rehana "straddles cultures and languages" (Lauret-Taft 3), and other contradictions overcoming in the end of the novel the "ambiguous feelings about the country she had adopted" (*AGA* 47).

Anam shows how Bangladesh Liberation War offers an opportunity to women to rebuild their own life and redefine themselves—an opportunity to start afresh, to do and to be, to assume a new identity and to appear in new roles. It is not merely the time of emergency, but also the time of emergence of women with new roles. Anam's novels "trace the emergence of personalities following the conflict, the different ways people are shaped, either scarred or surviving; the strong and the fragile" (Sethi 78). Women's engagement along multiple lines catalyses their collective metamorphosis in the milieu of war, blasting the dead continuity and opening up new windows for them and for others.

For Anam as a novelist, chronicling the post-war scenario and the unwholesome side of war has been a prolonged exercise from the time she writes. Hence, she is predisposed to history in a substantial way and thus, her rendition of history and its events remains fairly true to the former. The book champions and celebrates, and holds to humanity and its restoration. Anam's purposeful and strategic transfiguration of the conventional target-subject from a passive sufferer to an active participator help us understand her craft comprehensively and thoroughly. Moreover, as Saikia puts it:

Women's memories enable us to see the inner experience of the war in people's lives. Their stories humanize the narrative and their speech and silence transcends an individual experience to make it a collective encounter and we are urged to face the inhuman acts of violence and to remember the sites of inhumanity. The story of human resilience despite the losses women suffered creates a different human perspective which is recounted in their stories (109).

The human and humane acts are exemplified till the end of the novel. In the last part of the novel "Saltlake," we are brought to West Bengal and to the Refugee Camp at Salt Lake run by Red Cross where Maya, her friends, Sultana and Mukul offer their service to take care of the refugees "trawling through the streets" (237). Dr. Rao has come to Calcutta from Kashmir for doing the refugee work and Rehana is "trailing Dr Rao through the ward, taking notes on the new patients, writing down their medications and prescriptions (239). Even the shopkeeper who was once a refugee heartily offers "Ten per cent discount,' 'Ten per cent refugee discount'" (236). Thus, Anam "foregrounds the ordinary kindnesses that emerge in the context and aftermath of the war" (Ranasinha 117).

The Agency of Women in the Biafran War: A Study of *Half of a Yellow Sun.*

Chimamanda Ngozi Adichie was born in 1977, seven years after the end of the Biafran War. The Civil War in Nigeria is known as the Nigerian-Biafran War or The Biafran War. The war continued for three years, beginning on 6 July 1967 and ending on 15 January 1970.

The government of Nigeria and the state of Biafra which wanted to withdraw from Nigeria took part in this violent struggle. The Civil War was the outcome of the Nigerian government's effort to counter the effort of the Igbo people of the eastern region to separate from Nigeria. Nigeria got independence from the colonizing United Kingdom on October 1, 1960. The geographical mapping of the regions now we know as Nigeria was created by the British colonial administration in 1914, not by native peoples themselves. After independence, ethnic conflict emerged in Nigeria. Four large ethnic groups exerted their domination in four regions respectively – the Hausa/Fulani in the Northern region, the Yoruba in the Western region, and the Igbo in the Eastern region. The Igbo people failed to co-exist with the Federal Government of Nigeria dominated by the Northern people. There was mass destruction or ethnic cleansing of the Igbo people and they felt threatened by the dominance of the Northern clan. Thus, the national unity of Nigeria was at stake since its independence. All efforts to bring about Nigeria's political, economic, and cultural solidarity failed, chiefly because of the narrow fight for power at the regional or federal level.

The regional interest and identity overshadowed national interest. Each region was afraid of the dominance of the other – Southerners feared the Easterners, the Westerners feared Northerners, and Northerners were scared of Southern domination. Amid this atmosphere of fear and suspicion, faulty and unsound elections were held in 1964 and 1965, in which each party played all sorts of dirty games. The dysfunctionality and defectiveness of the then Nigerian government became apparent after only five years and thereafter, the new-born country sank in the mire of corruption so much so that people started calling the ministers "ten percenters". These corruptors who stood in the way of the young nation were exposed and dethroned soon enough by writers and in January 1966, there was a violent coup by the military officers leading to a horrid and bloody civil war in which the Easterners strove to separation from Nigeria and formed the self-governed and independent state of Biafra.

Adichie had not lived through the war. Although she does not have the first-hand experience of the war in "The Story Behind the Book," she makes it clear that she has heard stories of the war from her parents, and from her grandfathers who died as war refugees. Adichie admits:

> I grew up in the shadow of Biafra. I grew up hearing 'before the war' and 'after the war' stories; it was as if the war had somehow divided the memories of my family. I have always wanted to write about Biafra not only to honor my grandfathers but also to honor the collective memory of an entire nation (Borum n.p).

Adichie belongs to the new cohort of women writers who are born after the Nigerian Civil War; she rectifies the insufficient or inadequate representation of women in war fiction. In male fictional accounts, women's active involvement is either not articulated properly or the characters are portrayed with commonplace and stock roles. For example, Chinua Achebe's *There Was a Country: A Personal History of Biafra* (2012) is found to be lacking in chronicling women's part during the Biafran war. Laure Clémence ZANOU CAPO-CHICHI in the article "Women's Roles during Biafran War in *Half of a Yellow Sun*" quotes Chijioke who while studying "the connection between literature (narrative) and life (history) in Adichie's *Half of a Yellow Sun* shows how Adichie casts insights into the characters' human feelings" (151).

In *Half of a Yellow Sun*, Adichie breathes new life into the exposure of Igbo women's role from all social classes. Adichie's female characters rise above the roles traditionally ascribed to them. Kainene, Olanna, Mrs. Muokelu, and the others have different drives, motives, impulses, and stimulus. Some of them are forced by personal experiences; some are driven by and obsessed with idealism; some are consumed and motivated by patriotism; some get knotted in the tortuous helix of Biafran war unwillingly and unknowingly.

Adichie lays emphasis on the individual experiences that reflect the collective. Individual experiences and personal sensibilities of women who live through war override other aspects. But there is a possibility of the accounts becoming one-sided or biased. Adichie's purpose is to show us the other side of things. Her major contribution is the extension of the 'self.' So far, things have been considered exclusively through the male perception. She has included the female. There is a strong focus on women's subjectivity and the internalisation of all experiences.

Adichie acknowledges her indebtedness to more than dozen representative collection of books that have helped her in writing the book: Chinua Achebe's *Girls at War and Other Stories* (1972), Flora Nwapa's *Never Again* (1975), Chukwuemeka Ike's *Sunset at Dawn* (1976), Cyprian Ekwensi's *Divided We Stand* (1980), Elechi Amadi's *Sunset in Biafra* (1982), Eddi Iroh's *The Siren in the Night* (1982), Kalu Okpi's *Biafra Testament* (1982), Ossie Enekwe's *Come Thunder* (1984), Nwapa's *Wives at War* (1984) and Anthonia Kalu's *Broken Lives and Other Stories* (2003). Hugh Hodges in the article, "Writing Biafra: Adichie, Emecheta and the

Dilemmas of Biafran War Fiction" points out that "the majority of them are histories or political studies" (1). Adichie in *Half of a Yellow Sun* owes a lot to her literary predecessors, e.g. the war experience of Meka the teenage soldier in *Come Thunder* resembles the experiences of Ugwu in *Half of a Yellow Sun*. Adichie's Richard Churchill is perhaps inspired by Alan Grey in *Destination Biafra*. Similarly, in *Half of a Yellow Sun* the experiences of Olanna and Ugwu come close to the experiences of Chukwuemeka Ike in *Sunset at Dawn* and Flora Nwapa in *Wives at War*; but at the same time, Adichie responds to her precursors by adding a lot to them. The mark of distinction is articulated by Hugh Hodges in the following lines:

> That is, precisely because *Half of a Yellow Sun* dramatizes its own incompleteness, its inability to fully comprehend (in both senses of the word) the Biafran War, it negotiates the dilemmas implicit in fictionalizing war more successfully than most of its predecessors. (3).

Unlike the other novels striving for what Eddie Iroh calls "an unbiased, total assessment of the whole great tragedy" (Hawley 18), Adichie focuses on the portions of the war through the lens of teenagers, middle-class people, and women, and attempts to "redress the gendered bias of discourse on the war" (Adams 288). Adichie has not attempted to give a complete, total, and big picture of the Biafran War, as the presentation of totality presupposes a privileged and pansophical perspective, and consequently, the human dimension of things would be inevitably lost. Rather, Adichie focuses on the limited, minor, or marginal human perspectives. Her rendering of the war is not from the perspective of the privileged: "The only 'facts' that matter are those that effect survival on a daily basis: hunger, suspicion, fear" (Hodges 3).

About Adichie's *Half of a Yellow Sun*, *The Chicago Tribune* observes that "A novel that [uses] fiction to its best advantage, telling the stories of ordinary people... – ineluctably caught in savage circumstances of chaos, breakdown, and violence... what Adichie's novel offers is a compassionate, compelling look at the nearly unfathomable immediacy of war's effect on people" (i).

Adichie herself acknowledges:

> I wrote this novel because I wanted to write about love and war, because I grew up in the shadow of Biafra, because I lost both grandfathers in the Nigeria-Biafra war, because I wanted to engage with my history in order to make sense of my present... (Kimber 66).

The novel is not dried up and stagnated by facts of political events. Rather, it is a human story which overwhelms the political events. Adichie has further said:

> All the major political events in the book are 'factually' correct. But what was most important to me, in the end, was emotional truth. I wanted this to be a book about human beings, not a book about faceless political events (Tunca 25).

Adichie's *Half of a Yellow Sun* about life in Nigeria during the Biafran War of the 1960s is the story of five characters – fifteen-year-old Ugwu, university professor Odenigbo, sociology teacher Olanna, her urbane twin Kainene and Kainene's English lover Richard; all these characters are stranded in the tumultuous early sixties and late sixties of the Biafran War. The novel is divided into four parts: Part I and III take place prior to the war in the Early Sixties; Part II and IV take place during the BW in the Late Sixties. In the novel, Adichie resuscitates the experiences of women, their positive contributions, their self-sacrifices. Her female characters rise above the taken-for-granted stock roles. Kainene, Olanna, Mrs. Muokelu, and others are shown as people who are compelled by either personal causes or by nationalist causes or by sheer ideological causes to become active participants in the rising of the yellow sun i.e, the freedom of Biafra.

Olanna is a university-educated Igbo woman whose household becomes one of the focal points of the narration. Along with her partner and husband Odenigbo, a professor of mathematics at the University of Nigeria in Nsukka, their daughter Baby, and the young houseboy, Ugwu, Olanna experiences the displacement and deprivation that characterize many of Africa's Civil Wars. Olanna's domestic space serves as a microcosm of the war's impact on the people, on the state of Biafra, and on the nation itself, metaphorically and metonymically.

Olanna is Chief Ozobia's daughter; yet, she does not mind standing in line to get food for her daughter, and her family. She "can blend easily" (88). She has spent years abroad, has done her M.A. from London University; she is proficient in English, French, and Latin. On her visit to Uncle Mbaezi at Kano, "she wished she were fluent in Hausa and Yoruba like her uncle and aunt and cousin were, something she would gladly exchange her French and Latin for" (50).

She cares not only for her own kind but also for uncle Mbaezi, aunty Ifeka, cousin Arize and former lover Mohammed. She is equally concerned about Ugwu. She is a beacon, a source of strength for Odenigbo. She firmly believes that "things were in order, the way they were meant to be, and that even if they tumbled down once in a while, in the end, they would come back together again" (49).

Olanna comes out and helps others to come out of their stereotypical mindsets. Arize has the idea that men of Abba origin are ugly. According to her, Odenigbo is ugly because he is from Abba. Olanna defies it and proves it wrong that Odenigbo is not ugly: "Good looks come in different ways" (51).

"Mestiza consciousness" necessitates the "writer to begin writing in her 'home(ly)' dialect and right where she is" (Torres 8). Through Olanna, and other women characters, Adichie has stressed on the "homely dialect". As a "mestiza", Olanna "straddles" English and Igbo language, and by straddling language she straddles cultures and ways of life – "African and Western, native and foreign, tradition and change" (Wenske 77). To be on the border of each side and to balance both become possible not only because of Olanna's Western education: "the old and new are not only balanced in the mobility that is afforded by education and language" (Wenske 78). The balance arises out of Olanna's strong awareness of the presence of the two and out of her malleable consciousness.

Ugwu the domestic help of Olanna's lover Odenigbo is mesmerized by Olanna's English in the first meeting with her: "Master's English was music, but what Ugwu was hearing now, from this woman, was magic" (*HYS* 22). Besides, Olanna's Igbo is as magical and spontaneous as her English: "Her Igbo words were softer than her English, and he was disappointed at how easily they came out. He wished she would stumble in her Igbo; he had not expected English that perfect to sit beside equally perfect Igbo" (*HYS* 23). Ruth S. Wenske strikes the right chord in observing that "the efforts of Adichie's protagonists to speak Igbo in their home reflect their attempt to bridge the gap between the educated elite and the rural majority" (79). What is more, in her "competence" and "performance" of both English and Igbo Olanna exemplifies a keen desire to coalesce the European and African so that the binary can be reconciled a new inclusive identity can be formed.

Binarism and conflict surface between Olanna and her lover Odenigbo. They have opposite beliefs about Christian religion. While Olanna is a theist, Odenigbo is just the opposite. In Part Three: The Early Sixties, section twenty three of the novel, when Odenigbo jibes at her "social-service faith" (253), a dialogue between them follows:

"I do believe," she said. "I believe in a good God."
"I don't believe in any gods at all."
"I know. You don't believe in anything."
"Love," he said, looking at her. "I believe in love."
(*HYS* 253)

Though Olanna points out to Odenigbo that love is as irrational as the Christian God, she believes in acts out of love – love for herself, love for those around her, and for her homeland and her culture.

In addition, there is in the novel the "victim/agent" duality which is strongly brought to the fore in Olanna. She is a victim of the war not only because her life and the lives of her near and dear ones are screwed by the war but also because she witnesses the brutal victimisation of war. But she does not merely cease to be a victim. Adichie also records her agency during the war. Olanna surpasses the "victim/agent" binary by "straddling" the binary i.e., by becoming both victim and agent.

That the women and children are the worst victims of the Civil War becomes clear from the exposure of Olanna to the experience of a train trip. Olanna catches sight of a woman hugging and caressing a calabash, came near her and showed the latter the head of her daughter:

> The train was a mass of loosely held metal, the ride unsteady as if the rails were crossed by speed bumps, and each time it jolted, Olanna was thrown against the woman next to her, against something on the woman's lap, a big bowl, a calabash. The woman's wrapper was dotty with splotchy stains that looked like blood.... The train swerved and Olanna bumped against the calabash.... The woman with the calabash...said..."Take a look", she said again. Olanna looked into the bowl. She saw the little girl's head with the ashy-grey skin and the plaited hair and rolledback eyes and open mouth. The woman closed the calabash. 'Do you know ', she said, 'it took me so long to plait this hair? She had such thick hair.... She thought about the plaited hair resting in the calabash. She visualised the mother plaiting it, her fingers oiling it with pomade before dividing it into sections with a wooden comb (*HYS* 148-149).

The train, instead of suggesting life, action, and progress, stands for death, disaster, violence. It is the carrier of war, casualty, peril and hazard that are to follow. The big bowl, the "calabash" is the crucible metaphorically implying the hurly-burly and the turmoil in Nigeria. It presupposes the lives of the common people hamstrung and encumbered in the blood, mire, and violence of the Civil War. Olanna's looking into the bowl suggests that women have witnessed the tribulation, the dire disaster, the evil eye of war, the kiss of death from close quarters. The word "jolt" hints at the terrible blow, the gruesome repercussion, and the shocking quake of war. Olanna's "bumping against the calabash" testifies to the lives of those ordinary Nigerians who get entangled in the war willy-nilly. The mother's complaint to Olanna that "it took her so long to plait the hair" pins down and anticipates the loss and wreckage, the hard times, the bruise, the burden, the injury, the stress, the anxiety, the harrowing torment of the mothers and other women.

Olanna experiences, with utter disgust and discomfort, the smoky, empty street, and the pungent scent of burning when she visits Sabon Gari with Mohammed. The familiar street looks strange and unfamiliar. The compound gate is in pieces demolished to the ground. There lie scattered in dust, splinters of wood, packets of groundnuts. Coils of smoke wind in serpentine fashions while flames billow with grit and ash. The house along with Aunty Ifeka and Uncle Mbaezi is dead: "Aunty Ifeka lay on the veranda. The cuts on her naked body were smaller, dotting her arms and legs like slightly parted red lips" (*HYS* 144).

In Part Four, section twenty-five, Adichie records, through Olanna's experience, the sustained air raids and aerial bombardments, the atmosphere of violence, and of fear. The aerial bombardments make the city a sinister place buried in ruins and shadows, and pushes the civilians into hideouts for their safety. To secure their security, Odenigbo with the help of the neighbourhood men builds a bunker. Even the sound of thunder brings to Olanna's mind the threat of an imminent air raid and scares her to death. The thought of her Baby's security worries and unnerves her. Mrs. Muokelu, the teacher of Elementary school at Akwakuma, adds to her anxiety when she tells her about how soldiers took away the children forcefully. Olanna is so much flustered and panicked that she starts dreaming about the imaginary loss of her child:

> She had a recurring dream: She forgot about Baby and ran to the bunker and after the bombs had fallen, she tripped on the burnt body of a child with its features so blackened that she could not be certain it was Baby. The dream haunted her. She made Baby practise running to the bunker. She asked Ugwu to practise picking Baby up and running. She taught Baby how to take cover if there was no time for the bunker—to lie flat on her belly, hands wrapped around her head. (*HYS* 262)

The dream keeps coming at Olanna. She is relieved when Baby starts coughing in the rainy season. Olanna had this strange belief that since Baby has caught a cold and is sick, she is safe from air raids. She relies on the justness of the gods. Both the sickness of Baby and her insecurity are war-time misfortunes. She is affected by the former means that the latter will not bother her: ". . . since Baby was sick, she could not be harmed in an air raid" (*HYS* 263). The next line proves how fragile her belief is and how helpless Olanna is and how derelict are those whom she represents: "A cough was something Olanna could exercise control over, an air raid was not" (263).

Later, when Olanna takes Baby to Albatross Hospital, she meets Dr. Nwala who warns her that "The mud will stain your dress" (263). The slimy and sticky substance is a powerful symbol of war and it suggests that the life of Olanna and her community will be embroiled in the mire of war. The wartime crisis is glaringly reflected in the condition of the hospital. The hospital corridor is dim. They have run out of medicine. It smells of urine. Women are waiting along with their babies to be treated: "Women were sitting with babies on their laps, standing with babies on their hips, and their chatter mixed with crying" (263).

The external ravage and devastation have created havoc in her mental landscape. The internalisation of the external is visible in her hallucinatory "Dark Swoop". Whenever she hears of torture, murder, and rape, the "Dark Swoop" keeps descending on her, haunting her. The country seethes and so does the terror-oppressed, traumatised mind of Olanna so much so that she starts seeing hallucinations:

> A thick blanket descended from above and pressed itself over her face, firmly, while she struggled to breathe. Then, when it let go, freeing her to take in gulp after gulp of air, she saw burning owls at the window grinning and beckoning to her with charred feathers". (*HYS* 153)

Even the sound of thunder gives Olanna a panic attack: "Her greatest fear was that Baby would die. It was there, the festering fear, underlying everything she thought and did" (249). During continuous bombing, she along with Baby, Odenigbo, and Ugwu hides in the Bunker, and is oppressed by the fear of death. At that moment only death seems to be the only reality:

> Death was the only thing that made any sense as she hunched underground, plucked some soil, rubbed it between her fingers, and waited for the bunker to explode. ...She was floating away from inside herself. Another explosion came and the earth vibrated, and one of the naked children crawling after crickets giggled. If she had died, if Odenigbo and Baby and Ugwu had died.... (*HYS* 265)

Olanna tries hard to recuperate. She is tired of fear. She strives to breathe. Even during violent conflict, she gets married. When Richard asks about her, Olanna replies "We are fine" suggesting that "she had made peace with what had happened" (164). When Odenigbo mentions that there are no clouds in the sky, Olanna replies with dark humour that the weather is appropriate for air raids and both of them burst into laughter.

On her wedding day, "Olanna sat in front of the crooked mirror. Her hair was held up so that all of her radiant, flawlessly smooth face was exposed" (192). The "crooked mirror" reflects the evil time, but in the mirror gets reflected an indurated and seasoned face that is strong enough to brave the "crooked" time.

Although they flee from Nsukka and come to Abba and build bunkers to take shelter during an air raid, we see Olanna exerting herself to the full in Part Four of the novel:

> The war would continue without them. Olanna exhaled, filled with a frothy rage. It was the very sense of being inconsequential that pushed her from extreme fear to extreme fury. She had to matter. She would no longer exist limply, waiting to die. Until Biafra won, the vandals would no longer dictate the terms of her life. (*HYS* 265)

On the spur of the moment, everybody is seized by the frenzy of winning the war at any cost. Fascinatingly, Olanna with annoyance pauses and muses on things she has forsaken:

> ....nobody talked about the things left behind. Instead, they talked about the win-the-war effort.... Win the war. It was difficult for Olanna to visualize a war happening now, bullets falling on the red

dust of Nsukka while the Biafran troops pushed the vandals back. It was often difficult to visualize anything concrete that was not dulled by memories of Arize and Aunty Ifeka and Uncle Mbaezi that did not feel like life being lived on suspended time (*HYS* 179)

Olanna has an even approach, a solidarity in her consciousness in which past and present, the nation and her near and dear ones juxtapose and get equal priority. She does not have a herd mentality. She supports from her heart the cause of Biafra and actively indulges in the 'win-the-war effort'. But she unlike others cannot brush aside those she loved and lost, the memory of whom keeps on surfacing and weighing on her mind. Moreover, while others are eager for war, Olanna refrains from such a desire. Olanna's heart is so heavy with personal loss that it is difficult for her to even conceive of war at present.

During the civil war, women become soft and easy targets. They are victimised, but they survive and put forward resistance in their own way. The depiction of female victimization, and the ensuing female resistance adds not only a human dimension to the violent war-story, but also takes us homeward and inward. The domestic internalisation of war attributes more credibility to the effect of war on women's inhabited domestic space.

During war, women have undergone such violence as military raids and rape. Susan Brownmiller in *Against our Will: Men, Women, and Rape* says that rape is "an unfortunate but inevitable by-product of the necessary game called war" (32). Rape in this novel has both literal and metaphorical significance. Literally, lots of Igbo women become easy preys to sexual assault and rape. For instance, Anulikpa is raped by the federal forces: "They forced themselves on her.

Five of them.... They nearly beat her to death" (*HYS* 421). There were occasions when "They raped pregnant women before they cut them up" (*HYS* 191). Metaphorically, rape implies the vulnerability, humiliation, intimidation, and demoralization of women and the nation (Biafra) as well, and all that women stand for. It implies the exertion of domination, clout, and subordination over the females. Thus, "the body of a raped woman becomes a ceremonial battlefield" (Brownmiller 38). Georgiads Mboya Kivai in discussing rape in *Half of a Yellow Sun* makes an apt remark:

> Rape is an expression of power and authority. It is a form of violence and most of the perpetrators of the crime are men. Men desire to rape women in order to assert their authority over them. Rape can even be a symptom of inequality and the desire on the part of those who wield power to assert it on the powerless. It is an action rooted in masculine behaviour that serves to perpetuate patriarchal order. The basic argument here is that in Adichie's novels rape has a deeper political significance than just men forcing themselves on women sexually. The several episodes of rape identified by Adichie serve to communicate the plunder, misuse and destruction characteristic of the ruling class. It is the men who are depicted as powerful and they rape women who are seemingly powerless... (Kivai 87)

The penis is used as a political weapon by which such male characters as High-Tech and his mates nominate themselves as men of power and as part of the dominant ruling class. Ergo, they rape any female person they bump into. This assertion of power and dominion takes place when in Part Four Ugwu rapes the girl at the bar and the others with him provoke and feed the fire of Ugwu:

> When he finally went back inside, he stopped at the door. The girl was lying on her back on the floor, her wrapper bunched up at her waist, her shoulders held down by a soldier, her legs wide, wide ajar. She was sobbing, 'Please, please, *biko*. Her blouse was still on. Between her legs, High-Tech was moving. His thrusts were jerky, his small buttocks darker-coloured than his legs. The soldiers were cheering. 'High-Tech, enough! Discharge and retire!'.... 'The food is still fresh.!' 'Target Destroyer, aren't you a man? *I bukwa nwoke*. On the floor, the girl was still. Ugwu pulled his trousers down, surprised at the swiftness of his erection. She was dry and tense when he entered her.... (*HYS* 365)

By getting hold of the girl's body through rape, Ugwu and the other soldiers desperately try to get a hold over their newly won authority. They "must prove their newly won superiority—prove it to a woman, to themselves, to other men" (Brownmiller 32). Through the use of force, they need to show off their might—an act that indeed underscores the weakness and fragility of men. Beneath the sheer euphoria of the triumph over female body, underlies a sense of anxiety and of defeat. In fact, opines Brownmiller, "men appropriate rape of 'their women' as part of their own male anguish of defeat" (38).

In conjunction with rape, victimisation of women, and especially the Igbo women takes place through multiple other forms of violence. Like rape, the exercise of violence—both external and internal—is inflicted on women and children who become the soft targets and easy victims of their aggression. Such acts postulate nothing but suppression and exercise of power. Adichie incriminates the policy of Igbo annihilation and in particular, women's persecution in the Northern parts of Nigeria after Major Kaduna Nzeogwu's coup, actually known as the Igbo anti-corruption coup. To cite one notable example from *Half of a Yellow Sun*, Odenigbo's relative Obiozo from the North recaps that he sees the dead body of "a mother and three children, lying on the road to the motor park" (144). In another instance, Enugu eyewitnesses "A pregnant woman [being] split open in Kano" (144) whereas in another gruesome occurrence, Olanna's blood relation, Aunty Ifeka is brutally murdered. On her return from Kano, Olanna describes:

> ...the vaguely familiar clothes on the headless bodies in the yard, the still-twitchy fingers on Uncle Mbaezi's hand, the rolled-back eyes of the child's head in the calabash and the odd skin tone— a flat, sallow gray, like a poorly wiped blackboard—of all the corpses that lay in the yard. (*HYS* 153)

Alice is another war victim. Mama Oji suspects her to be the saboteur as her origin is unclear. Although initially she has lies to Olanna about her origin, she later on confesses, of course being influenced by Olanna's reassuring words, that actually she is from Asaba. Before the war, she finishes her Teachers' Training and starts to work in Lagos where she meets an army colonel. The colonel purposely keeps Alice in the dark regarding his married wife abroad, gets involved in a physical relationship with her, gets her pregnant and gives her the false promise of marriage. He kept avoiding Alice on the pretext of being busy in war. During the war, Alice comes with her baby to Enugu where the colonel, after the return of his wife from abroad, abandons Alice and her baby dies.

On July 28, 1969, Obafemi Awolowo, Nigerian Minister of Finance remarked that "All is fair in war, and starvation is one of the weapons of war". During the Biafran War, Igbo economy and the food production completely broke down. Obi IWUAGWU in his article "FOOD SHORTAGES, SURVIVAL STRATEGIES AND THE IGBO OF SOUTHEASTERN NIGERIA DURING THE NIGERIA CIVIL WAR" quotes E.B. Ipke who points out that five major factors are responsible for the breakdown of Eastern Nigeria—"the influx of refugees, total economic blockade, mobilization of men and materials for the Biafra Army, military operation resulting in population displacement, and the capture of the food surplus areas of the Cross River Basin especially Ibibioland, Bende, Abakiliki and the Rivers areas by the federal troops in the early months of the war" (280-81).

Of the five factors, the crucial one is the economic blockade. On June 1, 1967, Federal Government prevented Biafra from exporting palm and crude oil by imposing blockade on the former. This resulted in acute hunger and starvation. The price of protein foods rose by leaps and bounds. In 1968, the cost of a chicken was five Biafra pounds, while the price of a young goat rose to twenty-five pounds.

The dearth and deficit of food made life difficult and hard on everyone, especially women who stayed home. Mothers started procuring food items available from local resources. Olanna who hails from an aristocratic background never feels the dearth of food until the war breaks out. During the war, Olanna realises for the first time in her life what food crisis means. In Chapter –II, Section 13,

Ugwu cooks Jollof rice for Baby with fresh tomatoes from the garden. He also promises that he will make fruit salad for Olanna with Orange and milk. Before the onset of the war, life was easy and food was available in abundance. Life was slow and simple. Richness and ripeness were all around: "She [Olanna] watched the outline of the mango trees in the next yard; some of them had fruit drooping down like heavy earrings. The sun was falling. The chickens were clucking and flying up into the kola nut tree, where they would sleep" (*HYS* 185).

During the war, it becomes hard for Olanna to find any protein food for Baby. Mrs. Muokelu with much difficulty brings for Olanna some dried egg-yolk from a relief center on Bishop Road. The fried egg yolk Baby eats looks "soggy and unnervingly bright-colored on the plate" (267) which proves that something has gone abnormal and that things are not as they were and as they ought to be.

For food, Olanna has to stand for a long time in a queue in front of the relief centre which was, before the war, a secondary school for girls. There are many days when she comes back with nothing. Sitting on the veranda and looking up at the thatched roof, Olanna and Ugwu recount the days of their affluence: "Do you remember, Ugwu, how we used to throw away soup with meat after only a day?" (284).

The awkwardness and helplessness faced by Olanna at the relief centre and later on, when the soldiers chase her and snatch away the tin of beef from her, are indicative of womenfolk's helplessness and vulnerability during the war. Olanna is present on the scene when the Nigerian soldiers want the village girls in exchange for food: "Come marry me now, I go give you rice and beans" (412). The kinsman of Alice who is Olanna's neighbour at the time when she moved from Nsukka to Umuahia presents himself as a symbolic figuration of the wretchedness of the condition Asaba, her hometown:

> The vandals took our town many weeks ago and they announced that all indigenes should come out and say 'One Nigeria' and they would give them rice. So people came out of hiding and said 'One Nigeria' and the vandals shot men, women, and children. Everyone. (384)

In Chapter 28, Adanna the daughter of Mama Adanna falls ill. Her belly gets swollen and the colour of her skin becomes light and sickly. Mama Oji and Mama Adanna think that it is Malaria, but Olanna diagnoses it as kwashiorkor and suggests Mama Adanna: "You need to find crayfish or milk;" but Mama Adanna refuses and instead, decides to resort to anti-kwash, i.e., anti-kwashiorkor leaves, a kind of native herb which women like Mama Obike believe to replenish protein deficiency:

> Olanna was surprised by how quickly she hitched up her wrapper and began to wade into the bush on the other side of the road. She came back moments later holding a bunch of slender green leaves....Leave Mama Adanna alone. The anti-kwash leaves will work as long as she does not boil them for too long. (339)

Olanna's major concern is to keep her family safe. But she is not selfish. She has done what she can for others. Whenever women come knocking on her door for work and for food, she offers them "*garri* soaked in cold water before telling them she had no work" (285). She puts her resistance in her own way. The day following the air bombing, she goes to the school with sturdy steps and teaches her students the significance of the Biafran flag:

She taught them about the Biafran flag. They sat on wooden planks and the weak morning sun streamed into the roofless class as she unfurled Odenigbo's cloth flag and told them what the symbols meant. Red was the blood of the siblings massacred in the North, black was for mourning them, green was for the prosperity Biafra would have, and, finally, the half of a yellow sun stood for the glorious future (281).

She instils so much of rebelliousness in her students and with such intensity that one of the students Nkiruka declares "I want to kill all the vandals, miss" (281). The purpose of Olanna's vexillology classes is to invoke patriotism and instil national consciousness among children. After doing this, she feels "as if she had finally become an equal participant in the war effort" (267).

As to Olanna's wartime contribution, she along with Mrs. Muokelu, arranges private lessons for children who are taught mathematics, English, civics, and gratis, almost on a daily basis. She is very accommodative, unselfish, and altruistic. She realizes that the children are the future of Biafra. She envisages:

> … how hunger was stealing the memories of the children. She was determined that their minds be kept alert; they were Biafra's future, after all. So every day she taught them under the flame tree, away from the horrible smells towards the back of the buildings. She would have them memorize one line of a poem…. (*HYS* 388-89)

Adichie provides a universal character to the suffering of women in war and depicts the inhumanity and savagery of all wars through the character of Richard, the writer in love with Olanna's sister Kainene. In his book on Nigeria, Richard refers to "the German women who fled Hamburg with the charred bodies of their children stuffed in suitcases, the Rwandan women who pocketed tiny parts of their mauled babies" (81). Later towards the end of the novel, a redhead, while conversing with Richard about the American policy, says: "People are dying in Sudan and Palestine and Vietnam. People are dying everywhere" (374).

Adichie, in the mentioned novel, also unearths another aspect of the whole problematic by exploring the different approaches taken by the rich and the poor women respectively towards war. Poor Igbo women of Abba play active roles with great commitment during the Biafran War while the rich men's wives contribute to the war indirectly. The rich women are afraid of losing their jewellery, but the poor women donate their whole lot to Biafra. There is a moral split among the rich and poor in Abba. Olanna finds it out after she joins women's groups. While she is reluctant to part with her belongings, women who are economically underprivileged donate and sacrifice all they have thereby vindicating the poor Abba women's single-minded purpose and resilience. All this makes Olanna's commitment to Biafra strong. She learns that supporting Odenigbo, who favours Biafra, is equivalent to contributing to the greater cause of Biafra. So, she stands by him as a devoted wife and as a lecturer in Sociology as well.

Cynthia Cockburn in her essay "The Continuum of Violence: A Gendered Perspective on War and Peace" argues that the tendency for war to disrupt everyday life is peculiarly significant for women who in most societies have a traditional responsibility for the daily reproduction in their community lives in ways that are both class and gender-specific. Odenigbo focuses on the wider issues of the nation while Olanna is preoccupied with the domestic realities- making a home, feeding her family, and raising her child: "His eyes saw the future. And so she did not tell him that she grieved for the past, different things on different days, her tablecloths with the silver embroidery, her car, Baby's strawberry cream biscuits" (*HYS* 262).

Olanna thus laments the loss of those objects that had allowed her to take pride in her household. She longs for them not only for herself but also for her daughter, clearly feeling that she has failed in some essential way to be a good mother. That is perhaps the reason why during the hard times of war, Olanna performs the role of a "national actor" (380) by becoming, for small children in the refugee camps, their godmother, educating them about their new yellow Sun i.e, their new country.

Thus, in the wake of the Civil War, the non-combatant civilians, especially women, assume new roles and take on new responsibilities. Unlike the official version of history that has traditionally overlooked, obscured, and ignored women's active participation in the war, Adichie unearths through the instauration of the characters of Olanna and others how non-combatant civilians have contributed much to the shaping of the history of The Nigerian Civil War known as the Biafran War.

Women are the absent warriors who remain at home. One side of war is aggression, destruction, and violence and the other side of war is recompensing these losses. Women have an innate proclivity towards taking care, being kind and protective. So, during the war they remain at home. They take care of the families thereby adding to the strength of those who fight. They take care of health—both physical and mental. They teach and they pacify the aggression. Hence, women are also soldiers, but not in the traditional understanding of the word.

During the Biafran war, Kainene is shown to be another stronghold for her family members and for the Biafran people. She single-handedly manages her father's business with determination and courage. She is "the sort of person who did not need to lean on others" (103). She is affectionate, very supportive, sympathetic, nurturing and enterprising. When she apprehends the fall of Port Harcourt, she buys land at Orlu and builds a house where she invites Richard, Olanna, and her family and safeguards them. Unlike other women who elicit a panic-stricken reaction and response to war, Kainene's reaction to the same and her ensuing shift to Port Harcourt is calm, cool and composed. For her, war is like any other phenomenon, and a part of life: "She was scanning a newspaper and nodding her head to the Beatles on the stereo and she made it seem normal, that war was the inevitable outcome of events and that moving his things from Nsukka was simply as it should be" (*HYS* 175).

Kainene runs a Refugee Camp at Orlu and tends the refugees to provide food and keep them safe from getting harmed. When there is a shortage of supply of garri because the blockage of roads, "Kainene . . . [launches] a Plant Our Own Food movement" (389). She pulls things together in producing foods for the refugees. Olanna is surprised at her enterprise: "When she joined the men and women and children in making ridges, Olanna wondered where she had learned to hold a hoe" (389). Kainene stands up vehemently against the sexual oppression of Reverend Fathers Marcel and Jude at the Refugee Camp and disposes them off. She dispenses her contribution to the war efforts with courage, conviction and determination.

More often, women have to take the financial burden and the responsibility of running the household. For example, when Mrs. Muokelu's husband gets seriously wounded in the battle and loses one leg, she quits teaching in the Primary school and decides to start a business to provide for her family and for her husband's relatives from Abakaliki whom she had sheltered: "My husband has returned from the war front with one leg. What can he do? I am going to start *afia attack* and see if I can buy salt. I can no longer teach" (276).

Olanna witnesses both sides of life during war. She is from a well-to-do family. She had seen the sunny side of life prior to the war; but the war provides her with the opportunity to look at the slimy side of life too. Because she experiences the two sides of life, she goes beyond them and attains a consciousness that has a place for all—both friends and foes.

Whenever someone is in need, Olanna goes beyond herself to help others. When Mama Adanna comes begging for a soup, she gives her half a cup although she has not enough soup. She even gives a tin of sardines and dried milk sent to her by Prof Ezeka for Ananna to be cured of kwashiorkor. She looks at Ugwu not as a houseboy but as someone who has ties of blood with her. When he is forcibly taken by the army, she unhesitatingly leaves no stone unturned for getting him released. Forgetting about Baby, she spends her last money to let him off. Later on, being angered at the carelessness of Ugwu, she says to him: "I bribed that soldier with all the money I have. Now you will produce what I will feed my child" (252).

In "mestiza consciousness" the force of binarism is "swallowed" and "neutralised" (Torres 8). Through Olanna's mediation via her "mestiza consciousness", the binarism between "individual / collective", "Western/ Nigerian", "new" point of view, / "old" point of view, "new elite" / "rural majority" gets balanced. Olanna assimilates binarism, appropriates it and thus disconcerts it through her individual and personal feats.

In the novel, Olanna makes a journey. The Biafran crisis and the crisis of the Igbo community do not narrow Olanna's consciousness, rather expands it. In the beginning. she is concerned about her own cause but in course of the novel she starts devoting herself in the "collective cause" (Vuletic 114). Informed by an inclusive consciousness through which difference and binarism are transgressed, we observe throughout the novel the empathetic agency of Olanna. By and by, she has appropriated the Igbo ways and the contradiction within herself. An illustration of her appropriation is found when she performs the native ritual "*dibia*" which was rubbish and nothing but "supernatural fetish" (*HYS* 105) to her. She laughs at Ugwu whenever he mentions it. But when Kainene goes missing, Olanna takes the help of the "*dibia*" with a hope that it will bring her sister back: "She drove to the River Niger to throw in a copy of Kainene's photo" (433). Again, Olanna has rejected Ugwu who holds that Baby is the reincarnation of her mother: "People just look alike, Ugwu, it doesn't mean they reincarnate" (*HYS* 252). The same Olanna declares towards the end of the novel: "Our people say that we all reincarnate, don't they? *Uwa m, uwa ozo*. When I come back in my next life, Kainene will be my sister" (*HYS* 433). "The shift in Olanna's perception of the present also implies a shift in the historical frames within which she imagines herself" (Vuletic 114).

Ogechukwu A. Ikediugwu in the article "Feminist Inclinations in Chimamanda Ngozi Adichie's *Half of A*

Yellow Sun and *Purple Hibiscus*" has characterized Olanna and Kainene as motherists for their caring, cherishing life-giving nature. Ikediugwu quotes Christine Odi who, after Acholonu, has credited motherists with the following traits:

> A motherist is a defender and protector of family values, seeker of truth and true knowledge, courageous yet humble, loving, tolerant, powerful yet down to earth.... She is one who is willing to protect the natural and cohesive essence of the family, the child, the society and the environment (9).

Women are the binding force between the home and the world. At the time of crisis, they pull themselves, their family, relatives, friends, and the society at large out of the fire. Despite remaining anchored to limited space, they induce a far-reaching impact on the war-devastated society. During the Nigerian Civil War, women concretise motherism that is typical of their gender which allows them to express themselves in a positive and constructivist way during the time of difficulty and to come out of the culturally cocooned space in which they are conventionally posited. Their pluralistic consciousness, or "mestiza consciousness" thus cuts across class and gender hierarchies and nestles all, irrespective of their differences.

Chapter III

Racism and Beyond: A Study of *Americanah* & *The Bones of Grace*

This chapter divided into two sections concerns two novels – Chimamanda Adichie's *Americanah* (2013) & Tahmima Anam's *The Bones of Grace* (2016). Both the novels can be put in the category of "migrant bildungsroman" as in both these texts, the lead characters migrate to places other than their birthplaces for academic purposes and wade through distinct phenomena centering around issues like racism and ethnicity. During their stay abroad, they learn many important things about racism and return home with inculcated senses of utter disillusionment.

The discussion in the first section of this chapter is on Adichie's *Americanah*. In the novel, the protagonist Ifemelu gets exposed to racist discrimination in the USA; the discrimination is nothing but an essentialist construct, a discourse of 'othering' by which the White Europeans generate the racist ideology to establish their ethnic superiority over the nonwhites. Based on their presumptuous sense of superiority, they stratify mankind into the divisive categories of white/black, superior/inferior, lucky/unlucky, creamy/non-creamy and many more. Ifemelu is from Africa. In her native land, no one tells her that she is inferior because she is black. She grows up in a race-less society—a society where the American form of racism is conspicuous by its absence. Ifemelu's identity that is formed in Africa is challenged and goes through a series of negotiations and transformations when she arrives to study in the USA. At home, her identity was independent; but in the USA, it becomes dependent in the sense that the whites tell her who she is. She identity and persona are defined and established by the whites. Her 'self' is delimited, demarcated, and circumscribed by them. In such a precarious scenario, she experiences the "peculiar sensation, the double-consciousness, the sense of always looking at the self through the eyes of others" (Du Bois 3). She finds ways "to attain self-conscious humanhood, to merge [her] double self into a better and truer self" (Du Bois 3). Finally, she rejects her duality and returns home.

Tahmima Anam's *The Bones of Grace* is discussed in the second section of this chapter. The novel moves beyond race, but hinges on the question of identity. The lead character Zubaida Bashir is from Bangladesh who comes to the USA for her study and becomes a fossil expert. Initially, she has faced the problem to socialize. But she overcomes it and settles in the new setting as she makes more friends. She has a little problem with the alien culture and vice versa. The source of her problem is she herself. She has been harboring a deep crisis since her mother has told her that she is an adopted child. Zubaida has many historical counterparts e.g. Aristotle who, according to one of Zubaida's friends, was also adopted. But this does not alleviate Zubaida's crisis. It motivates Zubaida to look after her real identity, and at the end of the novel, while at home, she gets to know her real identity. She learns that she is not at all princess Zubaida. Rather, she is born to an ill-fated and destitute mother. The novel lays bare the contours of the shaping and making of one's identity which takes place in a complex process. Structured in an epistolary fashion and narrated with "humanising prose", the novel books and brackets different episodes in the life of Zubaida — going away from home, falling in love with Elijah, taking part in the fossil dig of a "walking whale", returning home, marriage with Rashid, discovery of her true identity etc. And in a prolix scale, the novel presents the peculiar precarity of Zubaida's condition.

Ifemelu's Dialogue with Racism and Her take on it in *Americanah*

> "...if you're white, you' re all right; if you' re brown, stick around; if you' re black, get back!"
>
> (*Americanah* 163).

This popular rhyme is quoted by Ifemelu in *Americanah* and it depicts the place the Black people have in the American social hierarchy which the present chapter strives to discuss. This chapter showcases Adichie's novel *Americanah* and endeavours to comprehend the "dried-in-the- raisin" and the endlessly "deferred dreams" of the Africans, or to be more particular, of the Nigerians in America. The novel depicts racial discrimination and organized subjection of the 'other' in the U.S. via the experience of the lead character Ifemelu whose blog is the chronotope of the experience of African-Americans. The blog is the expression of racial exploitation, the mindset of the racists, and is a dialogic receptacle where the heterogeneous experience of racism is thoroughly explored.

Racism has been defined by The OED Supplement

(1982) as "the theory that distinctive human characteristics and abilities are determined by race". As per the record of *The OED Supplement* (1982), its first advent in the English language takes place in the 1930s.

Racism falsely assumes, and institutionalizes practices, and internalizes the idea that color determines quality, and that the white is superior and the black is inferior. The darker one's skin is, the more wretched she or he is. Onyeka F. Iwuchukwu in the article, "Racism and Identity in Onwueme's *Riot in Heaven*" aptly puts:

> Racism is a concept and practice of discrimination whereby a particular race assumes a position of superiority when treating the other race as inferior or less human: while this may be understood as commonplace, it remains a fact that the most often practice of racism is White superiority where Blackness determines inferiority (Iwachukwu 7).

Robert Miles and Malcolm Brown in their book *Racism* argue that the actual meaning and use of the term 'racism' ensues from the concurrence of two vital proceedings. The first, according to them, is "the growing body of scientific evidence that undermined the idea of 'races' as natural, discrete, and fixed subdivisions of the human species" (59) and the second is the historic "reaction to the rise of Fascism in Germany" (59). The racist ideology, though had its presence in earlier times, was however rampantly perpetuated and legitimized by Hitler and the German Nazis through their categorical "identification of Jews as an alien and inferior 'race'" (59).

Race and racism are fictions without having any biological and scientific legitimacy. They are rather the social and moral phenomena inherent in stereotypical attributes and imaginings. Even when we use the very words race and racism, the words presuppose an unquestionable validity of their existence. Richard John Perry in the Preface to *"Race" and Racism the Development of Modern Racism in America* quotes C. Loring Brace, according to whom, race is a four-letter word that "is not only a useless concept but also is positively pernicious" (ix).

Race is a natural given whereas racism is a biological construct. Following this argument, one can say that race is like sex—natural or biological. Hence, the race of an African is different from that of an Australian or an American. There should exist genetic differences among an African, an Asian, an Australian, or an American. They are indeed biologically different. But racism is not like race. Racism is like gender—a social construct and a discriminatory practice based on skin colour. According to racism, one's genetic fabric does not designate one's race; his or her skin colour does. In racism, skin colour becomes the ultimate yardstick of measuring men and women. Racism is the 'artifact' that is considered to be the 'fact'. Racism is –

> The clustering of people on the ground of physiognomy or physical characteristics for the purpose of social apartheid is very much a cultural crop, the production of a particular cultural background. It is part of a mindset, an axiomatic position that is based on the wrong assumption that biological 'race' is real. (Perry 2)

Racism is the "tar baby" which sticks to our mind and from which it is difficult to escape. The term, "tar baby" became popular through *Uncle Remus* by Joel Chandler

Harris. It means "something from which it is nearly impossible to extricate oneself" (*Merriam-Webster* 77).

Racism is a kind of oppression. With all other figures of oppression, racism too shares a common thread; it occurs both on the individual and institutional level. Though the whites are against racism, they still enjoy some institutional benefits as a dominant group that other colored minor groups do not have. The government, the workplace, schools, and such other institutions endow the whites with some added advantages which are called 'white privilege':

> It's true that white supremacists, as well as white trash, sometimes and perhaps often think, say, and do viciously racist things. But so do good middle-class white people, and that is the point. There are no saints to be found. White liberals are just better at pretending that there are. (Sullivan 58)

Quite relevantly, racism has been defined by Robin DiAngelo in *What Does It Mean to Be White? Developing White Racial Literacy* (2016) as:

> A form of oppression in which one racial group dominates others. In the United States the dominant group is white, therefore racism is white racial and cultural prejudice and discrimination, supported intentionally or unintentionally by institutional power and authority, and used to the advantage of white people and disadvantage of people of color (108).

Each human being possesses unique characteristics or oneness that smacks of his individuality. No two human beings are the carbon copies of each other in all aspects. So, the human difference is infallible and absolute and the human variation indeed comes up with almost boundless prospects for branding distinctions. However, the human distinction is arbitrary, erroneously erratic in a scenario where the human beings, groups, or categories of people are judged solely on the basis of social and physical yardsticks.

Broadly speaking, racism is a form of 'othering,' a social shaping of individuals into categorized subjects, the process of identifying and discriminating fellow human beings on their outward difference.

Chimamanda Ngozi Adiche, a globally acclaimed novelist, shifted to the U.S. from Nigeria, and her athletic, vigorous writing in her *Americanah* (2013) "explores what it means to be African, and what it means to be African-American, with extraordinary depth" (Reese 2018). Adichie in her discussion with David Remnick on "On Facing Racism in America" in The New Yorker Festival in 2017 remarks that "America is a country that is steeped in racism" and when she "she steps out into the world, into the American world", she is indeed "stepping out into racism" (NYF 8).

Issues of racism have been addressed in many American texts. There are multiple examples: for instance, Samuel Langhorne Clemens' *Adventures of Huckleberry Finn*, Chloe Anthony Wofford Morrison's *Paradise* are hotbeds of racism. What sets Adichie's "uncompromising new" novel *Americanah* apart is its unambiguous and uncompromising portrayal of the hidden undercurrent of racism in the sophisticated façade of American democracy and her thoroughgoing depiction of the African women's experience and handling of racism and its effects through the inculcation of what I have categorically called in this book as the 'mestiza consciousness'. In her depiction of racism, Adichie is neither 'pretentious' nor 'selective' like many other Black fiction writers of the past and the present; rather she is vigorous and direct in her unearthing of the clandestinely racist undercurrents of the American society. In her interview with Chitra Ramaswamy, she states categorically that she is well aware of the 'rules' and 'tropes' of writing about race, but does not follow them. During the interview, she further makes the following relevant remark:

> Writing about race should be lyrical and poetic and never quite definite. Very Proustian. And at the end the reader should feel exactly the same as they felt at the start. That's the way to do race in literary fiction. I could have done that, written a safer book. The reviews would have been better. People wouldn't be complaining. But I wanted it to be true (Ramaswamy 17).

However, although the subject matter of her writing is of preeminent importance, her treatment of the theme is engagingly cool, fluffy, and lightweight. While reading the novel, we feel heavily concerned and at the same time cannot but laugh at times.

Americanah reconnoitres the Nigerian immigrant Ifemelu's experience as a student in the USA—a Nigerian female student who comes there with and all-inclusive and cosmopolitan consciousness, yet has to affront the racial constraints. Being an immigrant, she has to encounter and confront the preponderances of race and racism while meeting with both Americans and non-Americans. What emerges through her trials and tribulations is a biting satire of the American society and in this context, critic Raboteau comments: "*Americanah* is social satire masquerading as romantic comedy" (2013). The trajectory of romance and race crisscross in the novel. But the novel is exclusively centred on romance and love, but its dimensions extend towards the broader concerns of racism as critic Akbar comments: "Ifemelu and Obinze's romantic trajectory offers the book a formal structure but it is Adichie's exploration of race and migration that is its heart" (Akbar 89).

The title *Americanah* is a slang used in Lagos to refer to those Nigerians who return to Nigeria with an American spell and American hangover. The novel studies the experience of the home-returned immigrants in both the overt and covert racist fabric of the American society and thoroughly exposes the racists in America. The novel sportively narrates multiple layers of racism that operate beneath the sophisticated and civilised façade of the American social fabric.

The title also indicates the "borderland consciousness" of Ifemelu . She is neither a Nigerian nor an American but a synbook of the two. Ifemelu has neutralised the psychological trauma of racism by constructively resisting it and "by holding onto cherished values from her Nigerian background while identifying with the vibe of her new American society" (Amonyeze 3). This synbook is not merely "adaptive biculturalism" (Amonyeze 3) but an acceleration of Ifemelu's "mestiza consciousness" which gets largely projected onto her blog.

Gloria Anzaldua declares that "mestizos are a synergy of two cultures" (63). As a mestizo, Ifemelu is a "liminal individual" who is "neither here nor there; they are betwixt and between" (qtd. in Amonyeze 5). She struggles to reconciliate with the strange ways of racism, goes through "fluctuating loyalties", and finally, "grapples fully with the conflict" (Yerima 4). She declines to be pinned down to stereotypes of racial othering. Blessed with "mestiza consciousness", Ifemelu poses a challenge to the ideology of racism and overcomes the constraints of culture. Adichie through her persona and through her fictional representation seeks "to create fresh memories and secure a new place in history" (Amonyeze 6).

At the beginning of *Americanah*, Ifemelu—a newcomer to the US—once goes for shopping with her Nigerian childhood friend Ginika, who is accustomed to the ways of the world in the USA. During her payment at the counter, she asks the cashier whether the name of the salesgirl who helped her is Chelcy or Jennifer. The cashier enquires: "Was it the one with long hair? . . . The one with dark hair?" (126). Thereupon, Ifemelu gets surprised: "Why didn't she just ask 'Was it the black girl or the white girl?' (126). Her friend answers with a laugh: "Because this is America. You're supposed to pretend that you don't notice certain things" (127).

Hair in the novel becomes signifier of one's ethnicity and identity, and hence a crucial determiner in identity politics. That hair is integrally wedded to one's identity and that Adichie is tied up in knots with hair is underscored from the very opening pages of the novel. Towards the very beginning of the novel, Ifemelu has to head for Princeton from Trenton for braiding her hair as "It was unreasonable to expect a braiding salon in Princeton—the few black locals she had seen were so light-skinned and lank-haired she could not imagine them wearing braids" (*Americanah* 8).

Ifemelu's sojourn from Nigeria to the USA and from Trenton to Princeton brings her close to the day-to-day experience of racial discrimination of the blacks in the USA, particularly the migrants. Moving from a region and place where race is not at all a big 'issue' to a place where race is a seminal issue, Ifemelu tries hard to put aside her asymmetries as she realizes that her usual "dark kinky hair" is neither classy nor fair. She crosses the path with "racism as a structure, that is, as a network of social relations at social, political, economic, and ideological levels that shapes the life chances of the various races" (Bonilla-Silva 39).

The journey is extremely vital and decisive for Ifemelu as it opens avenues to the dynamics and the "polyphony" of race discourses in America. While on the train, Ifemelu makes acquaintance with a white man who sits still next to her. According to him, there too much razzmatazz about race: "Race is totally overhyped these days, black people need to get over themselves, it's all about class now, the haves and the have-nots" (*Americanah* 11). This view of the white man is used by Ifemelu in her blog. She draws on it in the starting sentence of a post named "Not All Dreadlocked White American Guys Are Down".

On the way from Princeton to Trenton, she meets a man who says: "Ever write about adoption? Nobody wants black babies in this country, and I don't mean biracial, I mean black. Even the black families don't want them" (9). He tells her that he and his wife had adopted a black child and their neighbours looked at them as though they had chosen to become martyrs for a dubious cause (*Americanah* 9). It is hard to imagine that the babies who are yet to see the light of the earth are not free from the nasty entanglements of racial hatred. The situation is so hostile that people are afraid of adopting black babies.

Everybody believes America to be the land of bliss and promise but Ifemelu finds that it is not so at least for the blacks: "'It's wonderful but it's not heaven'" (122). She finds it hard to get a two-bit job though she possesses the necessary skill and qualification. A restaurant refuses to hire her for the position of a hostess. Even the job of a babysitter is denied to her for some unknown reason. Ifemelu finally figures out that it is her skin color that becomes her actual impairment.

Ifemelu's experience as an émigré approximates Adichie's own familiarity with the experience of going away from Nigeria at the age of 19 to take admission in a college in the US. Ifemelu comes out of Nigeria for 13 years; but in case of Adichie, it was four. Critic Raboteau writes: "Having spent a good chunk of time living in America as an adult and being a hawkeyed observer of manners and distinctions in class, Adichie is uniquely positioned to compare racial hierarchies in the United States to social striving in her native Nigeria" (2013). Regarding the racial discrimination of African women in America, critic Crenshaw writes: "Because of their intersectional identity as both women and of color within discourses that are shaped to respond to one or the other, women of color are marginalized within both" (Crenshaw 98).

Shan, the sister of Ifemelu's boyfriend bellows her complaint on the difficulty the Black writers face in America: "You can't write an honest novel about race in this country. Black writers... have two choices, they can do precious or they can do pretentious" (*Americanah* 292). Quite contrary to the declamation of Shan, Adichie's novel is devoted to the deliberation of race and "is neither precious nor pretentious, though it is polemical in its angriest moments, and satirical at its best" (Akbar 77).

However, Adichie herself confesses: "Talking about race in the US, it very easily becomes about demonising" (Brockes 2018). A prime example is Mrs. Kimberley who despite being a "a liberal, well-meaning American and so well-meaning that she doesn't know how to deal with race" (Brockes 2018) is miscomprehended to be a racist. She takes Ifemelu into confidence and offers her the babysitting job.

It is due to her lack of sensitivity to the issue of race she is misunderstood.

Racism effectuates in the disintegration of the self, results in low morale, disorientation, and distress. *Americanah* chronicles a newly developed 'racial consciousness' in Ifemelu who stands against it, discover herself anew, recovers from the shocks of daily, eye-opening racial encounters, asserts herself full-fledged and ultimately, returns home frustrated. In the face of the tons of pressure, she does not let herself in the flow, keeps her head up against systematic and collective oppression. She does not leave the ground as long as she has been in the USA. In an interview with Lisa Allardice, Adichie appreciates this do-not-give-up spirit of women: "I do see in women a sense that 'We're done, this is it ... No.' and it gives me hope" (Allardice 67).

The novel is an exegesis of racism in US society. *Americanah* is, indeed an "honest novel about race…with guts and lustre" (Evans 05). We the readers get an African perspective on race and can have a defamiliarised rendering of the society in the West. The novel takes exception to the reader's outlook on race as it wholesomely displays the structures of "new racism"—a term conceived by Martin Barker "to capture how racism has adapted over time so that modern norms, policies, and practices result in similar racial outcomes as those in the past, while not appearing to be explicitly racist" (DiAngelo 51). Adichie explains this new form of racism in an interview with Synne Rifbjerg in 2014 at Copenhagen:

> Race is the major organizing principle of American history and American life, really, and it is the one thing that Americans are most uncomfortable about. It is a subject that they circle around. It is a subject that

> they invent codes to talk about. It is a subject that I think is still very unfinished. It is a subject that many Americans prefer to think that it has to do with the past, but it is very much the present and I think it is also the most misunderstood, the most pretentiously contentious social subject in America (Rifbjerg 60).

The whites are of the view that there are hardly any racists and that racial bias has ceased to exist "since the 1960s, and that most whites are color blind" (Bonilla-Silva 39). The novel interrogates the euphoria that rises in a society marked by the apparent absence of the so-called racial discrimination. This euphoria was on its highest point when in 2008, Barack Obama got elected as President of the United States of America.

Obama in the novel represents non-binarism. He is at the same time 'Caucasian', 'African', 'African-American' and 'Asian'. He stands for the confluence of culture. He "being a metisor, a hybrid of cultures gives a fillip to the quest for an amalgam of cultures and the evolvement of a new cultural outlook that unites all" (Akingbe 43). The novel showcases the upsurge of this euphoria in Manhattan in the following lines:

> Obama supporters who were dewy-eyed with wine and victory, a balding white man said, "Obama will end racism in this country," and a large-hipped, stylish poet from Haiti agreed, nodding, her Afro bigger than Ifemelu's, and said she had dated a white man for three years…. (*Americanah* 253).

The positive anticipation regarding the end of racism turns out to be bald and bare. The unprecedented euphoria in America that Obama's coming to power in the White House will stop the existing, miasmatic, and epizootic social curse of racism in America is stripped of truth. Ifemelu immediately replies that it is a lie. The only reason people keep saying this is to "comfort others". The truth is, to use the remarkable words of W.E.B. Du Bois from his *The Souls of Black Folk,* that "the problem of the Twentieth Century is the problem of the color-line" (5). The novel dismantles the illusion that American society has successfully cleansed itself of racism after Obama becomes the President.

The American White people practice a "new racism" that is the clandestine and subtle form of racism that emerges after the Civil Rights Movement. It is racism without being racist. It is the falsified hypobook that racism does not exist at all. It is the assumption that if one does not talk about racism, it does not exist. Adichie shows how racism persists, percolates, guises, and takes insinuating forms and becomes conspicuous by its apparent absence. Americans pretend that racism has ended and look the other way, as if, they cannot see how it has a huge part in their society. *Americanah* displays before us the American safari of a budding Nigerian neophyte, Ifemelu, who runs into and gets to know the subliminal racial structures in America that is perennially hidden beneath the artificial and sophisticated fabric of the long-cherished American democracy. When the novel ends, Ifemelu does clearly enunciate the way and how racism operates in the USA.

We get a hint of the neo-racism or the new kind of racism in Ifemelu's post, "Job Vacancy in America – National Arbiter in Chief of "Who Is Racist"":

> In America, racism exists but racists are all gone. Racists belong to the past. Racists are the thin-lipped mean white people in the

> movies about the civil rights era. Here's the thing: the manifestation of racism has changed but the language has not. So if you haven't lynched somebody then you can't be called a racist. If you're not a bloodsucking monster, then you can't be called a racist. Somebody has to be able to say that racists are not monsters. They are people with loving families, regular folk who pay taxes. Somebody needs to get the job of deciding who is racist and who isn't. Or maybe it's time to just scrap the word "racist." Find something new. Like Racial Disorder Syndrome. And we could have different categories for sufferers of this syndrome: mild, medium, and acute (275).

In "So What's the Deal?" Ifemelu puts forward the propagated belief among the white people that race is but a construct. But the stereotypical representation of Black people as evil carriers of diseases and infections is still indelible in their imagination:

> They tell us race is an invention, that there is more genetic variation between two black people than there is between a black person and a white person. Then they tell us black people have a worse kind of breast cancer and get more fibroids. And white folk get cystic fibrosis and osteoporosis. So what's the deal, doctors in the house? Is race an invention or not? (264)

Ifemelu unearths the underlying hypocrisy, the hiatus between theory and practice. It is highly ironic that those who proclaim that race and racism do not exist, end in practicing racism. The question seeks to expose the duality and to subvert the methodized, institutionalized mould of thought about the Blacks.

What the Americans practice is "aversive racism" (Gaertner 377). It is a new-fangled, covert, subtle, implicit and often unconscious kind of racism that is evidenced on an individual level; it is different from traditional racism that manifest through overt, conscious, and ostensible discriminations and is generally evidenced at collective or institutional levels. Those whose attitude smacks of aversive racism see themselves as liberals and well- educated; they do not empathize but sympathize with the sufferers of old times and uphold the doctrine of fraternity, equality; but in reality, they foster aversion to the blacks and races other than white. Their expression of aversion is very discriminating, insinuating, and subtle and is akratic in the sense that they act against their better judgment.

According to Adichie, there is a memorable racist episode in chapter 16 of *Americanah*. Ifemelu has been babysitting in the household of Mrs. Kimberley and her husband Don. While Kimberley and Don are not at home, a carpet cleaner arrives. But the moment he sees Ifemelu, a black woman, he gives a typical racist reaction: "He stiffened when he saw her. First surprise flitted over his features, then it ossified to hostility" (*Americanah* 146). The moment he comes to know that Mrs. Kimberley Turner is the owner of the house and the black girl Ifemelu is a low-grade domestic help in the Turner household, the previous reaction disappears. Ifemelu observes "the swift disappearance of his hostility. His face sank into a grin. She, too, was the help. The universe was once again arranged as it should be" (*Americanah* 147). Adichie herself had to face the same embarrassing situation when she worked as a babysitter in a well-to-do family in the outskirts of Philadelphia:

> I remember opening the door and his face was such a cliché; he looked at me and his whole face fell. You know: I can't believe I'm working for a black person. And he had such an attitude. And then when I said, 'Mrs. So and So said you were coming', he changed and suddenly was my friend. (Brockes 98)

The glaring reality about race and partisanship in America becomes manifest in an argument among Georgina, Emenike, and Alexa. Emenike strikes the right note when she says: "It seemed to me that in America blacks and whites work together but don't play together, and here blacks and whites play together but don't work together" (*Americanah* 241). The conversation moves to a comparative analysis of class and race in America and other countries and Obinze picks up on it: "A white boy and a black girl who grow up in the same working-class town in this country can get together and the race will be secondary, but in America, even if the white boy and black girl grow up in the same neighborhood, the race would be primary" (*Americanah* 241).

The novel shows that even in the wake of globalization, post-racist, and post-Obama times, the American society is still a color-blind one. In their "social imaginary" (James 33), they have not shut the door on racial discrimination. Ifemelu proves this in the following passionate and intensely cutting rejoinder to a California guy in Manhattan:

> The only reason you say that race was not an issue is that you wish it was not. We all wish it was not. But it's a lie. I came from a

country where the race was not an issue; I did not think of myself as black and I only became black when I came to America. When you are black in America and you fall in love with a white person, race doesn't matter when you're alone together because it's just you and your love. But the minute you step outside, race matters. But we don't talk about it. We don't even tell our white partners the small things that piss us off and the things we wish they understood better, because we're worried they will say we're overreacting, or we're being too sensitive (*Americanah* 254).

The dual or manifold consciousness of the Afro-Americans has beautifully been captured by W.E.B. Du Bois in his theorization of double consciousness. The Afro-Americans "ever feels his two-ness, — an American, a Negro; two souls, two thoughts, two unreconciled strivings; two warring ideals in one dark body, whose dogged strength alone keeps it from being torn asunder" (Du Bois 2). It is true that Ifemelu is caught in a double situation, double identity and double consciousness: "Uneasy in a club of other "Nigerpolitan" returnees who pine for paninis and good customer service, she's the quintessential outsider — or in other words, an artist. In America she was black. Back in Nigeria, she's an Americanah" (Raboteau 09). But this doubleness does not "dedouble" or fragment her identity and her consciousness. It will be wrong to say that Ifemelu is stuck eternally in her doubleness. She makes a decision in the end of the novel and comes home.

Ifemelu's chancing upon "apartheid" experience and sectarianism as an African becomes a site for Adichie to delve into and elaborate the evolving discourse on racism in America. In Ifemelu's consciousness, the discourse of racism takes on a cheeky and saucy cast that gives the third degree to America's so-called liberalism. Ifemelu came to the USA with her eyes and frame of mind sweepingly open and was shocked to realize that it is in contrast to her homeland. Ifemelu puts under the microscope various aspects of racial issues in her lifestyle blog that she writes anonymously called "Raceteenth or Various Observations About American Blacks (Those Formerly Known as Negroes) by a Non-American Black". Ifemelu's questioning of the racial customs in America via her blog and her intervening involvement with the existing social mores in America opens, in the words of Bernard Ayo Oniwe, "a possibility for challenging the implicit promise of the post-prejudicial world due to the influence of globalization" (70).

Ifemelu speaks dauntlessly on the subject of racism partially because she discourses from the vantage point of an outsider. She is not the 'always-already' black subject in the USA. Racism with its tooth and claw is yet to be ideologically inculcated in her consciousness. She originates from a place where the race is not an issue: "I came from a country where race was not an issue; I did not think of myself as black and I only became black when I came to America" (Adichie 290).

Ifemelu perceives succinctly the brusque, easy-going and offhand nature of racism in daily life in the company of Curt who being white does not 'see' but takes a gander of things. Curt only spots racism that is open-and-shut and conspicuous. He is a guy who can "grasp one thing" but can be "tone-deaf about another similar thing" (*Americanah* 255). Once an Asian woman in a spa has refused to shape the eyebrow of Ifemelu because they "don't do curly" (289).

Curt has threatened the manager of the spa that he would shut the place down. While Curt stands by Ifemelu, he is oblivious of the fact that he indulges in chauvinism and a different kind of racism. Ifemelu takes the edge off and brings Curt around: "Maybe they've never done a black woman's eyebrows and so they think it's different, because our hair is different, after all, but I guess now she knows the eyebrows are not that different" (*Americanah* 256).

In Part 4 of the novel, Ifemelu experiences many examples of everyday racism in the company of her white boyfriend, Curt. From almost every white person–common white people on the street, friends, and acquaintances of Curt, the host of the restaurant, "the owner of the bed-and-breakfast in Montreal", the aunt and the mother of Curt, Ifemelu receives ill-favoured and unwelcome responses. When Curt introduces her to his friends as his girlfriend, they look surprised and give her the "why her" look (290). For them Cut has chosen the wrong girl. Only a white-skinned girl can be the girlfriend of a white-skinned boy. They do not understand why Curt has picked a black girl. Earlier, a white woman saw Ifemelu's " hand clasped in Curt's" and the white woman hid her face with the palm of her hand, as if , it was a shameful sight and gave "the look of people confronting a great tribal loss" (*Americanah* 256). For them, in the company of a black girl, Curt has lost the purity of whiteness. When Curt clasps Ifemelu, kisses her, and introduces her at the party, everyone gives strange and funny looks: "The looks had begun to pierce her skin. She was tired even of Curt's protection, tired of needing protection" (*Americanah* 256). Ifemelu gets the same surprise when Curt takes him to Vermont to visit his aunt, Claire who overenthusiastically talks about "Kenyan safari, about Mandela's grace, about her adoration for Harry Belafonte

...to over-assure that she likes black people" (*Americanah* 256). Even when she is introduced to Curt's mother, she gives her the ""Why her?" looks"" (290). She glances at Ifemelu and gives her the look, as if, Ifemelu should be grateful enough to her as she is liberal enough to allow her to the household: "She mumbled that some people were still looking for reasons to complain even though America was now color-blind" (*Americanah* 256). Curt's mother goes even one step further when she "shot an eyebrow-raise of accusation at Ifemelu, as though to say she knew very well who had turned her son into a pathetic race warrior" (*Americanah* 256).

With Curt, Ifemelu has strange experiences of racism without the whites being overt racists. While reading a copy in Ifemelu's apartment called *Essence*, Curt makes a biased comment that the magazine solely features black woman: ""This magazine's kind of racially skewed"" (*Americanah* 257). To prove Curt and his kind wrong, Ifemelu almost hauls him to the bookstore at Inner Harbor, showing him copies of many women's magazines and also showing him how in thousand pages of those magazines, only three to four women have featured. And quite interestingly "all of them are biracial or racially ambiguous, so they could also be Indian or Puerto Rican or something. Not one of them is dark" (*Americanah* 258), and none of them is as black as Ifemelu. Ifemelu fuming, raging, and seething inside himself, pops the question, "Now, let's talk about what is racially skewed" (*Americanah* 258). On the same day in the evening, Ifemelu composes an e-mail to Wambui reflecting on "digging, questioning, unearthing" (293) the incident at the bookstore about the magazines, things she did not open up before Curt, "things unsaid and unfinished" (293).

Ifemelu's friend Wambui's positive reply to her

email encouraged her to get going with a blog so that the "raw and true" (293) observations of Ifemelu can extend to more and more people whose stories of racial victimization has gone unheard. Ifemelu "longed for other listeners, and she longed to hear the stories of others. How many other people chose silence? How many other people had become black in America? How many had felt as though their world was wrapped in gauze?" (*Americanah* 258). Though she is new to the world of blogs, she takes it on and subscribes to Word Press, and her blog, *Raceteenth or Curious Observations by a Non-American Black on the Subject of Blackness in America* comes into being.

Adichie's protagonist becomes a blogger and the blog Adichie brings into existence for Ifemelu in the novel evinces both Adichie's and Ifemelu's tenacious allegiance to the political and social causes. Adichie mentions the kick behind interpolating the personal website of Ifemelu: "I wanted this novel to also be social commentary, but I wanted to say it in ways that are different from what one is supposed to say in literary fiction" (Guarracino 2). Ifemelu sets the blog going as a whatchamacallit leeway for projecting her experiences of the everyday reality and to come across with her observations on the discriminatory practices like racism she experiences as a "female flaneur" (Elkin 2016). In the essay, "Afropolitanism as Critical Consciousness: Chimamanda Ngozi Adichie's and Teju Cole's Internet Presence" it is fairly observed, "It negotiates the hierarchization of cultures and criticizes the white-centeredness of the US environment depicted in the novel, and chronicles everyday incidents of racism" (Coetzee 39).

Blogs are considered to be a biased, one-sided, and non-interactive platform. A blog does not just present a list of references or associations rather pose a personal perspective. One of the key problems is how to keep this perspective neutral when it narrates other's perspective. Ifemelu's Blog is a straightforward online dairy, linking one's thought to others with unwittingly witty effects that are almost impossible in other known media. Her blog becomes a deictic and synecdochic platform, establishing an association with many social, cultural, and personal quotations. The speaker/writer breaks social dictums stealthily and implies many implied propositions as purposed by her.

The true makings of the blogosphere (and other computer-mediated communication) lie in undercutting the taken-for-granted fabrics of ideas. One positive side is that it immediately gives access to the given situation and the immediate access creates a difference in how one reads. We 'surf' that is we do not dive deep and do not scan the text of a blog. We are carried casually and sparsely across the sea of references. The blogger does not always call a spade a spade but leaves it opens to us to adjudge for ourselves.

The blogs link various incidents and emotions, texts, and contexts and tell us more of what is already known to us. Ifemelu's blog is a sort of hypertext providing extensive references to the discourse of racism associated with ideas related to it. It provides us a mental graph and the thought waves of Ifemelu, the African Americans, and of Americans mainly on racism.

For Ifemelu, blog is a dynamic and democratic space in the sense that it brings all together irrespective of class, caste, creed, gender, and race. Through it, she can make sense of the present situation, the here and the now. "Race entraps, beguiles and bewilders her because it's an imaginary construct with actual consequences" (Raboteau 56). Through Ifemelu's vantage point in the blog, we achieve a vantage point and come to think of a world in which we all – the texts and the contexts, the subject, and the object are integrally interrelated. Her blog thus coalesces different ways, discourses, locations and structures of power on to the same surface.

In "Raceteenth," Ifemelu's tone is cocky and point blank. She observes with gut sensitivity, and dispassion. A crumb from her entry entitled, "To My Fellow Non-American Blacks: In America, You Are Black, Baby" proves the point:

> Dear Non-American Black, when you make the choice to come to America, you become black. Stop arguing. Stop saying I'm Jamaican or I'm Ghanaian. America doesn't care. So what if you weren't "black" in your country? You're in America now. We all have our moments of initiation into the Society of Former Negroes. Mine was in a class in undergrad when I was asked to give the black perspective, only I had no idea what that was. So I just made something up. And admit it — you say "I'm not black" only because you know black is at the bottom of America's race ladder. And you want none of that. Don't deny now. What if being black had all the privileges of being white? Would you still say "Don't call me black, I'm from Trinidad?" I didn't think so. So you're black, baby. (193)

"Raceteenth" is not merely an inventory of "Various Observations" (11). There is more than meets the eye. It is, as if, a balance sheet of expostulations and grievances. It is an observatory sketch of race relations and dynamics of racism from the point of view of one who has eye-witnessed racism in America. Besides needling the state of affairs, it highlights the purport of complying with it. The blog discovers the art of maintaining solidarity among the blacks in America and the art of living among the whites. Such an example is this post: "You must nod back when a black person nods at you in a heavily white area. It is called the black nod. It is a way for black people to say, "You are not alone, I am here too"" (221). The art of living among the whites is best expressed in the following post:

> If you are in an Ivy League college and a Young Republican tells you that you only got in because of Affirmative Action, do not whip out your perfect grades from high school. Instead, gently point out that the biggest beneficiaries of Affirmative Action are white women (194).

Ifemelu's exhortations and prescription can be placed at the disposal of the whites too. The post named "Friendly Tips for the American Non-Black: How to React to an American Black Talking About Blackness," talks about the way the whites should speak about race:

> Dear American Non-Black, if an American Black person is telling you about an experience about being black, please do not eagerly bring up examples from your own life. Don't say "It's just like when I ..." You have suffered. Everyone in the world has suffered. But you have not suffered precisely because you are an American Black. Don't be quick to find alternative explanations for what happened. Don't say, "Oh, it's not really race, it's class. Oh it's not race,

it's gender. Oh, it's not race, it's the cookie monster." You see, American Blacks don't WANT it to be race. They would rather not have racist shit happen. So maybe when they say something is about race, it's maybe because it actually is? …. Don't preface your response with "One of my best friends is black" because it makes no difference and nobody cares and you can have a black best friend and still do racist shit and it's probably not true anyway, the "best" part not the "friend" part….Don't say it's just like antisemitism. It's not. In the hatred of Jews, there is also the possibility of envy — they are so clever, these Jews, they control everything, these Jews — and one must concede that a certain respect, however grudging, accompanies envy. In the hatred of American Blacks, there is no possibility of envy — they are so lazy, these blacks, they are so unintelligent, these blacks. (284)

Does it dig at the Blacks in America? Is it self-reflexive? Is it iconoclastic and tongue-in-cheek? Does it sound all-seeing and all-knowing? The answer is that the clout of this sardonic, brusque weisenheiming does not make any definite statement. The meaning of it will vary from person to person.

In the blog "Understanding America for the Non-American Black: American Tribalism" Ifemelu elaborates tribalism as a "racist label imposed on non-western populations" (*Sociology of Race* n.p.) which "is a negative reference to groups seen as inferior and insular that resist and oppose other forms of organization and political authority claimed as legitimate and found in nation-states...." (*Sociology of Race*). She elaborates:

> In America, tribalism is alive and well. There are four kinds—class, ideology, region, and race. First, class. Pretty easy. Rich folk and poor folk. Second, ideology. Liberals and conservatives....Third, region. The North and the South. Finally, race. There's a ladder of racial hierarchy in America. White is always on top, specifically White Anglo-Saxon Protestant, otherwise known as WASP, and American Black is always on the bottom, and what's in the middle depends on time and place. (Or as that marvelous rhyme goes: if you're white, you're all right; if you're brown, stick around; if you're black, get back!)... You see, in America's ladder of races, Jewish is white but also some rungs below white....The longer you are here, the more you start to get it. (*Americanah* 163)

"Blogging reveals to what extent Ifemelu will eventually be capable of reflecting upon the dialectic of racial oppression" (Cruz-Gutierrez 257). In Ifemelu's entry, "A Michelle Obama Shout-Out Plus Hair as Race Metaphor" she states that hair is "the perfect metaphor for race in America" (294). "Coarse, coily, kinky, or curly"(294) hair is characteristic of the black woman; these are their natural hair and native to them. But what is natural to the Blacks is not natural to the whites in America: "When a Negro woman has natural Negro hair; people think she did something to her hair. Actually, they have not done anything to their hair" (*Americanah* 259). Ifemelu gets angry: "You should be asking Beyoncé what she's done"

(*Americanah* 259). Ifemelu asserts with a mixture of pride and mockery: "I have natural kinky hair. Worn in cornrows, Afros, braids. No, it's not political.... I just don't want relaxers in my hair—there are enough sources of cancer in my life as it is (*Americanah* 259). In the same jesting take-off, Ifemelu refers to Michelle Obama and observes what would have happened had Michele gone natural while appearing on TV: "She would totally rock but poor Obama would certainly lose the independent vote, even the undecided Democrat vote" (*Americanah* 259).

In "Understanding America for the Non-American Black: American Tribalism" Ifemelu elaborates tribalism, "racist label imposed on non-western populations" (*Sociology of Race* 76) which "is a negative reference to groups seen as inferior and insular that resist and oppose other forms of organization and political authority claimed as legitimate and found in nation-states...." (*Sociology of Race*). Moreover, the post exposes the dynamics of power in the race ladder:

> In America, tribalism is alive and well. There are four kinds—class, ideology, region, and race. First, class. Pretty easy. Rich folk and poor folk. Second, ideology. Liberals and conservatives....Third, region. The North and the South. Finally, race. There's a ladder of racial hierarchy in America. White is always on top, specifically White Anglo-Saxon Protestant, otherwise known as WASP, and American Black is always on the bottom, and what's in the middle depends on time and place. (Or as that marvelous rhyme goes: if you're white, you're all right; if you're brown, stick around; if you're black,

> get back!) ....You see, in America's ladder of races, Jewish is white but also some rungs below white....The longer you are here, the more you start to get it. (*Americanah* 163)

Ifemelu opens to view a "race ladder" in which the whites are at the top and the Blacks like Ifemelu are at the "bottom" and the ladder spreads out to gender, nationality, social, economic, and political statuses. For Ifemelu, the being of such ladder/s is preposterous, and pushing off or deracinating the ladder/s is nothing but inconsequential and counterproductive. In one of the posts, Ifemelu opines: "Racism should never have happened and so you don't get a cookie for reducing it" (*Americanah* 267).

Ifemelu's account in the blog stated previously pitched into the "American Non-Black," may sound unfavouravble to the whites. Ifemelu purposefully turns the dynamics of power in the ladder of race inside-out by giving a hint of what will happen if there is an overturn of the power structure. She issues us a set of don'ts and then the dos:

> What's the do? I'm not sure. Try listening, maybe. Hear what is being said. And remember that it's not about you. American Blacks are not telling you that you are to blame. They are just telling you what is... Sometimes people just want to feel heard. Here's to possibilities of friendship and connection and understanding. (285)

The last sentence put out the fire of Ifemelu's speech, purging her previous incendiary words of viciousness and malice. She does not blame the whites for the misery and she does not instigate the blacks into violent and active rebellion, but invites them to see things as they are and presents before them the immensity and gravity of the situation. The Whites and Blacks should not see fire and smoke in their dreams and should not be at loggerheads. Besides proactively nursing collectivism, tolerance, and fare forwarding, the white people must try to give an audience to the Blacks. This, Ifemelu hopes, will prevent the further reinforcement of disunion, and clinch fair result for all races, leading to the procurement of peace, harmony, and to the procreation of "possibilities of friendship and connection and understanding" (323).

Americanah directs us to the engaging aspect of blogging and at the same time focuses on the way Adichie has equalized and socialized her writing. Besides Ifemelu and the pursuer of her blog, Adichie and her readers also moot and toss around race related issues in the novel: "The blog evolves into a site where opinions are created and negotiated, a place of dialogic cosmopolitanism' that enables a 'different conceptualization of democracy'" (Coetzee 2017). It has been remarked in "*Americanah*: Ifemelu and Her Blog":

> Ifemelu uses her blog to turn racism on its head. In the process of addressing the many stereotypes and clichés befalling blacks, she in turn establishes many similar judgments about non-blacks. It seems to me that Ifemelu, intentionally or not, uses her blog as a way to fight back, to offer not only a defense for blacks, but also to give them an argumentative voice in the matter, and to point out that they are not the only race to be judged or ridiculed or objectified. (Shampoe 45)

Ifemelu's blog attributes voice to the voiceless; it gives voice to the American and non-American blacks alike who share her experience and yearn for their painful voices to be heard and in this scenario, the blog becomes for them the sanctuary. The harsh and cutting tone of her posts gives the expression that she is subject to endure many unpleasant bouts in America. The blog also renders her the opportunity to both engage and estrange from the repulsively racist way of life around her.

At the beginning of the novel, the blog is implicated through passing references, and later on, it is divorced from the 'normal' through the use of different typeface and offbeat arrangements. In the end, it makes the breakthrough on the online platform and becomes known as "The Small Redemption of Lagos". The way the blog progresses, it becomes a form of abolition of all differences with an alarming gesture. The blog becomes a very violent and cutthroat zone. At the same time, the blog lets her vent her viewpoint on race that is not otherwise possible and turns into an area where the slanders and vilifications can be squeezed out with indulgence and without check.

Ifemelu is borne to the daylight of separatism from a warm, desegregated dark place, but finds herself in the thick of American social and cultural ambiance, during the 1980s and 1990s in a racist community. She undergoes a mechanism of socialization that fails, tries to adapt herself to the strange social setting which chisels her perception of herself concerning others. She comes up against a preexisting cultural state of affairs which does not alter her but creates something in her – an advantaged angle and a powerful perspective rich with new cultural spoils.

Adichie makes Ifemelu alive and lets the sunshine of racial egalitarianism pass through her blog and raise her up as a convincing character—a homebody. Ifemelu is a keen and sharp-eyed observer so much so that she is sometimes over-critical. She is judgemental of everything except her. And at the same time, she is forgiving and undiscriminating. These strong points and weak points combined together in her prevents her from becoming a flat stereotype; rather, they make her an exceptionally unordinary, around a round female lead whose synthetic complexity and unsettling ontogenesis throw a curve. Listening to Ifemelu is to see both sides of the coin.

Without the blogs and Ifemelu's critical ethnic gaze at American society, the novel would have ended as a love story. The meat of racism has been served on the bread of love with bite and candidness. The novel arouses anger and love at the same time; it has the sinew and bent to metamorphose our existing mindset. Adichie counts on us to amplify our viewpoint and make the world a better place.

In Ohio, Ifemelu gives her first "diversity talk" ever titled "How to Talk About Race with Colleagues of Other Races" to a small company of only white and she throws light on that racism is a mixed bag and its kind and nature varies from place to place: "The first step to honest communication about race is to realize that you cannot equate all racism". Ifemelu realises the end result of racism and understands the way the ball of racism bounces.: "All individuals have already become racialized; race is thus a fait accompli. On this view, what is required to deal with exasperations of race is not the abolition of race but an acknowledgment of the contributions of racial diversity" (Warnke 66). Since there is no escape from racism, it is better to find ways to deal with it and throughout the novel, she strives for recognizing the racial diversity.

Ifemelu proposes to respect the culture of others and finds herself in the "other". On the face othering, she starts othering the whites but ends in a reconciliatory and inclusive discourse. Through her Adichie recognises the need for interdependence and reciprocity with the understanding "that one's culture is multiple, metis and that each human experience and existence is due to the contact with other, who in reality is like ... oneself" (qtd. Akingbe 41-42).

According to Shan, Ifemelu does not have a hyphenated identity and that is why she can coolly and carefreely talk about and write about African Americans. Shan tells Grace:

> "You know why Ifemelu can write that blog, by the way?" "Because she's African. She's writing from the outside. She doesn't really feel all the stuff she's writing about. It's all quaint and curious to her. So she can write it and get all these accolades and get invited to give talks. If she were African American, she'd just be labeled angry and shunned. (*Americanah* 293)

Shan is far from right. While it is true that Ifemelu is an outsider, she is not merely that; she is an insider too. She is both subjective and objective, both an outsider and an insider at the same time. She is a mouthpiece of those who are "lost in translation". The blog reflecting her concern lends a "touch of humanity and pertinence of life" (305). It leads us to a movement and invites a response from us, making us think differently and unravelling the 'personal' that is mooted in something impersonal. The blog not only holds up a statement to Ifemelu's individual positioning, but also attributes believability to her statement. Through the blog, she makes "a daring effort to penetrate beyond the veil of illusion and unfold the grim truth" (Warnke 67) and, to display the litmus test the African-Americans go through daily.

Ifemelu's tone is razor-sharp, quick-witted, droll and chucklesome, and off and on, her upright and upstanding umbrage provides a route via her blog to inflammatory polemic. However, the pep and bounce of Adichie's wit and the irony is not at all affected by these and makes the novel a "thing of joy".

The blog becomes the Bakhtinian dialogic space, "containing many different voices, unmerged into a single perspective, and not subordinated to the voice of the author. Each of these voices has its own perspective, its own validity, and its own narrative weight within the novel" (Robinson 2012). More so, it becomes a "polyphonic space comprising of mélange points of view, the multiplicity of perspectives and voices....Each character has their final word, but it relates to and interacts with those of other characters" (Robinson 39). The blog is a text within the text with racial "heteroglossia," on discourses of race and racism at odds with each other where "the dominant discourse is interrupted by other voices" (Robinson 39).

Ifemelu's writing makes her 'famous' and it reverses her fortune. When she arrives in America, she was a marginal being without any distinct identity recognizable in America. But "thanks to the blog...she begins to live a far more assimilated life" (Akbar 98). Blogging endows the element of metafiction in the novel. The blog is, as if, a novel within the novel in which the writer is character and vice versa. Blog in this novel has multiple functions, pointing out the pigeonholes and at the same time blurring the boundaries of difference. Ifemelu's blog becomes the melting pot, a crucible in which the disparities boil and get amalgamated. Thus, the blog through a merged representation of different existing ideologies of race becomes a synecdoche of "mestiza consciousness".

Bernard Ayo Oniwe argues that despite presenting the problems of racism in America through Ifemelu, no definite answer to the problem comes out of it:

> *Americanah* gives fresh illuminative point of observation and commentary on race and racism in America, from the vantage point of a black African immigrant…the intriguing and celebrated observations and speculations made on race by Ifemelu… come with a caveat; they are not projected as solutions to the problem of racism (Oniwe 71).

But Ifemelu's reaction does offer solutions. Ifemelu's solution echoes the Victorian poet Matthew Arnold who in "Dover Beach" offers mutual love and trust as a solution to twentieth century crisis of faith. Ifemelu evinces:

> The simplest solution to the problem of race in America? Romantic love. Not friendship. Not the kind of safe, shallow love where the objective is that both people remain comfortable. But real deep romantic love, the kind that twists you and wrings you out and makes you breathe through the nostrils of your beloved. And because that real deep romantic love is so rare, and because American society is set up to make it even rarer between American Black and American White, the problem of race in America will never be solved. (*Americanah* 259)

If Ifemelu had found a solution to the problem of racism in America, the moot question is why she had to return to Nigeria then? Niyi Akingbe & Emmanuel Adeniyi in "'Reconfiguring Others': Negotiating Identity in Chimamanda Ngozi Adichie's *Americanah"* look at it as Adichie's failure in her experimentation with transculturalism. It is perhaps the success of 'hostile racism' in America. She leaves not because she fails but because America fails.

Ifemelu ends where she began, a space free from the socially profane four-letter word– race. Home is a space that ultimately disembarrasses her for her skin colour: "home is the only place where there is no race… when [she is] home, facing [her] body, that [she is] most free of race; it is there that [her] mind offers [her] liberation" (Hooks 184). Unlike Aunt Uju who throws on American makeup, going through in the words of Aimé Césaire "mechanization" or "thingification" (Kelley 2015), Ifemelu strives to give up American makeups. Ifemelu understands that race screws up things and is at odds with cultural synbook. Ifemelu is left with no alternative. To disapprove and negate her natural self would have been similar to rejecting the racelessness and to welcome discrimination and quinine of all sorts. Going back home is definitely a gesture of rejection of American racism. Racism in America is not conducive to the nurturing of Ifemelu's transcultural and cosmopolitan bodhi and most important of all "mestiza consciousness".

Mestizas are "transgressors". Ifemelu transgresses "racial stereotyping" (Akingbe 52), and the binary constructs: outsider/insider, Non-American/ American, Black/white, us/them. She deals with these one-sided constructs and the ensuing ambiguities and conflicts with an all-encompassing discourse and with "a mode of identity that is secure on neither side" (Torres 10).

Through Ifemelu's "borderland consciousness" Adichie responds to the tenacious, negative impact of racism, and to the reductionist cultural compartmentalisation by "creating a 'counter culture of the imagination'" (qtd. in Amonyeze 6).

Beyond Race: Quest for Identity in *The Bones of Grace*

If *Americanah* is a race novel, Tahmima Anam's *The Bones of Grace* (2016) moves beyond race. The protagonists in both novels - Ifemelu in *Americanah* and Zubaida in *The Bones of Grace* are in search of their identity far away from their motherland. Though from Asian countries and though brown-skinned, Zubaida does not have to face racism on and off-campus. Rather, her white boyfriend is very much impressed by her. Unlike the other two novels of Anam in which the third person omniscient narrative is used to give voice to the collective, in this novel the first-person narrative is used to refer to the unique problem Zubaida faces. Besides facing a unique problem, Zubaida, in course of the novel, develops a new consciousness, the borderland consciousness or "mestiza consciousness" through which she overcomes her problems and the different points of crises in her life: we see different 'intersections' of Zubaida's identity and how she "accepts and sustains her contradiction" (Hernandez 10).

The Bones of Grace (2016) is the last novel that completes Anam's Bengal Trilogy, the other two being, *A Golden Age* (2007) and *The Good Muslim* (2011). The novel is epic in scope as it deals with the odyssey of Zubaida, the archeological search of her identity and the identity of individuals of her kind. Her search takes her to a grand tour and we are taken from Chittagong to Cambridge to Pakistan to Dubai until she discovers and makes us see that we the humans have made ourselves and that she too is not an exception: "To know this is to be empowered to make her imprint on the world around her" (Kapoor 78). Zubaida's story goes beyond the personal and becomes a story of the generations of women and the new nation Bangladesh as well. Zubaida's "story resonates powerfully within the saga of three generations of women personifying Bangladesh's evolution from the clarity of revolution to the confusions of assimilation with the larger world" (Anam 05).

Through nine sections – "The Preludes", "The Dig", "Homecoming", "Prosperity Shipbreaking", "The Testimony of Anwar", "The Arrival of You", "Looking for Mother", "Return to Grace", "The Last True Story," *The Bones of Grace* effloresces gracefully with the weaving of Zubaida's life journey, her dig into the past for personal and archeological discovery, the journey of Anwar, the breaking of the ship named "Grace", the healing of the bruises, breaks, and damages of the Liberation War. The different strands mirror each other and exist parallelly in Zubaida's consciousness. Her self becomes the site where things get produced, reproduced, assimilated and she ends up with new ways of contending with her problematic identitarian states.

The novel "tells a much more intimate story, a story of one woman's journey into finding her past or finding her roots" (Chakraborty 08). Zubaida is a bit of an outlier, an outsider in many ways, partly because she has lived abroad, partly because she is adopted and she is trying to find herself and so she is kind of pushing against those national narratives (Chakraborty 08). The novel moves away from the nationalist narratives which mainly gaze on the tropes of conflicts, casualties of war, violence, human sacrifice, etc. The novel rather raises questions "about history, about belonging and identity" (Chakraborty 08). In the novel, Anam exemplifies that:

Identity is not an already given thing but

rather it is a process. It is not something fixed that we carry around with ourselves like a piece of luggage. Rather, it is constituted and changes with changing contexts. It is articulated and expressed through identifications within and across different discourses. (Brah 143)

The novel is an epistolary one. Letters, sometimes scripted in the mind, sometimes on paper, and sometimes spoken aloud sculpt the structure of the novel. Zubaida writes series of letters to her pianist lover Elijah Strong. They have spent a very short time together and as a result, she has not been able to tell him everything about herself. There remains "silences and ellipses" (*TBG* 27). That is why, she decides to tell him her story through letters. The novel begins with one such imaginary letter addressed to Elizah in which Zubaida recounts the first time they got acquainted with each other.

The epistolary mode provides Zubaida with the immediacy to take full control of the narrative, enabling her to make her story very convincing and to "structure a sympathetic yet empowered version of her consciousness that ultimately helps her deal with her everyday existence" (Dell 54). The technique takes us to her subjective world and creates a close affinity between the writer and reader. The usefulness of the letters as the narrative mode is summed up by the pioneering epistolary novelist Samuel Richardson in the Preface to *Clarissa*:

All the letters are written while the hearts of the writers must be supposed to be wholly engaged in their subjects so that they abound not only in critical situations, but with what may be called instantaneous descriptions and reflections....must be the style of those who write in the height of a present distress; the mind tortured by the pangs of uncertainty than the dry, narrative, unanimated style .... (5)

Like Tahmima Anam herself, Zubaida belongs to the third generation. Anam in the interview with Samhita Chakraborty mentions her complete identification with Zubaida. Though she can identify with Maya in *The Good Muslim*, they have a generation gap and difference in experience. Anam and Zubaida belong to the same generation and Anam's crisis and doubt of identity are projected onto Zubaida:

But with Zubaida, also because she is the same generation as I am, her ambivalence and her questioning her identity and her sense of not quite belonging to any place is definitely something that comes from me. So I feel that we have a lot of things in common. But obviously, I wasn't adopted and so all those questions are amplified in her life. (Chakraborty 09)

Though Anam is interested in the political happenings in Bangladesh, Zubaida is least interested in the political happenings of the war. She lacks the nationalistic craze. The collective past does not pull her in. The wave and thrill of the Liberation War do not affect her as it affected her parents and grandparents who were active participants in the Liberation War. Hers is more of a personal quest. Her interest is riveted to her birth and origin. She takes pride when her parents are referred to as "muktijodhhas" ("freedom fighters"), but she holds grudge against the War as it is instrumental in causing the irreparable crack in her life:

> If Zubaida is in thrall to anything then it is her individual past, the riddle of her birth which she must solve. And finally, when she has been able to piece together all the disjointed parts of the fossil as well as herself, she feels confident enough to place her heart in the immortal pages of history, hoping that one day Elijah, the love of her life, will come back. (Afrin 19)

Zubaida is a true "mestiza" as she moves through many transitions, liminalities and inbetweenness in her life. Zubaida the narrator in "The Preludes" makes it clear that she is "adopted" and that her biological identity is uncertain. Throughout the novel, the protagonist has been in search of that root. She is "always suspected" since childhood. She remains "sandwiched" between her parents. The image of the bones recurs in the novel. The fossil hunt and the discovery of the bones are metaphors of the search for her roots:

> The recurring image of the fossil, Diana, and the metaphor of digging, altogether, function as reminders that Zubaida's odyssey entails a search for her identity, her roots, her past which is mired in hidden truths, and a quest to rekindle the embers of a seemingly dead love, a pursuit to re-penetrate the consciousness of the man whom she had loved and lost. (Afrin 18)

She looks upon herself as being different from others. She cannot be like other women, like her mother, the "angels in the household" who are there at the backstage and whose identity and contribution cannot be undermined and who are the epitomes of loyalty and goodness in a typical Bangladeshi setting: "These are the kinds of wives that pre-dated me, Elijah. Invisible, magic-wielding, food-stretching, loyal to the last breath. This is the world ... with people ... who always exceeded what was expected of them, no matter how small their mandates" (*TBG* 263).

The constant physical shift of Zubaida from Dhaka to Boston to Pakistan and then to Cambridge takes place during her journey that she undertakes to fulfil her academic ambitions—a journey during which she connects to different kinds of people. She moves like a nomad and lacks permanent grounds to put her feet into. That she does not have any root to attach to and that she is separated from her lover Elijah makes her think that she is incomplete.

Zubaida has the desire to fly "beyond the country, to a place of pianos and cold winters and childhood" (*TBG* 393). Though Zubaida is rootless and without any fixed identity, sometimes consciously and sometimes unconsciously, she wants to have an identity and foster a desire to belong which gets manifested in her actions and her interactions with the various phenomena:

> Zubaida's conscious agency and unconscious subjective forces are enmeshed in her various activities and life experiences throughout the novel. These provide the site on which she develops a sense of belonging, a sense of 'identity', and thus articulates its difference from other people's way of doing things. This desire to belong can be called a 'homing desire'. (Brah 142-143)

Zubaida is born to an unknown mother and is adopted by Maya and Joy. When she grows up, a relationship develops with Rashid, the son of her parents' friends – Dolly and Bulbul. The married relationship of

Zubaida and Rashid comes to a halt as Zubaida gets drawn towards Elijah Strong. Though Zubaida has spent years in Bangladesh, she feels that she is a wanderer: "My heart is a nomad, still, after so many years of being in this country, child to the parents" (*The Bones of Grace* 84). Her parents fought for the country at the expense of many near and dear ones. They throve with the country and developed a deep attachment to it so much so that "there is a memory at every turn, affection for every change in season, roots in the ground so deep you would have to tear them apart to separate person from the place, body from the soil. But not me" (*TBG* 85). Critic Brah comments: "At given moments of her life, Zubaida is positioned across multiple processes of identification which shift and configure into a specific pattern. The particular identity processes have become salient and motivating for her and leading to action" (Brah 144).

Zubaida is ambivalent; she is in a state of "having either, or both, of two contrary values or qualities" (*OED*), and is striving towards "assimilation of contraries". Her life goes on "with an acceptance of a concurrent void and with a willingness to descend into that void wherein, as it were, one may begin to come into confrontation with a spectre of invocation …in an alien territory and wilderness [that]has become a necessity for [her] reason or salvation" (qtd. in *The Location of Culture* 56). Zubaida defends her irresolution by referring to the strangeness of her lover Elijah Strong: "I was reminded again of your strangeness, and also of the way you were both more sure of yourself than anyone I had ever known and yet also unmoored as if you had never managed to find something to attach yourself to" (*TBG* 271).

Zubaida fits into the Adzalduan definition of a "new mestiza" in her resilient acceptance of contradictions and ambiguities, in her ability to cope with and juggle her crises. Moreover, "she has a plural personality... she operates in a pluralistic mode – nothing is thrust out, the good the bad and the ugly, nothing rejected, nothing abandoned. Not only does she sustain contradictions, she turns the ambivalence into something else" (Anzaldua 101).

Zubaida is a "restless being" (339). Her "past was a mystery" (52). She is desperate to hold on "to every piece of [her] past, unable to forget, or let go, of a single thing" (79). At home and outside home, Zubaida is a misfit. She goes on looking for people like her:

Me, I couldn't look at another living person and see something of myself, the angle of eyes, a gait, a particular texture of hair ... In a culture where people commented freely on everyone's looks, people rarely said anything about mine, because a simple phrase, "how beautiful you are", couldn't be followed by, "just like your mother (42).

She wants to dissolve: "the loneliness of being only in one body when the spirit wanted nothing but communion" (119). Torn by her ambivalence, Zubaida comes out with the same reaction her mother would have shown:

> I would jump out of my own scissored self
> and traverse the difficult and treacherous
> chasm of history, and though I didn't realize
> it at the time, because all I could feel was the
> missing-limb ache of your loss, the start of
> this journey prompted a small, electric joy
> (*TBG* 309).

If the first source of Zubaida's ambivalence is the adopted situation, the second source is her sheer lack of will: "My ambivalence was compounded by my lack of determination to stay in your country" (*TBG* 18). She is divided in her loyalties. She could not resist the temptation of staying in a country "where people cared about the bones of animals that lived far before memory or human ambition" (*TBG* 19). At the same time, she is unable to turn her back on the place where her parents fought bravely and lived, the place of her origin. To think of abandoning the place would be similar to Judas's kiss: "To construct my loyalties in any other way would constitute a betrayal, and I was, above all things, aware of my commitments" (*TBG* 19).

Zubaida's response to Bangladesh is a mixture of love and hate. She wishes she could hate it but she is "forced to love" it. It is a place where everyone like her has tried to get away from. Living here is "like running into a burning building" (84). What she loves about the country is the "monsoon air", "the smell of the paperbacks in the winter", "lying on her grandmother's bed", "the taste of egg and paratha". She loves the country but it is confined to the few objects and the few people. She has more reasons to dislike the country than the ones to love it: "The love exists, but its domain is small, located in the particular bodies of particular people" (*TBG* 84-85).

Before her visit to Dera Bugti, the digging site in Pakistan, she has imaginary anticipation that a visit to this place will never take place and this perhaps foreshadows the fact that "this was the start of a downward cascade" (*TBG*). The fact is that it is through her toppling into "alien territories" again and again, she has articulated the hybridity of her culture. In *The Location of Culture*, Homi K. Bhabha remarks that "it is the 'inter' – the cutting edge of translation and negotiation, the *in-between* space – that carries the burden of the meaning of culture" (56). Zubaida has tried relentlessly because as a woman, as an adopted girl, as Elijah's worthy partner, she is burdened with the pressure of proving herself to others, to herself, to her "sheltered childhood, to her parents and even to Elijah" (63). "Identities are not a priori givens;" there are "multiple processes are involved in the construction" of Zubaida's identity (Brah 144).

The acute self-searching takes her to the osseous question: "To whom did these long bones belong, the tone of my skin? Not to the ancestors collaged onto my history" (*TBG* 42). Home seems to be a torturous and inescapable prison for her. She starts developing repulsion for the immediate environment she is in and for her parents too and suffers from utter self-disgust. The dig has not been a success. Zamzam who helps in the dig dies. Her mission fails. She has to return home. She is exhausted: "'I'm on the verge of a spectacular failure" (*TBG* 88). She is no longer "the person I used to be" (121) and has become "an injured animal … [in] the zoo" (301). It seems that Zubaida has reached a dead-end which is perhaps necessary for her to begin from the beginning. Critic Salma opines: "Anam shows that achieving freedom often entails a process of complete destruction" (Salma 178).

Zubaida feels that she is a part of everywhere she has been to and yet she is nowhere. She is and is not a "part of all she met": "[I] had spent much of my life parcelling myself out, giving a little to this person, a little to that, and there was no one to connect the dots, no one to understand the sum total of all parts …" (*TBG* 339-40). This is best expressed by her while she refers to her amphibian existence in Bettina:

> 'Amphibian' was our code word for people like us. Bettina was Argentinian, born in Queens, had grown up in Buenos Aires when her parents had decided to un-immigrate themselves, gone to college in Paris, taken

several years off and backpacked through China, where she had been bitten by monkeys, and landed up here, in Cambridge, by which time her parents had returned to their place in Astoria, chastened by the more exciting side of the planet. 'Amphibian' signalled people in between, people who lived with some part of themselves in perpetual elsewhere. (*TBG* 14-15)

She is Muslim; but she behaves in a non-Muslim way. Yet, during her research visit to Pakistan, she wears a burka. She is Bangladeshi; but regarding her choice in marriage and religion, she seems to be against the mores of Bangladesh: "I could love whomever I wanted, and marry or not marry them, or change my religion, or get divorced multiple times and have children with three different fathers if I wanted" (13). Though Zubaida claims that she is an amphibian, she does not live merely "a double life, reflecting her dual life strategy" (Zug 2020). She has multiple identities that exist parallelly and she tries more than one strategy to cope with the multiplicity.

Zubaida may be said to approximate the "rhizome" (The term used by Gilles Deleuze and Felix Guattari in their 1987 book *A Thousand Plateaus*) identity that is unstable, heterogeneous, and that develops simultaneously, horizontally. Her identity consists of a series of 'assemblages' that constitute the multiplicity of his identity. Her "descent is not clear, as is the process of differentiation" from one identity to other. Like a rhizome, "she is always in the middle; she develops new identity wherever she is; her identity is not predictable and it does not follow a linear pattern of growth and reproduction" (Adkins 23). We get enough evidence of her 'rhizomatic' personality when she mentions in one of her addresses to Elijah that she does not have a lineage. Her existence is unlike that of a tree; it is not at all punctuated by "to be" but engendered by the conjunction "and ... and ...and ..." (Adkins 24). The "horizontality" and "a-linearity" of Zubaida's identity reaches new height as she discovers her lineage and achieves towards the end of the novel a "borderland consciousness", and consequently her dualities overlap. Though trapped initially, the working of Zubaiba's consciousness finally "breaks down duality", "heals the split", "transcends" it in favour of a "collective consciousness" or "mestiza consciousness" (Anzaldúa 80).

More than one phenomenon help shape and develop the "mestiza consciousness" in Zubaida. The first one is the whale skeleton named Diana. The second one is Zubaida's lover Elijah. The third is an abandoned ship named Grace and the last one is Zubaida's sister's daughter Shona.

Zubaida has multiple strings of attachment, many centres – Diana, Elijah, Grace, and Anwar/Shona.Zubaida wants to use the ship and the whale as connectors and pointers to the various identities that she has to draw; and like a "mestiza", she uses them to discover new lines to transverse and originate new identities She is haunted and defined by her past which she cannot brush aside. She grows up harboring the deep-rooted fear in her that her parents will get rid of her: "they would somehow take me back to where I was from, return me" (*TBG* 289). Though her parents never display any lack of love whatsoever throughout her whole life, she cannot get over this fear until the end. It is her adopted condition coupled with the feeling of rootlessness along with her dreadful distress which drives her to find attachments or secure zones of belonging.

Amongst the many loci that are found in her complicated

and trouble-ridden life, one centre or locus is Diana that perhaps can be taken as the symbolic compendium of the bones of the "walking whale". The bones of the *Ambulocetus* found at Dera Bugti were collectively named Diana after the Roman goddess by the sedimentologist Jimmy. It is the metonymy of Zubaida's existence: "Diana is the reason I left this town, and Diana is why I have returned. I think of her as a spirit of comings and goings, a beacon that leads me across continents and through time. I live in hope that she will lead me back to you" (3). Just as Seamus Heaney dug his past with his pen, Tahmima Anam vis-a-vis the palaeontologist Zubaida has dug their past through fossil hunting.

The fulcrum of the novel and the climactic phenomenon in the life of Zubaida are encapsulated in her journey from Cambridge to Dera Bugti in Pakistan for the "archaeological dig" at the underbed of the Tethys Sea for salvaging "the fossils of *Ambulocetus natans* – a rare type of walking whale" (Kapoor 45). Undoubtedly, Anam has resourced her knowledge in anthropology (Anam completed Ph.D. in anthropology from Harvard) which "is the most open to questioning what the truth is and looking at the truth subjectively, understanding [that] the truth is contextual" (Kapoor 47).

The bone is the backbone of the novel. Metaphorically, the bone is tantamount to "mestiza consciousness". It is the inspiration for Zubaida, the stimulus of her writing: "[A]s I held Diana's bone in my hand that day, a flood of words came to my mind, and I rushed home and wrote them down. I have been living in a state of waiting... for this moment, this opportunity for reckoning" (*TBG* 3). Zubaida has worked with bones and she has to work further with bones literally and metaphorically. As Diana is not complete, there will be some ellipses and hiatuses in her history which she herself has to fill fictionally:

> But the bones I had studied, pressed down by millennia, were always partial. I would work with fragments and imagine the whole, fill in the parts that had been broken by history, and this was how it should be because our knowledge of the past could only ever be in pieces, left there for us to put together (*TBG* 360).

Fragmentation and ambivalence are destined for Zubaida. The onus of putting things together, turning parts into a whole, and thereby overcoming fragmentation and ambivalence falls on her which she does favourably with "mestiza consciousness".

At a symbolic level, the bones become her "talismans, reflecting the future and the past" (403). While looking at the bones intensely, an epiphanic moment arises in which she not only visualises the lives of animals that came before and after Diana but also the people she has intimately loved and lost. The bones become the essence of her realisation and learning experience: "Everything that endures is in the atavism of her bones, fifty million years of history encased...." (*TBG* 403). Moreover, the bones stir her muted self, and function as her creative stimulus: "I held Diana's bone in my hand that day, a flood of words came to my mind, and I rushed home and wrote them down" (*TBG* 3).

The condition of the tetrapod whale "who both walked and swam... a creature embracing its duality, its attraction to both the lure of the seas and the comforts of the land" (*TBG* 20) metonymically expresses the ambivalence of Zubaida and her attractions to the multiple points:

> There was nothing for me but those skulls and bones and taxonomy and strata, Hutton's earth, with 'no vestige of a beginning, no prospect of an end', that was what I chose: the earth with its hot centre, and its rocks that threw up history and bones, enduring bones, skipping back to a time when I couldn't be found (*TBG* 37).

Whales prefer to go back into the sea. Like them, Zubaida goes back to go forward. Unlike others, she decides to dig into her past as it assisted in "bucking history she countered" (*TBG* 48). In line with *Ambulocetus*, Zubaida forensically presents her evolution:

> What we do know is that the whale was first a coyote, then a water-curious amphibian, and finally, the creature that would rule the seas and become the stuff of our myths, our ocean-totems, our outstanding beast, and the one who reminds us that long before our time, beings were made on a grander scale, their bones as big as cities. The whale is the fragment of that grandeur, of life writ on a canvas so large it is almost beyond the imagination. And for this to have happened, a transgression had to be committed, an abandonment of limbs, an adventure into water, and the courage to bid farewell to the past, whatever such voyaging may have cost, whatever longings and loves were left behind in the rubble. (*TBG* 396)

Zubaida draws strength from the past. *Ambulocetus*'s story echoes her story. She is full of "randomness" (395), always unpredictable and at her will. She grows and develops, adapts, evolves, and carves out a new path for herself. Her story is also to be and to become through many places, many identities, and many phases—each surviving, showing possibilities of never giving up:

> The story of *Ambulocetus* is the story becoming, of transformation, of leaping between one sort of being and another sort of being and another sort of being, of leaving history behind for the wide swathe of the possible. It is not the story of extinction. (*TBG* 390)

The paleontological quest of Zubaida and her personal quest go hand in hand. She not only searches parts of *Ambulocetus* to combine them and make a historical breakthrough and die a palaeontologist; but also, she searches for her fragmented and discombobulated parts scattered indiscriminately so that she can assemble them together and know herself as a composite biological 'being.' By imagining herself as a composite whole, she wants to make peace with her restlessness: "I would work with fragments and imagine the whole, fill in the parts that had been broken by history, and this was how it should be, because our knowledge of the past could only ever be in pieces, left there for us to put together" (360).

As a palaeontologist, Zubaida firmly believes that knowing the root is essential and that the bones are indispensable in tracing the roots of the sea-creatures: "… the souls of those ancient creatures were in their bones" (360). Similarly, she understands that the real 'she' is not the adopted 'she.' Hence, to know who she is, she must get to the bone of things. And through Zubaida, Anam who lives far and far away from Bangladesh, waters her root, revisits Bangladesh imaginatively, continues, and replenishes her relationship with it.

There is an intimate connection between the past and the present, between the anthropological "dig" and the personal dig, between the bones and the living beings. At Dera Bugti while the dig is on, Zubaida processes Daina's remains which are freshly found out; she reflects on how Diana remained a mute witness to the bygone ages. Her remains harshly remind that we are nothing but tiny mortals: "Diana in my hand is a miracle, a testament to everything we are as humans – the scientists who uncover the past, the artists who imagine it…we realise that we are mere pinpoints in the long chapter of our own history" (54).

And this has a direct bearing on the plot construction of the novel, on the narration, and on the novelist's carefully deliberated structuration of her own work. At the end of the day, she thinks of her story she is narrating to Elijah: "Piece by piece, I put it together. All the other voices clamour to be heard – my mother, and Anwar, and Mo, and the other life I might have had if things had taken a different turn" (54). Here through the discovery and pairing of the bones, we find the key to the novel's skeletal structure and how different strands of the story are woven and turned into a great 'book of life.'

Apart from Diana, another such centre in the life of Zubaida is Elijah, perhaps the strongest one. She is obsessed with Elijah. He is the one to lean on, one who keeps her in thrall, one who frees her, liberates her, one she can hold on to and open her heart to. Zubaida voyages through her life like a ship voyaging through the turbulence of waves, and of the many havens in which she takes shelter during her voyage, Elijah Strong proves to be the most reliable one. He is there in the prelude, in the bridge, and the coda of the novel. Although he is physically present in the few pages of the novel, we see his silhouette on every page of the novel.

Zubaida candidly expresses the importance of Elijah in her life: "I remember you on the cusp of every major event in my life" (402).

Elijah becomes a symbolic mirror on which Zubaida's "mestiza consciousness" gets reflected; it is in his propinquity that Zubaida's multiple identities or lack of them merge and get reflected. He is the sum total of Zubaida's parts, an alchemic solution and a panacea for her:

> Hello, Zubaida, Putul, Abbasid princess, orphan, provenance unknown. Hello Mrs. Rashid, meet the inside of your thigh, meet your mate, this man only this man, your only mate in the world, your only relation, because you know no one whose blood matches your blood, well, here is a man whose presence obliterates the need for blood, because you are made of the same things, you are nothing and everything alike, because your taste in his mouth is all the closeness you will ever need, the bed is hard beneath your bodies, the bed of a person who has never left this country, the smell of this country is the smell of the sun on the paddy....(*TBG* 277).

He is the rock, a tree-like guy with the help of whom Zubaida gets the courage to face her dilemma. He has left his unfading presence so strongly near Jubaida that even when he is not tangibly present near her, Zubaida can feel his vibes instinctively.

Elijah Strong, to whom the entire novel is addressed, is Zubaida's ineluctable 'other.' She always looks to him for solace and for inspiration during the tortuous moments of her aloofness. He is what she has always aspired to be.

He is her mirror. Elijah is like her and at the same time unlike her. He feels that like Zubaida, he "had been born in the wrong family" and that there are things which he could only confide in Zubaida. They were nothing, yet everything alike" (14). When Zubaida gets dissociated into parts which she is unable to bracket together, it is only in Elijah's presence that she can reconnect those fragmented parts into a composite whole and consider herself as a human being:

> I realised that I had spent much of my life parceling myself out, giving a little to this person, a little to that, and there was no one to connect the dots, no one to understand the sum total of all the parts, the orphan, the scientist, the daughter of revolutionaries. Except you, of course. (*TBG* 340)

They have differences. "With nothing to resist Elijah floated like a fallen leaf" (11) while Zubaida had to carry her splintered and burdened soul with her. Zubaida wants those things which irritate Elijah. While Zubaida is apprehensive, ambivalent, complicated, and nonchalant, Elijah is still, resolved, decided, and rooted. Zubaida mentions the difference: "I had never seen a gaze like that, so direct and so unambivalent. Most people like to be in at least two places at once, but you- you were standing there as if roots had grown around your feet" (*TBG* 9). Elijah is not the opposite of Zubaida but the ideal; in him, she discovers an image to look forward to. Moreover, Zubaida feels that she is adopted literally and metaphorically. She is without an identity. She does not have any lineage or bloodline to fall back on. Elijah has all she does not have: "What would you do with this messy history, Elijah? Your chamomile-scented home, your overfed cat, lemonade in the refrigerator, and that family tree, so august, no mystery blood, no revolutions" (*TBG* 86).

The reflection of her own image in Elijah causes both love and hatred. She loves the image of Elijah, a thing that parallels the Lacanian "mirror stage":

> The mirror stage is a drama whose internal thrust is precipitated from insufficiency to anticipation—and which manufactures for the subject, caught up in the lure of spatial identification, the succession of phantasies that extends from a fragmented body-image to a form of its totality that I shall call orthopaedic—and, lastly, to the assumption of the armour of an alienating identity, which will mark with its rigid structure the subject's entire mental development (qtd. in Felluga 180).

Zubaida indeed seeks "spatial identification" but fails to do so. She had created a false notion of attachment and love with Rashid; for a time, she had thought her love for Rashid to be real; this love turns out to be the opposite in the end. Zubaida fragments the notion of herself. She looks at herself in parts: "I couldn't look at another living person and see something of myself, the angle of eyes, a gait, a particular texture of hair, or identify the things I hated about myself, the smallness of my breasts, the weakness of my ankles. The kink in my hair had no echo" (42). She wants to form an "orthopaedic" identity, to unify her parts into a whole which gets reflected in her search for Diana's bones, and in her attempt to meld it piece by piece. And throughout the novel, despite finding her footing in Elijah and later in Shona, she remains an estranged figure. This is voiced by her at the end of the novel when she truly discovers her past identity: "And I had to confront the fact that, even though something of the mystery of my life has now been solved, the fundamental aloneness of it will always be with me, like a scar that flattens and fades but refuses to disappear" (402).

It seems that Zubaida does not want to get implanted permanently anywhere. She could have lived permanently with Elijah; but she chooses not to develop roots. Elijah holds his hand out for her; but she avoids his hand for she fears that it would attach a sense of stability and permanence to her: "I worried if I spent another minute there, on those steps with you, I would be rooted forever, that I might live and re-live this moment for the rest of my life" (*TBG* 47).

In the section "Return to Grace" while the intimacy between Elijah and Zubaida becomes public, Rashid's mother Dolly holds Zubaida responsible for her unfaithfulness to Rashid and to his family and with a sense of utter annoyance and disillusionment, she refers to Jubaida's "bad background" (*TBG* 369). While it rains heavily outside, Dolly starts unraveling Jubaida's origin and discovers that she was born in Mymensingh to a poor and helpless mother whose husband abandoned her and sold her for twenty thousand rupees. Rashid's father Bulbul later informs Zubaida that her name was Mohona and she had a twin sister named Meghna. Zubaida listens to Dolly with absolute placidity as she is afraid that "this new knowledge might disappear from her mind...history might be altered, so that all this truth telling could be reversed" (*TBG* 371).

Zubaida finds herself positioned in an existential interface and finds it difficult to comprehend and accept the intricacy of her complicated and divided existence. It is no wonder that she develops an interest in an intermediate "creature embracing its duality, its attraction to both the lure of the seas and the comforts of the land" (20). But Elijah mentions her duality on her face: "You are an intermediate species, like *Ambulocetus*" (34). Moreover, when Zubaida solicits Elijah's help regarding finding her origin, Elijah refuses to help: "it has to be you" (278).

Elijah is for Zubaida the binding force. He is her healer. In him, she discovers her potential deliverer. She falls in love with him for needs—to get relieved from her feeling of insecurity, from the haunting and nagging fear of rejection from all quarters due to her inherent and essential doubleness, to get respite from the bouts of depression that captivates her and finally, to succor her fear-stricken temperament. In Elijah, she finds the promise to all her needs:

> When you fall in love, because suddenly there is a thread connecting your life and all the lives that went before you and all the lives that will follow. Even when we were together I was filled with a sense of the dread, not for the parting that would occur, but simply because I had a periscope into life, the vast and intimate sadness of it, for the first time, and that is why I loved you because even the worst of the world was there to be discovered together, shoulder to shoulder with you my beloved stranger. (*TBG* 403)

Her relationship with Elijah becomes stronger with time; it grows "stronger, like liquor in a cask" (163).

It is Elijah who frequently emancipates Zubaida from her feeling of in-betweenness. He is the present who comes between Zubaida's past and future. He comes between home (Bangladesh) and the world (the USA), between adopted identity and real identity. He has a shaping influence on her: "You will always remain the making of me" (407). While Zubaida tries to memorize her childhood and ponders with excitement over the proposed visit to Dera Bugti "to find a complete skeleton of the ancient whale Ambulocetus natans", and while she imagines "the dig" and "the moment of discovery," Elijah meets her in a musical concert at Sanders Theatre. Whenever she feels empty, it is either Elijah's physical presence or the rumination of his memory that fills that gap:

> To find a complete skeleton of the ancient whale Ambulocetus natans, and my memories mingled with thoughts of packing away my apartment and the journey I was about to embark on, imagining the dig, the moment of discovery, the possible unveiling of a fossil that had already changed the way we looked at the relationship between the land and the sea, and in this interlude, between memory and the anticipation, a crack appeared, a pause in which everything slowed down, an in-between moment that was neither here nor there- and into that crack fell you: a man with piano hands and the smell of cold weather on his collar. (*TBG* 6)

In the novel, there is a reference to the feminist writer, educationist, Rokeya Sakhawat Hossain who is the hero of Zubaida's mother, Maya. Rokeya not only impresses Maya, but also Zubaida as the latter wonders: "And: how did she, trapped in her zenana, push her eye to that better place and see all that would someday come to be, and imagine the things we would never have...who had flipped the world round, making prisons into meadows" (*TBG* 116). With Elijah, Zubaida does not feel what she feels with her husband: " . . . in your presence...I was beyond pretty: I was majestic, a sovereign, like the Queen in Rokeya's story" (*TBG* 123).

Apart from his importance in Zubaida's life, Elizah is also important for the story. Since she is the first-person authoritative narrator of the story, Zubaida professes that she could have presented herself in a better light by telling false things under the garb of truth. But she has not done so because he is averse to falsity. Her account is authentic, and she does this for getting him back:

> I have been tempted to bend the truth, to paint myself a little prettier, but I know you hate evasion more than anything, so I have been relentlessly, brutally truthful. I have placed my ugly, complicated heart within these pages, and although the shame hasn't passed, I tell myself at least I have been able to face it. I have been able to look that woman in the eyes and say, yes, I was her. I was her and I am her. But this truth- telling, in the end, is not for me but for you. To bring you back to me. To give you something in return for the pain I threw at you like a shower of stones. (*TBG* 406)

It may be that Tahmima Anam, through her persona, messages us that the novel is not at all fictional but an authentic re-representation of what happened in her life.

Diana and Elijah are the cornerstones of her existence; the two overlap and orient her to discover and re-discover her: "Diana is here, and I have seen you, and now I can take account of the whole thing" (3). Both Elijah and Diana are most like and unlike her. They are, in fact, her double, and her anti-self through whom, by whom, and against whom she seeks her own self (Yeats and Finneran 162). Both, however, influence the way she looks at love, relationships, and life.

Anzaldua talks about "conceptual metaphors" which are instrumental in "redeeming and reclaiming voice, instinct, intellect, and sexuality" (Aigner-Varoz 60). Diana is such a metaphor. For Zubaida it is an "antirepressive" force through which Zubaida reclaims her identity and repressed sexuality. Elijah on the other hand is furthers the mestiza consciousness in Zubaida by serving as a mode of self-critique" (Aigner-Varoz 59). Through him, Zubaida gets to know herself and gets freed from the "oppression within her own psyche" (Aigner-Varoz 59). Together, Diana and Elijah pave the "path of knowledge and learning…and a way of balancing, of mitigating duality" (Anzaldua 19).

Anam adds the Anwar-Meghna sub-plot to make Zubaida's story more lively and prismatic. In her letter, Zubaida refers to Anwar who plays a crucial role to play in her life and without whom she could not have completed her quest: "I might still be in the dark about my past. I've only ever been hair away from utterly being alone in the world, Elijah, and it was Anwar who shone a light where once there was only darkness" (75). The novel not only depicts Zubaida's quest, but also of Anwar's as well. But Anwar's quest is also different in kind: "I wasn't the only one in Chittagong in search of a self … The whole time I was there … [Anwar] was right beside me, carrying around my secret like a talisman dangling from his neck" (252). Anwar "is a man who revealed to me the entire history of my being, and, having done so, released me from all the things I believed I couldn't do, wasn't entitled to, because my past was a mystery" (252).

Anwar loves Meghna, makes her pregnant, marries another woman to satisfy her mother's desire for grandchildren, and then leaves for Dubai as a construction worker, abandoning the pregnant Meghna in the lurch. But the fact that he has abandoned Meghna keeps haunting him ever since. When his co-worker Pahari dies, he returns home and goes out on a search for Meghna. He eventually bumps into Zubaida and mistakes her for Meghna whose twin sister she really is. In the end, Anwar learns from a prostitute that Meghna has ended as a prostitute and died, leaving a daughter.

With finesse, Anam compatibly dovetails Zubaiba with Anwar. The sub-plot helps Zubaida's story come to full circle: "I wasn't the only one in Chittagong in search of a self. I wasn't the only one who felt like the loneliest person in the world…he (Anwar) was right beside me, carrying around my secret like a talisman dangling from his neck" (252).

There are parallels and differences between the two. In the main plot, incidents take place in posh and upper-class surroundings. Zubaida is a paleontologist who studies at Harvard and her search for the past is tinged with anthropological references. But Anwar is a mere construction worker. His search for his lost love is primarily driven by guilt. His search unearths the misfortunes of the itinerant unskilled labourers like him and also exposes the dark underbelly of the new nation where helpless women have to take to prostitution to raise their daughters. But they are united in the search of their past, to recover what is lost. It is Anwar and Shona who complete Zubaida's "little quest to find her origin and even the wound of Elijah's absence" (361).

Zubaida owns Shona, the daughter of her sister, Meghna, and Anwar: "My sister's daughter was also my daughter" (393). The sub-plot helps us know Zubaida in a different light and elicits our sympathy for her. The mother in Zubaida comes out. Shona gives her a reason to live and becomes the surrogate daughter. Anwar-Meghna-Shona becomes her anchor to her past, her juju: "I know who I am now. I saw it the moment I looked into her face. I am her, and she is me. The restless being is at peace at last" (394).

In the novel, "Prosperity Shipbreaking" does not become a region where one can only find disintegration and destruction. It is definitely a place where ships are torn apart. But here Zubaida gets an opportunity to regenerate. Here she finds Shona, her biological sister Meghna's daughter with whom she can establish blood relation. Metaphorically, Shona is like the salvaged fossil of *Ambulocetus*. As the discovery of the whale *Ambulocetus'* fossils informs us about the former's evolution and habitat, Shona helps Zubaida understand the mystery of her birth. Shona is the key to her biological root, the antidote to her crisis.

One year of her marriage with Rashid passes and the next year she lives "in the shadow of the Grace" and watches how that "great leviathan strip . . . [s] down to her very bones" (125). Rashid is a guy who wants to settle. He is a guy who "fold . . . [s] his clothes neatly and brushed his teeth timely" (120). Rashid, the boyfriend-turned-husband of Zubaida, also plays an important part in the whole affairs. She always feels his tight grip on her: "I just kept feeling his hand under me, his steady presence, teaching me to swim, to belong, to fit in" (79). From the very first day of their marriage, what upsets Zubaida is the tone of condolement and mercy from Rashid's end: "I remembered the pity and absolution in his voice. It was only the first day and already I felt the depths of the mistake, touching me like the ink from a stray pen in my pocket" (135). The fact is that it is an open secret that Zubaida is an adopted girl which is why everyone in Rashid's family – Dolly, Bulbul, and Rashid himself – displays a collective attitude of excessive coddling towards her as a re-compensation for her grief. However, Zubaida continues to remain lonely, despite all the support and sympathy she receives from Rashid's family members as is not able to come out completely from the traumatic experience of her past life. In Rashid's snug, sheltered and upscaled house filled with pity and sympathy for her, she seems to be losing her previous self. It is difficult for her to reconcile:

> I would catch a glimpse of the person I used to be, was, in fact, just months ago, the sort of person who would travel across the world to dig whale bones out of the ground and in those moments I felt as if I was battling a phantom, a woman who haunted my otherwise perfect life. (*TBG* 121)

In their entire married life, just once Zubaida comes across "a complete absence of dissatisfaction" (128) when she gets pregnant. She hopes that she is going to get kin with blood-bond, one with whom she can grow an umbilical bond: "I thought about meeting a person who was related to me by blood, something that had never happened to me before" (127); but she miscarries and laments "the complicated forms of attachment that had been promised and taken away" (132) from her. This year is very important for her as in this year her birth and origin are stripped of its mystery. Zubaida comes out of Rashid's house to the shipbreaking site "Prosperity Shipbreaking" at the suggestion of her mother's friend Rubana to help Gabriela, the British researcher who feels the need for a native for her documentary on the shipbreaking workers."

At "Prosperity Shipbreaking," the very sight of the broken ships takes out "the sadness that already existed within her" (141) and magnifies it. She, in fact, takes the miscarriage hard and the loss makes "her longing acute in the multiplied hit of a desire for something that is a new, but very old" (142). However, she manages to brush off all might-have-beens and "her arrival at the shipbreaking yard coincide . . . [s] with the arrival of a new ship called *Grace*" (143). *Grace* is decommissioned because of the virus infection in it and it becomes "a footnote in the history of unlucky ships" (147). Zubaida gets what she had wanted. And *Grace* becomes instrumental in drawing Elijah close to her, Anwar and Shona, and it is thus a vital catalyst in the furthering of the novel's plot, in the progression of Zubaida's life, and in unveiling her true identity.

Zubaida is adopted by Maya and Joy and the adoption is arranged by Rashid's family including Dolly and Bulbul to fill the void, to fulfil the need for love in the lives of their friends, Maya and Joy. Zubaida who was adopted to fill the void carries one in her which she strives to fulfil. They turn Megna into Zubaida and she repays this debt for the rest of her life.

Zubaida possesses more than one identity which is encoded in more than one name she possesses. Mohona is her actual name given by her biological mother; the historical and regal name Zubaida is given to her by Maya and Joy who adopted her; Zee is the endearing abbreviation given to her by her boyfriend turned husband Rashid;

Putul is the name given to her by her paternal grandmother which is further abbreviated into Poots:

> Zee was the girl who married with a gold chain fastened to her head; Putul was the girl who hated the smell of henna on her hands and left home to find a new patch of air among the scrapheap of the world, Putul the bird who flew south in search of a warmer climate and a place to spread her wings (254).

Though she is born as Mohona to a poor woman whose husband abandoned her, she is endowed with the name Zubaida "after the Abbasid princes Zubaidah bint Ja'far" (253) marries Harun al –Rashid. The naming is not ironic because Anam's Zubaida is no less a princess. She lives like a princess and is the cynosure of *The Bones of Grace*.

Zubaida identifies herself with *Grace* and compares her condition with that of the ship. As is common with a fossilist, Zubaida starts seeing in her mind's eye the kind of bustling life the ship once had, the "disappointment at having spent so little time afloat, her sadness at being consigned to the scrapyard, her pain at being taken apart" (150). Zubaida has also an intuitive knowledge that the ship "would yield more treasures than she could know" (150). Zubaida does not believe in superstitions, but the ship and the piano in it gives her "a smoke signal" (158). The ship has a Piano for which the new owner of the ship finds no buyer. Zubaida invites Elijah, her pianist friend-lover from the UK. Elijah comes and the two meet for the last time. Anwar comes to the shipyard in search of Meghna and comes across Zubaida and works as a labourer in one of the shipbreaking sites. Zubaida also finds Shona who has tried to escape to Bangladesh hiding in the Piano. The ship is thus indispensable in bringing to Zubaida more than she has expected. It is as if for so long Zubaida has been in the sea of life and for the first time, she comes to the shore and finds what she has been searching for: "Once you get to the shore, everyone goes their own way" (158).

A metonymy of "mestiza consciousness", the ship becomes the melting pot of the past and present and of the different cultures she straddles in and it seems to be an anchor to her multiple existences. Further, the ship symbolises the memory of her good days. The ship is a metaphor for her floating identity and her existence: "Like houses and villages, boats stand for the basic social units of a family or community" (qtd. in Ballard 391).

The title *The Bones of Grace* refers to the remains of the abandoned ship called *Grace* which was brought to a shipbreaking site in Bangladesh. The title also refers to the bones of *Ambulocetus* found at Dera Bugti. The son of the local chief Zamzam who helped in the "dig" called the bones so: "These are bones of grace, Zamzam said...." (68). The bones are found after much sweat and exertion. They are as if god-gifted. They have dignity in terms of their ontological archaeological and anthropological values. Moreover, their discovery gives Zubaida the identity she has been seeking and encourages her in her personal "dig".

The image of the whale and the ship are crucial in the novel to understand Zubaida's constant mental and physical shift and variation, her dilemmas and impasses regarding the determination of her identity, her constant entanglement with such dilemmas, her negotiations, appropriations and her subsequent instrumentality in the complex developments around her.

Elijah, Diana, Anwar pave the path towards the discovery of the "I" in her. They are undoubtedly her 'others.' But sometimes she herself becomes her 'other': "I would have been looking around the corner for myself, the subject and the object at the same time" (*TBG* 36).

The novel itself is a human agency. Zubaida's being and becoming is a human agency. The anthropologist-cum-novelist Anam and paleontologist-cum-narrator Zubaida assert the significance of the human agency in the following lines: "...we are in the age of the Anthropocene, when humans rule the world, dictate the conditions and possibilities of life, shorten or lengthen the survival of the planet . . . we live on a planet shaped by humans. Not by nature, not by time, or history, or dinosaurs, but by us" (*TBG* 398).

Zubaida forgives her parents when she comes to know that her adoption is "born out of a need to love and be loved, I could see that now and I believed it... that their solution for the damping of their sorrow had collapsed around them and left them no option but to settle for someone else's child" (*TBG* 336).

Zubaida accepts that she is far from being complete. She does not make any effort to hide her incompleteness. As she muses on her life and on her inevitable presence of indecisiveness, the lack of fixity dawns on her: "I thought again and again about ... all the choices people made about their loyalties, and I knew that, no matter what I did, there would always be that tug in another direction, a headwind that would cast a sweeping and overwhelming doubt" (*TBG* 89).

Diana is not complete. Grace is not complete. She is not complete. With vision and mental picture, Zubaida scribes and brushes her life and strives to make it complete. She leaves her mark in every place she visits, has relations with those places and she is desperate to make a whole out of the parts. The archaeological 'dig' helps in the revelation of the evolution of the whales. Zubaida's personal 'dig' helps in the revelation of her evolution – her love, her longing, her ambivalences, her insecurities, her transgressions, and her revelations regarding her true identity. She faces her lacunae and presents it truthfully which emancipates her from all her negativities—her incompleteness, her ambivalence and her rootlessness. Like Diana, she is "incomplete yet magnificent". She becomes the essence of the novel, the bone, the backbone, the "bone of grace" in the novel.

As there is no factual description and empirical evidence about her mother, Zubaida imaginatively recreates an image of her mother (Fatema Ansar) which "resembles a life, a history, something she can hold on to" (400). As it is the epoch predominated by the human, "there is nothing more human than to dream" (401). In her dream, Zubaida looks at her mother as a woman who was a victim of "the heel of fate" (399). She was a woman who welcomed her poverty and did not hold any grudge against fate. She bore her misery with an eye to the moon imagining "the other lives she might have had" (399). She married a man who met his death from snake-bite soon after the marriage. It was the first disaster that fell on her. The second blow of fate fell on her when the in-laws refused to provide for her. The third blow was the birth of twin girls – Mohona and Meghna. With heavy heart, she had to give up one daughter, Mohona who later became Zubaida. Despite a series of misfortunes, she "dreams too big for her life, the first act of will she had ever committed giving her a small measure of happiness. It wasn't much, but it was something" (400). This imaginative construction is necessary for her as it is a means a recovery from her wounded past.

Towards the end of the novel, Zubaida is past regret, insecurity, fear and most importantly she is past her ambivalence and the "amphibian" state. She has achieved mestiza consciousness. And in the light of this new consciousness Zubaida seems to be at peace: "I had no one else to blame, no one to murder in my sleep" (217). She does not blame anybody for her strangeness: "I had always had my adoption to blame on my sense of not belonging" (265). She has somehow joined and shaped all available hyphens and dashes in her life; she is a Diana born out of her fragments. But she is not satisfied with this task and this achievement. She wants to stand tall, to have an identity of her own, and to leave her signature presence in the pages of history:

> Now that I have pieced together not just the fossil but myself, I must tell you that this forensic approach no longer satisfies me, Elijah. It is no longer enough for me to uncover the truth. I want to make my tracks on the world, leave my own mysterious scratchings on the walls of history. (*TBG* 406)

Zubaida claims that from the beginning to the end she has not tampered with her story, that she has not "cut the tether to the truth" (406). She has "to tell the story exactly as it happened" (406). But she can manipulate the story of others with the brush of imagination: "I can start with a true story and I can make the rest up, blunt the edges of a tragedy" (406). The novel ends proleptically. In the end, Zubaida hopes an imaginary unison with her mother and with her lost lover, those who will give her a sense of belongingness. She leaves behind the grim ghost i.e. the past and looks forward "past Diana and the glass flowers and Zamzam and Meghna and the war my parents fought, all of our ghosts behind us, and before us the terrible, dark world- belonging only to each other" (*TBG* 407). It is not only Zubaida who wishes to make a forward movement, leaving behind the past. It is also the wish of the novelist Tahmima Anam. The backward and forward movement charts the journey of her Bengal trilogy. Like a seer, Anam sees that the world before her is dark, and at the same time, assures us that the darkness can be dispelled with human bonding, love and belongingness.

Mestiza consciousness helps us comprehend fully the internal and external clashes of Zubaida's life, her "lived experiences" and the "implications of those experiences" (Hernandez 8). Mestiza consciousness is emancipatory in its premise as those infused with it get over the wrongs done to them and get freed from personal, social, political and other conflicts and contradictions. Infused with it, Zubaida is no longer a "nowhere woman". She gets freed from her conflicts and contradictions and is relieved of the burden of ambivalence and of her bipartite state.

Chapter IV

Women against Religious Extremism in *The Good Muslim* and *Purple Hibiscus*

"The disease of religious fundamentalism is not restricted to Bangladesh alone and it must be fought at every turn....I am convinced that the only way the fundamentalist forces can be stopped is if all of us who are secular and humanistic join together and fight their malignant influence. I, for one, will not be silenced" (Cummins 53).

This quote from the Preface of the Banngladeshi writer Taslima Nasreen's novel, *Shame (Lajja)* cited in Angela Cummins' "Taslima Nasreen and the Fight against Fundamentalism" refers to the extensive sway religious fundamentalism has on almost every social groups, especially women, and the position of women under its authority. The quote has a direct bearing on this chapter as it deals with women subjectivity vis a vis religious fundamentalism. The quote has a direct bearing on this chapter as it deals with women subjectivity vis a vis religious fundamentalism.

Fundamentalism whether it is Muslim or Christian

"claim[s] that [only] their version of religion is true" (Yuval-Davis and Sahgal 3) and for this, they are ready to shed their own blood and the blood of others. These fundamentalists suffer from a one-dimensional disorder. They cannot see beyond themselves. They cannot accept the ways of other than themselves. They are blind to reason and allergic to pluralism: "All fundamentalists, whether Muslim, Jewish, Christian or otherwise, are partners in the attempt to breed division, strife, racism and sexism" (Saadawi 13). Moreover, in the cog of the dogmatic iron rules of fundamentalism, women get pissed off. Irrespective of religion, and across the countries, fundamentalism is bent on a single goal. It is to control women by making them the standard-bearers of the society they belong to. The exertion of control on women also takes place by putting on their shoulder the onus of carrying a set of predefined and delimiting societal standards:

> Fundamentalism appears in many different forms in religions throughout the world, but at the heart of all fundamentalist agenda is the control of women's minds and bodies. All religious fundamentalists support the patriarchal family as a central agent of such control. They view women as embodying the morals and traditional values of the family and the whole community. (*WAF* 1)

Leading female characters in Tahmima Aanm's *The Good Muslim* and Chimamanda Adichie's *Purple Hibiscus* keep their struggle on against the force of ultraist religious beliefs which are detrimental to them and to their community.

Sohail in *The Good Muslim* and Papa Eugene in *Purple Hibiscus* "construct a particular version of Islam/Christianity as the only valid representation of [their] religion. Most significantly, [they] abstract [their religion and its practice] from history and project the particular amalgam of belief, ritual, and practice with a transcendental validity" (Chhachhi 14). This chapter focuses on how women characters – Maya in *The Good Muslim* and Kambili, Ifeoma in *Purple Hibiscus* register and refuse the fundamentalism of Sohail and Eugene with their plastic and plural consciousness ("mestiza consciousness"). Though Maya rejects Sohail's path, at the very end of the novel she understands it. For Maya, Sohail's failing is her failing. She identifies with her brother's ways and forgives him. Kambili's rejection of Papa Eugene's ways takes place silently. The orientation of her anti-fundamentalist disposition takes its root and blooms under the influence of Ifeoma and Father Amadi. In the first section of this chapter, *The Good Muslim* will be taken into consideration and in the second section, *Purple Hibiscus* will be taken into consideration.

Maya vs. Sohail: Rising Beyond "good" and "bad" Muslim in
The Good Muslim.

The Good Muslim published in 2011 is the second part of Tahmima Anam's Bengal Trilogy and is a follow-up of what is narrated in *A Golden Age*. In this novel, Anam "examines the consequences of war, the hazards of an uneasy peace, the gains and losses of nation-building..." (Hussein). The novel is "told largely from the perspective of Maya, whose idealism is tempered by experiences...." (Hussein). The novel is in three Books and spans from 1971 to 1992. The Liberation War is over. "Sonar Bangla" (Bangladesh) is trying to rise up healing its 'wounds. It is a time of homecoming and becoming:

> It was a winter of return, mothers waiting at home, preparing elaborate meals with the leftover war rations, straining their eyes to the road, jumping at the slightest sound. Inevitably, the moment of homecoming did not happen in the way they imagined...."
> (*TGM* 25)

The gap between expectations and reality is highlighted here. People of East Pakistan expected the Liberation War will bring in a "golden age of freedom" for them; but the jarring and catastrophic impact of the war is opposite to their expectation. The angst ensuing the Liberation war, and the challenges which are ahead of the nation and its people are clearly communicated in the beginning of the novel. Misery unleashed by the war is spiralling. The dream of freedom is Edenic into which war makes a snake-like crawl and brings in its wake an assemblage of more negatives and less positives. People have become subject to melancholia, reprisal, alienation and wreckage, turning the country into a kind of purgatory:

> Mourning and reparation, exile and return, losses both personal and political link the novel's past and present. Two patterns emerge ... the nostalgic colours of memory, when a nation dreamed of freedom and equality for all, interwoven with a dark, rough thread in which the brutality of war invades the psyches even of the dreamers and the idealists. (Hussein 187)

In the post-Liberation War scenario, the newly formed nation diverges into two roads– the secular and the religious. The moot question is which one is better and which one is 'good' and which one is 'bad'. The previous novel focused on the 'before', 'the during', the "home" (the Haque family) and the "world"(the Freedom Struggle), the struggles of Rehana to prevent things from falling apart, while *The Good Muslim* focuses on the 'after', the aftermath of the Bangladesh Liberation War, on the posterity, on the "roads taken" by the scions of Rehana and Iqbal Haque – Maya and Sohail: "...but after it was all over, the killing and the truce and the redrawing of the border, he had gone one way, and she another (*TGM* 15). It is through Maya's inclusive consciousness , Anam "disrupts" the binary among the religious/secular; the "good" Muslim and the "bad" Muslim.

Soumya Lal in the article, "Silence and the Ethics of Partial Empathy in Tahmima Anam's *The Good Muslim*" discusses "the crises of empathy" (1) between Maya and Sohail. And the crisis occurs due to the "alienating experiences of post-war trauma" and due to their "irreconcilable differences about religion" (2). Lal points out the limited range of empathy and talks about "partial empathy" which is incapable of completely comprehending the self of the other, which "does not dissolve all distances between the self and the other, even though it does enable some proximities (6). In case of Maya who is endowed with "mestiza consciousness", it is not partial but complete empathy through which she completely appropriates and identifies with the otherness of her brother.

The narrative is relayed to the readers mainly through Maya's viewpoint. Her narration flows back and forth in time, from the stroke of success in 1971 to its present. The structural and temporal skeleton of the novel is as per the following – Prologue:1971 December ; Book One :1984 February, 1972 February, 1984 February, 1984 March, 1972 March, 1984 April, 1984 May, 1972 April,

1984 June; Book Two: 1984 July, 1972 May, 1984 August, 1973 March, 1984 September, 1973 July, 1984 October, 1974 January, 1984 October, 1984 November, Headmaster Headmaster Headmaster, 1984 December; Book Three: 1985 February, 1985 February, 1977 November, 1985 February , The Following Day Cold and not a Speck of Light; Epilogue 1992.

The Prologue begins in December 1971 "eight days after the end of the war" (*TGM* 7). Sohail Haque, a "mukti yodhha" (freedom fighter) is returning home. It is a time of "post-war disillusionment" marked by "dying mustard", "scent of meat", "cry of grass" (*TGM* 7), abandonment and ruin, blood and mud. Sohail is presented as an exhausted and broken man. Before the war, he was gentle, tender-hearted and compassionate. He was a young university student, a literature and social enthusiast whose steadfast companions were Goethe, Rilke, and Marx. During the war, Sohail was troubled by the individual misery of men and women in his neighbourhood and by the misery of the nation. He decided to dive into the cause of the nation by taking part in the Liberation War, "to lie down on one of the bunks with a half-smoked cigarette" (*TGM* 8). After the war, we find him shell shocked. He has changed radically and has become a "religious fundamentalist". To Maya's utter surprise, Sohail has metamorphosed into a different being altogether. The question that arises is: Is it War that has taken a heavy toll on him or is it a matter of choice?

Book One entitled "All that is in the Heavens and on Earth" begins with Maya in February 1984. She is coming home to reunite with her family in Dhaka after more than ten years after the end of the War. All the while, she has been a country doctor, who had forfeited her early days' dream of becoming a surgeon. It is a time of change and on the way back home, she notices very many permutations: the home is not the same, the mother is not the same, the brother is not the same, and the country is not the same. The critical situation in the family is a looking glass through which the critical situation of the nation gets reflected:

> The family crises mirror the state of the nation. A dictator is in power; war crimes are still unaccounted for, and criminals are on the loose. The stories of women raped and abused during the war for an independent Bangladesh have been erased or marginalised in the search for a clean, linear history. Frantic forms of religiosity proliferate (Hussein 185).

In the previous novel *A Golden Age*, the light of the narrative falls on Rehana. In the earlier novel, she was active, assertive and very much concerned, having butterflies in her stomach; but in *The Good Muslim*, she is uninvolved, disinterested, non-resisting, resigned, and unperturbed. In *The Good Muslim*, the spotlight of the narrative is on Maya who:

> ...saw a great weariness in her mother's gesture. She sees that, whatever is happening upstairs, Ammoo has decided to ignore it. She is no longer the protective, panicky mother she had once been. Now she is in retreat from them, passively accepting whatever it is they chose to do: turning to God, running away, refusing to send their children to school. There was nothing of the struggle left in her anymore. (*TGM* 34)

The narrative veers to the siblings of Rehana whom Maya has taken over from and whose shoes she has stepped into; but whether Maya is the superimposition of Rehana or an upgradation is a different question. It is mainly through the subjectivity of Maya and Rehana, Anam presents an apperception of Sohail's psyche who becomes an ultraconservative, diehard zealot.

In *The Good Muslim*, the personal/familial, political and religious are interlaced. The novel is not merely a portrayal of the post-Liberation War situation. It is also an account of the struggle of the Haque family trying to heal the traumatic effect of the war. In the novel, Anam delves into her birthplace at a given span of time to seek and understand its extant state of affairs. Anam says: "My worst fear, my deepest fear about Bangladesh is... that it turns into a nation in which religion becomes the primary marker of identity...." (Roy 15). *The Good Muslim* comes out of Anam's concern for the fundamentalist turn Bangladesh has taken. Anam has problematized the idea of being a "good" Muslim and has investigated how due to the war the social, religious, and moral articles of faith of the Bangladeshis suffer a serious jolt.

Like her mother, Maya becomes the "national actor": "In Maya, Anam illustrates a politically active woman determined to participate when civil war breaks out" (Ranasinha 115). According to Sohail's friend Joy, Maya is "Maya-bee". Her words "sting like a bee" (*TGM* 41). But as far as the work is concerned, she is a bee too. She works day and night in the Rehabilitation Centre doing abortions, comforting, consoling and fighting for the rape victims who are named as "Birangonas" by the Great Leader, Sheikh Mujib. Ruvani Ranasinha sums up Maya's agency for the cause of the nation after the War:

> Maya performed abortions on some of the thousands of female rape victims named 'Birangonas' ....While the female victims remain shrouded in internalised

'shame', the perpetrators go unpunished. This inspires Maya to write for opposition newspapers and to participate in the larger political movement calling for Bangladesh's unnamed dictator to prosecute war criminals who live with impunity in neighbouring Pakistan. (113-114).

On her way home, Maya brings with her a mango seedling which she looks forward to seeding down in the garden plot of her home ground, the place where she haunts as a child. It resembles Tahmima Anam's homecoming through Maya and the sapling is the metaphor of the novel itself: "The question is, can the sapling – and Maya – be transplanted in a garden and a country changed beyond recognition by all that has happened?" (Roy 14).

Maya comes to know from her mother that Sohail has joined Tablighi Jamaat ("The Congregation of Islam"), an Islamic group of preachers. They are "an ultra-orthodox Islamic sect which preaches that Muslims should replicate the life of Muhammad" (Taylor 2009). Their slogan is: "Oh Muslims become true Muslims". They "copy Muhammad in all his customs, even it is reported, eschewing beds for sleeping and toothbrushes for cleaning teeth; they use a twig" (Taylor 2009). It has its headquarters in Shona, the house once used for sheltering the "mukti yodhhas". Sohail and his wife Silvi hold religious gatherings upstairs and in the mosque, they deliver religious addresses to men and women regarding "everything there was to know about being a Muslim. God, men, morality. Purdah and sex. The life of the Prophet. His wives, Ayesha and Khadija, and Zaynab. The raising of children. How to be one of the faithful" (*TGM* 22).

The trauma of the Liberation War drives Sohail to take refuge in radical Islam but he falls into "the snare of literalism" of Islam. He is a both a believing Muslim and a practicing one. He is a "fundamentalist in the sense that [he] take[s] the Koran to be the literal Word of God, as dictated to the Prophet Muhammad through the agency of the Angel Gabriel" (Ruthven 52). The deceased father gets embodied in the Symbolic father, Allah to whom Sohail's life is firmly anchored. Sohail's biological father Iqbal Haque is dead. In the absence of his biological father, Sohail turns to the political father, Sheikh Mujibur Rahman. But very soon he is frustrated with the war and Sheikh Mujib and finally turns to the symbolic father who "is to be conceived as 'transcended' as an irreducible given of the signifier" (Wilden 271). For Sohail, what outweighs everything else is the symbolic, the spiritual Father. For him, Allah is "the archetypal Father [who] is the source of creation through the Logos or the Word, not the body, and is the source of order and consciousness. He is an invisible, disembodied presence hovering behind the material world" (Rosefeldt 17). Sohail jumps into this belief and is immersed in it.

Maya's experience and struggle as a young village doctor has enriched her and has made different kinds of faith manifest to her, so much so that she has lost faith in monism. In fact, she has lost faith in any particular religion or organized religion. During her stay in the village as country doctor, Maya is exposed to people who pray in the mosques; people who revere the Muslim Prophet and Christian saints with equal devotion; people who worship Bon-Bibi, the goddess of the forest; Bauls who are invited to sing in the village "who sang the songs of Lalon, turning the words of the Qur'an into song, a tryst between lovers, casting the divine as the beloved, the poet as His supplicant" (*TGM* 170). This exposure broadens her belief and makes it bent towards plurality.

While Sohail is obsessed with after-life, the dos and don'ts of religion, living in ritual-ridden spiritual and moral world, Maya is obsessed with life. She gives up name and fame and decides to become a gynaecologist without knowing that she is engaged in post-war overhaul:

> Somewhere along the way she had decided to become a lady doctor instead of a surgeon. She had seen how the women's faces changed when she entered the chamber, relaxing their grip on the examining table. At the time she told herself it was a practical matter. Anyone could become a surgeon, but a doctor for women, a doctor who could deliver their babies and stitch their wounds afterwards and teach them about birth control— that is what they needed. She didn't think of the debt she was repaying, that each of the babies she brought into the world might someday be counted against the babies that had died, by her hand, after the war. (*TGM* 13)

The way Maya reacts heretically, rationally and humanly to the extremely religious and sacerdotal view of Sohail, suggests that she rejects her brother's ways. Maya takes it as gospel truth that Islam brings them back to the ruthlessness and savagery of the Liberation War, wherefore it is to be annulled and struck out for her good, for the good of the family and the good of the nation:

> Maya had taught herself away from faith. She had unlearned the surahs her mother had recited aloud... had erased from her memory all knowledge of the sacred, returned her body to a time before it had

been taught to kneel, to prostrate itself… because [of] all the things she had witnessed, committed in the name of God (*TGM* 170).

After Sohai's homecoming, everyone especially Maya is eager to hear stories of his heroism, "that he planted bombs under country bridges and that he got away just before the flame hit the powder, and that the felled bridge cut off the army, and the people of north Tangail or Kushtia or Bogra were saved" (105). But Sohail does not have any such romantic story to tell; he has a grim and gruesome story to tell which he fails to give an account of. If he is to give facts and open his heart to Maya, he will have to tell her that he has murdered people and has participated in the brutal massacre. So, he chooses silence. But "Maya continues to follow him with her eyes, reproach him with a stony silence. Silence for silence" (105). The perceptive eye of Maya catches sight of the horrible spectacle that "death hovers inside him, the death to which he had come so close in the war, he and death in a tight corridor. Now it is like a bruise that won't heal" (*TGM* 106).

Indeed, much has changed after Maya's final homecoming. But the change is not only anticipatory, damaging and ruinous, but also positive and for the good:

The house was changed, but it had survived. And she had made it, two train rides and a ferry across the country, and she was laying her head on her mother's lap, and there was nothing to do now but remember all the times they had returned to this house, she and her brother, to find everything was the same and not the same, to find their mother waiting, waiting. (*TGM* 24)

In the dispirited and lugubrious post-war scenario,

this passage offers a positive direction. It suggests that the familial bond, the human bond can dispel negativity. And the bond is capable of impelling and recharging them with positivity and resilience so that they can revamp, rehabilitate and overcome the loss. As a result, it would not matter whether "everything was the same [or] not the same" (*TGM* 24). In addition, the passage "emphasizes Rehana's [Maya's too] constancy and, more abstractly, the inviolacy of the parent–child relationship, which can be read as a positive future- orientation... [and] retains a hopeful vision for the future" (Cilano72).

While Maya's experience as a country doctor during the war keeps her away from religion by a great deal, Sohail's bitter war experience makes him take religion in arms. In the post-war traumatic phase, Sohail falls completely on to the Qur'an which his mother Rehana lets him have who is apprehensive of her son's mental health. Sohail makes matters up and makes peace with the Qur'an. "The book believes he is good ...it is the greatest thing that has ever happened to him. He has found something, something that explains everything". The book helps him overcome his trauma; overcome his wife's death, and according to it, he arranges his son's education and even his mother's illness:

> The Book spoke to his every sorrow, to every bruise of his life. It spoke to the knife passing across the throat of an innocent man; it spoke to the day his father died, hand on his arrested heart; and it spoke to the machine-gun sound that echoed in his chest, night after night, and to the hollow where Piya had been. And every idea he had ever had about the world, it spoke to those too. That every man was equal before God –

how foolish of him to believe that Marx had invented this concept, when it was ancient, even deeper than ancient, embedded in the very germ of every being; that is what God had intended, what God had created. He wept from the beauty of it. (*TGM* 139).

While Sohail is tolerable to a point, his obdurate and callous choice regarding his son is hardly acceptable not only to Maya but also to us and Anam has shown "the real dangers of being so extreme in one's beliefs and having that be the only thing that matters" (Lissa 2011): "I feel I have a certain commitment to Muslims in challenging the stereotypes out there. I don't feel I am a religious person; my parents are Marxists and I grew up in a very secular household" (Roy 15).

Sohail is not the only fundamentalist in the novel. There are other characters in the novel who share his temperament and ideology. The villagers of Rajshahi where Maya has served as a country doctor, Masud, the husband of Nazia, Maya's first village patient are cases in point. The imposition of fundamentalism has heavily affected the women of remote areas who are economically weak. The curse of fundamentalism "women, especially poor women suffer the most" (Saadawi 12). At some point, the narrator describes: "A woman is believed to be like private part" (Rahman 11). She should not come out in public. At the village in Rajshahi where Maya has opened her private clinic, "there were rules about pregnant women, about where they could bathe" (19). Pregnant women are forbidden to bathe in public. On an excruciatingly hot summer day, Maya goes swimming with Nazia. The so-called protectors of the village complain to Nazia's husband Masud: "The men of the village had appeared in front of his house, shaking their heads. A pregnant woman in the pond? It was too much" (*TGM* 19). When Nazia brings forth a flat-nosed child with "Down's syndrome" that "looks like a Chink" (*TGM* 19), Masud thinks that she has violated the most important of the wifely duties i.e. maintenance of chastity: "In Islam, extra marital sex for men has become an inseparable part of life and society, whereas for women Islamic society upholds the value of virginity and marital fidelity" (Rahman 11). Without understanding the medical condition the baby is in, Masud suspects his wife, declares the illegitimacy of the child, and is bent on punishing her:

> The punishment was one hundred and one lashes. Masud came back from the meeting and spat the words at his wife. 'One hundred and one,' he said. 'That's what you deserve.' …. That Chink is not my baby. Lyingcheatingwhoreofawife….Raise the sari! Whore!....Shesh. *Finished*....And was that a smile in the man's eye? The one who was only following orders, protecting the village, the name of the village. (*TGM* 23)

Maya intervenes in vain. She is a mute spectator, counting the lashes. Of the lashes, one "shaped like a question mark" falls on her too. The question mark-like lash raises questions regarding the clout of fundamentalism, Masud's blindness towards reason and common sense, the helplessness not only of Nazia but also of Maya.

Maya is Anam's champion, her mouthpiece, and throws herself in with her and is well-disposed towards the viewpoint of Maya. Direct attack against religious extremism would have been unwarranted in the then context, especially in the context of Bangladesh. That is why, Anam has resorted to her fictional counterpart, Maya to do the same. Through Maya, Anam has been able to express her take on religion: "I got to say things through her that I maybe wouldn't on my own character. But that is the real joy of getting to invent people. You can exercise parts of yourself that you may not get to in real life" (Lissa 2011). Maya is unlike women like Nazia, who tolerate the punishment silently in the name of religion and thereby giving implicit consent to the exercise of fundamental practices. Maya's vigorous, anti-fundamental activism sets example for women like Nazia who get easily silenced and at the same time the version of her resistance and actions for change advocates the cause of women that is is in contradistinction to the official version which presents women as subject to "gender abuse": "Maya's activism, professional heroism provides a counterpoint to the stories of gendered abuse" (Ranasinha 114).

In *The Good Muslim* Anam is very much sympathetic to Sohail's immediate conversion to radicalism: "I have tried to explain why Sohail turns to this strict religious life because of the trauma of the war, and try to make him into a three-dimensional humane character rather than a person who we just sort of look from the outside and judge very harshly" (Roy 15). She has become successful because it is done through women's subjectivity. Anam says:

> I wanted to write a story about these two characters and their clashing concept of what it means to lead a moral life. Ultimately, I wanted the secular character to win because I think she's right, the brother is not. But other than that, things developed quite organically, and I tried to be as sympathetic to Sohail as I could (Roy 15).

All through the narrative, we find that Maya and Sohail

swing between two extreme ideological poles with a no-go and no-win situation. The "brother-sister duo symbolize... the clash between secularism and fundamentalism" (Nast 2017). While Maya is anthropocentric and androcentric, Sohail is theocentric, having a logocentric belief in religion. The polemics between them is apperceived at the end of the novel. The family becomes the crossroad of the dialectics between an urbane mode of Islam and an extremist mode of Islam among siblings. The "brutality of war invades the psyches even of the dreamers and the idealists" (Hussein 2011). War impinges on the two – Maya and Sohail and creates laceration and clash and their ways dichotomize and dissents to two different paths as ways and means of getting through and living through the bottom line of life.

Like Sohail, Maya too is a fundamentalist in her own way. Her fundamentalism is devoid of any religious connotation. She is a fundamentalist in her obdurate mooring to a set of exclusive beliefs for which she has to leave home, give up her initial dream of becoming a doctor, and for which her relationship with Sohail, her mother, Joy develops cracks and which clouds her judgment. Amrah Abdul Majid and Ahmad Jalaluddin in their article bring it up overtly:

> Both Maya and Sohail are extremists in their own sense – Maya, in her vehement rejection of Sohail's turn to religion, and Sohail, in his blind and unreasonable devotion to it. From this, Anam draws the interconnection between the supposed side of the divide by highlighting the porous relationship between them. It portrays the fair share of illogicality and reason, extremism and moderation and ethical and unethical

behaviours in both the religious and the secular (Majid & Jalaluddin 27).

Majid and Jalaluddin are right to a great extent about Sohail and Maya. But they fail to see that the "divide" they refer to moves on until the end where it ceases and the "porous relationship" between the siblings becomes impervious as at the end of the novel a new consciousness dawns on Maya in which the disunity of the split and vacuity gets married and saturated.

When Sohail comes and tells Maya that he has been praying, Maya takes it casually and brushes it aside by saying, "don't start talking religious mumbo-jumbo" (106). Maya cannot accept the sudden spurt of religiosity in Sohail. She thinks that either her brother is ill or in shell shock and that religion cannot be the cure of the disease Sohail is suffering from: "'you remember, don't you, what they did to us in the name of God?'"(107). Sohail gives a good rejoinder that religion is not evil by itself but it is the people who use it evilly: "Just because it was usurped for evil ends doesn't make it a bad thing" (108). The Book has made Sohail believe that he survives the war when many others could not for a reason. It is not sheer luck but the will of Allah and this he has failed to make Maya believe. Maya and Sohail fail to dissuade and persuade each other. Sohail "turns away" and Maya "turns to" her mother: "'He's going to turn your house into a mosque, didn't you hear?'" (109). Rehana who cannot see the fundamentalism of Sohail coming asks Maya to be excusing and easy with the ways of Sohail: "'Why, child, why do you have to be so intolerant?' ... 'He's going to pray; he's going to go to the mosque on Fridays. Don't be so frightened of it. It's only religion'" (109). By "only religion" Rehana means 'just', 'nothing more' and 'at the least' but ironically for Sohail, who needs to fold and sheathe his heavily appalled and upset heart with "a certainty, a path" it becomes entirely, wholly, purely and solely "only religion".

The other women in the novel are not free from the clutches of religious extremism. It is for women and by women, Sohail becomes drawn to religion farther and farther away from his former self, his former sets of beliefs and moves farther from Marx, Rilke, and *Lady Chatterley's Lover*. It is Rehana who gives the *Holy Book* to Sohail but her purpose is harmless. She thinks that Sohail will find the same solace she has been finding from the Book; she does what every mother would do for her son. It is the war and its by-products that have turned Sohail into a fundamentalist.

So many factors are there behind Sohail's conversion – "Piya, the war, the disappointing ordinariness of freedom" (145); but Maya has a strong conviction that Sohail's old self has been put to an end by his first love, Silvi who lives on the other side of the road, and who is the daughter of Mrs. Aziza Chowdhury, the friend of Rehana in times past. After her husband's death, Silvi keeps watching Sohail, and Maya keeps watching Silvi. Maya "knew that whatever direction her brother Sohail might be taking, it would be Silvi who pressed him further along the journey" (145). It is true that Rehana sets Sohail's religious ardour in motion; but it is Silvi who pushes him to the brink of extremism and whatever hope is left of Sohail turns into utter despair. Before the marriage with Silvi, Sohail is reasonable and feasible, but after their marriage: "There was only one. One message. One Book. The world narrowed. Curtains between men and women. Lines drawn in the sand. And Silvi, coated in black, reigned in her brother's heart" (*TGM* 149-150).

Sohail's religious detour is at the cost of his kith and

kin, as he starts overlooking more and more towards his familial obligations and responsibilities. For him, the world becomes a "grand design" (*TGM* 71). He turns away from "the death of his father, his wife...and it left no room for self-pity" (*TGM* 71). He is even apathetic to providing a good life to his only existing issue, Zaid. Besides sacrificing for the country during the war, Maya takes all pain for the family – the wellbeing of their mother diagnosed with cancer and the wellbeing of her brother's son Zaid whose mother is dead. But Sohail has "reconstructed the word 'family', and that she was nothing more than a girl he once knew" (*TGM* 71). For his mother and son, Sohail comes up with two arrangements which Maya is averse to: "Water from the Well of Zamzam" for the cancer of Rehana and Madrasa for Zaid.

Traumatised by the violence of war, Sohail has embraced religion tightly. Moreover, Sohail's religious bent is encouraged and augmented by his wife Silvi and his mother Rehana. What the war and women like Silvi and Rehana have done to Sohail, Maha has not been able to undo. In response to the extremist and fundamentalist choice of Sohail and others, Maya chooses a middle-of-the-road which is tolerant, nonpartisan, and peaceable.

Maya on her return expects to get back the impenetrable and cementing bond that was penetrated and worn out by the War years. In the absence of the father, both Rehana and Maya count on him especially Maya. She takes "Sohail's conversion, how he had morphed from an ordinary man into a Holy one" (Anam 51) personally: " . . . how fiercely she had needed him to be like her, how she had turned away when he had leaned towards God, taken it personally, as though he had done it to offend her" (Anam 18). The sense of Maya's loss and dispossession is figuratively put by Anam as: "... Maya noticed one of her teeth missing at the back of her mouth. Then the years opened up and took shape – the shape of that molar, craggy and smooth, big and small, a chasm" (Anam 18). The loss of teeth symbolizes the loss of a loved one, someone as close and integral to her existence as teeth is to her body. The cavity symbolizes the cavity in their bond, the alienation, the hollowing of the bond created by and during the interwar period.

Maya gradually discerns Sohail's separation. The sign becomes visible when he starts getting rid of Ibsen, Rilke, Lawrence, Fitzgerald, Waugh, *The Scarlet Letter*. All of a sudden, Sohail turns against books. He has decided: "His wife, a future without books" (205). But Maya is insistent:

> 'You put those books in crates, I'm going to
> take them out and lay them open for you.
> Every book you put away I will unpack and
> leave at your doorstep....I'm going to keep
> bringing the books back until you can't
> ignore them anymore'(*TGM* 205).

Sohail does not relent. He finds out another way to dispose of the books. While Maya sings songs of hope, Sohail piles up the books and burns them all, and at the same time, burns all the dogged hope Maya clings to.

Rehana holds Maya accountable for all this: "Did you listen? No. You mocked him.... You led him here, calling him a mullah. Why? You couldn't stand for him to be different'" (*TGM* 208). Outraged, repelled, and overwrought, Maya leaves home and renders her medical service here and there: "Rangamati, Bandorbon, Kushtia. She finally travelled back up, avoiding the city, weaving up the Jamuna, the Brahmaputra, and into Rajshahi, where she settled..." (*TGM* 210) until she returns home with which the novel kicks off.

Even after coming home, she finds things the same. The conflict between them surfaces once again and reaches the crux regarding Zaid's education. Maya wants Zaid to go to a normal school but Sohail sends him to Chandpur Madrasa while Maya is busy with Rehana's illness.

The agonizing, terrifying, traumatic, and pitiable condition of Zaid in Chandpur Madrasa and his heart-rending outcry and groan: "Abboo, Abboo, Abboo" enunciate the predicament and wretched condition of the children in the religious schools in Bangladesh:

> He is alone with the blanket and the plate, the grey light from a slit between the thatch and the wall, the scratch of rats, and as the lock is turned he hurls himself at the door and opens his voice to the footsteps fading with every moment, until there is nothing but his own voice, begging to be released, and his fist on the wall, and each cry echoing into the next: Abboo, Abboo, Abboo. At this moment he is more afraid of what is in the room, the aloneness and the rats and the line of light against the wall, than of what is beyond. He is wrong. (*TGM* 144)

Zaid is indeed wrong. He fails to foresee what tragedy lies beyond. He fails to foresee that he will be a victim of sexual abuse in this pit by the paedophile, sadist and pervert Huzoor. He does not foresee his death and millions like him; he does not foresee the country tilting towards fundamentalism.

If in the previous novel Rehana allegorizes the then Bangladesh and Maya and Sohail the Bangladesh of the future, in this novel Maya and Sohail allegorize the post-war Bangladesh and Zaid, the son of Sohail allegorizes the nation down the road and close at hand, the nation -to-be and to become in future. So, when Sohail decides to send him to Madrasa school, Maya objects as she cannot let her brother destroy the future. To this end, Maya visits Sohail at Ghost Road to talk to him. She expresses her serious concern over the safety of Zaid. The madrasa where Zaid has been sent is a vulnerable place, not at all a safe and secure schoolhouse for children. Maya urges: "The madrasa is not a good place, Bhaiya.'" She has also expressed her deep apprehension that the "Huzoor is doing things…the children have no defence against him" (215). But Sohail once again turns his back again by throwing away her biased and one-sided concern: "He is my son. I will ensure his safety" (*TGM* 215). It becomes clear to Maya that Sohail will not pay any heed to Maya's suggestion. He will not go personally to rescue his son Zaid from Chandpur madrasa, the nether world of education. Sohail will rather stick to his belief than pulling "his son from whatever hellhole he had sent him to" (215).

Maya herself undertakes the responsibility to save Zaid and all alone she sets out on an arduous, onerous, troublesome, and exigent odyssey or mission "ZAIDWHEREISZAID" up the river Jamuna to locate Chandpur Madrasa, and nearly rescues Zaid, but loses Zaid forever and ends in Dhaka Central Jail where she stumbles upon the truth regarding Sohail's metamorphosis or metanoia:

> Scraps of her life come back to her. Swimming in the pond with Nazia. The smell of sesame trees. The books burning in the garden. Sohail's voice. *I killed, Maya. I killed.* So that he won't become like me. It wasn't Piya, it was Silvi. It was the war. War made it too

late. *I killed.* Now she knew what it was, the heaviness of death. (*TGM* 230)

Zaid is no more, but he makes us see lots of children like him. During the journey, Khoka becomes a superimposition of Zaid. Although she has failed to save Zaid, she has succeeded in achieving her "anagnorisis". She stumbles and sees many stark facets and gains a special insight into her own life into her brother's life.

She thinks that she will never forgive Sohail for his unconcern; Silvi for wrenching her brother away from her; Joy for his unexpected departure. While in the Dhaka Central Jail, Maya, to borrow Lear's words, "stumbles when she saw". She realizes how mistaken she has been all along about Joy, Sohail, Silvi, and Joy. Joy when asked by Maya explains why he left for America all on a sudden without informing Maya who was so close to him. After the death of his father, his anger reaches boiling point. He was so enraged and infuriated and vengeful that he would kill anyone whether he is a Bihari or a Pakistani. On that account, his mother hurried him off to America because he might have taken out his wrath on someone. On hearing this, Maya gets the picture and figures remorsefully out: "And how cruel she had been. Stings like a bee" (*TGM* 231).

Joy brings to the Dhaka Central Jail Rehana who brings out to Maya all she knows about Sohail and Silvi: "'I've come to tell you something'" (232). Rehana unfolds that it is not Silvi who is to be blamed for what her brother turns out to be. After the war, "and after what happened in the war" (232).

Sohail who misses his deceased father intensely comes into contact with a father figure Haji Mudassar, the imam worshipped in Kakrail mosque and is influenced by him. Rehana further explains "and after what happened in the war" (232). Whilst Sohail returns after saving the life of Piya from the barracks, he chances upon a man and kills him mercilessly, assuming him to be the representative of those who raped Piya. Before Sohail stabs the man, he hugs him "as if he were his long-dead father" and "wrapped his arms around Sohail's knees and said *Bismillah ir-Rahman ir- Raheem*. The man begged for his life..." (*TGM* 234). But at that moment "in the glint of that knife he saw the eyes of the girl in the barracks, her head round and with a dusting of hair" and butchered the man "as he recited *God is Great, God is Great, God is Great*". After this momentous madness, Sohail turns doggedly to God.

That death costs Sohail his entire life and changes the course of his life. The blood guilt keeps "ticking within him". He starts avoiding everyone including Rehana because he thinks that had she given him the book earlier, he would not have committed the heinous deed.

Maya finally accepts her brother's ways with a comprehensive consciousness. Her ways become the bulwark of religious pluralism as she is aware of herself and others. "Religious pluralism... is a consequence of a world where everyone is increasingly aware of everyone else, where 'no one leaves anyone else alone'" (Ruthven 45). Her ways towards the end pioneers what a nation should be. For Maya's pluralistic ways, Tahmima Anam expresses her debt to Rabindranath Tagore. In "Rabindranath Tagore's Legacy Lies in the Freedom-Seeking Women of His," she says:

> In my novel, there is a character whose brother is slowly becoming a religious fundamentalist. She tries in every way she can to remind him of his life before he

found his faith, and finally, as he begins to pack away his western clothes and books, she decides the only thing to do is sing to him. She sits outside his bedroom door and plays the Tagore songs they have loved since childhood. She holds up those words - patriotic, pastoral, devotional - against the narrowing of his mind. And that, ultimately, is Tagore's lasting legacy: a raised hand against all forms of rigidity, a love of country that is born out of its landscape and seasons; and a spiritual universe that encompasses a plurality of forms (Anam 89).

That Anam is hugely influenced by Rabindranath Tagore's "freedom-seeking women" who embodies his vision of unity and pluralism and that the character of Maya is also based on the same vision is made clear by Anam herself in the above lines.

Is Maya a failed idealist? Her idealism does not fail. The set of ideals she firmly follows gets eased and soothed by the unfolding of events by and by when she is exposed to different shocking revelations. She has her blind moments but the moment she realizes her mistakes, she lets things off easily, stops bearing malice, wipes the slate of grudge, takes everything and everyone in arms, and fares things forward. She becomes a rock-solid character, a charismatic and winsome character with a never-failing charm.

The novel not only manifests Maya's individual growth, but also the biography of the spirit of a country, and its suffering. The novel is regarding the journey of lifeline and return of inclusiveness. We can view the voyage as making its way past social religious compliance; it is a course of revelation and identification of the 'self' in the time of concurring with the past. In the novel,

Anam ... presents it [Maya's acceptance] as an act of healing for those who have been silenced for too long. And she shows her chastened heroine finally accepting Sohail's choice as the act of healing necessary for him. Maya cannot follow her brother's path, and it continues to grieve her, but she has come to understand it: She recognises the wound in his history . . . because she has one too (Smith 38).

For Zaid's death perhaps Maya is responsible. Sohail could have saved and could have secured his son's safety in his own way which might not have ended in death. This will haunt Maya forever as the murder of Sohail haunts him. This is Maya's scar which she takes care with her all-encompassing consciousness.

For critics like Cara Cilano, Maya and Sohail cannot connote: "how can secularist nationalists, like Maya, who are akin to van Schendel's 'renewal nationalists' contend with the influx of the "religious nationalism" embodied in Sohail's changed views?" (Cilano72). But towards the end of the novel, Maya understands in "clear light of day" that Sohail, Zaid are an inseparable part of her; their disappointment is her disappointment; their agony is her agony. She finds the essential harmony between the different ideologies and in her subjectivity, the duality, the asymmetry collapses and mutates to seamlessness and organic symmetry. It is the "mestiza consciousness". Piya names his son Sohail and Maya names her daughter Zubaida cloning the name Zaid. In Maya's consciousness, the binary of the good and bad, the past and the present, the secular and the fundamentalist, Sohail and Silvi merge, and this newly developed consciousness consummates the harmony of contradictions.

Is Religion Any Good for Women?: Being and Becoming of Kambili in *Purple Hibiscus*

This section shows how women subjectivity can be a reactionary shield to the continued raid of religious propaganda and fundamentalist ideology of religion which constantly controls and interpellates the fertility of liberty. There is a steadfast assertion of an areligious viewpoint, a diverse liberating feminist intervention which is contraceptive to the birth of fundamentalism, the harmful hurdle to the overall wholesomeness, to the woman question and the cause of women. The concern of the chapter is how women in Chimamanda Adichie's *Purple Hibiscus* come to face and overcome different kinds of abuses perpetrated on them in the name of religion.

The backdrop and milieu of a novel, different elements, components, aspects, and the style of speech harmonize to make a complete whole. Adichie has accomplished this in her first published novel, *Purple Hibiscus*. The setting of the novel is the political turmoil in Nigeria and the storytelling is done in the first-person narrative mode through young Kambili, who is 15 years old and who dwells with a father who is authoritarian, oppressive, and dogmatic, a mother who is almost always emotionally drained, distressed and drooped and a brother quite inappropriate to the domestic set up as unlike the other members of the family; he is a nonconformist, and a dissenter. Cheryl Stobie in "Dethroning the Infallible Father: Religion, Patriarchy, and Politics In Chimamanda Ngozi Adichie's *Purple Hibiscus*" points out the heart of the matter:

> In the novel *Purple Hibiscus*, the Nigerian author, Chimamanda Ngozi Adichie, examines issues of faith in the private

and public domains. She highlights the devastating effects of patriarchal control and intolerance within the family, the Roman Catholic Church, education, and the State. Her impulse is reformist, and she offers alternatives to absolutism by endorsing respect, tolerance, forgiveness, and hybridity. She promotes a progressive view of religion, spirituality, culture, and gender roles. Countering the presentation of the 'infallible' father in various guises, Adichie espouses values associated with femininity, and she includes a luminous epiphany of the Virgin Mary. While dark events are depicted in the novel, it also holds out the prospect of redemption and hope (1).

There are two worlds in the novel – Papa Eugene's rule-ridden and "ritualized world" which is not conducive to the blooming and blossoming of Purple Hibiscuses i.e. full-fledged blossoming and blooming of the consciousness of Kambili, and the world of Aunty Ifeoma in whose garden, there are "experimental" hibiscuses: "rare, fragrant with the undertones of freedom, a different kind of freedom....A freedom to be, to do" (*PH* 15).

The house Kambili lives in is ruled by her father who is esteemed in the church and their community. In the house, the father reigns supreme. The door to free will or exerting one's own choice or will is very tightly shut. From her early days Kambili was brainwashed by her bigot father with religious extremism and this "conservative indoctrination has left her in a state of limbo" (Nwokocha 15). So much so that on her first visit to Aunt Ifeoma's house when her cousins deviate from the Christian ritual by amalgamating the Christian with Igbo practice she gets terrified and splintered: "I felt as if my shadow was visiting Aunty Ifeoma and her family, while the real me was studying in my room in Enugu, my schedule posted above me" (*PH* 94).

When the novel begins, the house bound by chains and iron rules is disintegrating. The first chapter titled 'Breaking Gods' sounds iconoclastic. The very opening words allude to Chinua Achebe's title *Things Fall Apart:*

> Things started to fall apart at home when my brother, Jaja, did not go to communion and Papa flung his heavy missal across the room and broke the figurines on the étagère. We had just returned from church. Mama placed the fresh palm fronds, which were wet with holy water, on the dining table and then went upstairs to change. Later, she would knot the palm fronds into sagging cross shapes and hang them on the wall beside our goldframed family photo. They would stay there until next Ash Wednesday, when we would take the fronds to church, to have them burned for ash (*PH* 6).

The transgression of Jaja of Eugene's order and Eugene's indignant response narrated in a grave, solemn, and ritual manner strikes the keynote of the novel. The above paragraph also points to the present, the past, and the future – how the past was, how the present is, and what the future will be. We are introduced to the religious drill and the rituals which will go round in the years to come. But Jaja gets in the way and breaks not only the train of traditional thoughts but also the possibility of temporal continuity of rituals in a merry-go-round fashion by absenting himself from the communion. The father "flung" missal and "broke the figurines" in response to Jaja who "flung" rituals and "broke the Gods" i.e., challenged the supreme religious authority as well as the supreme authority of his father in the home, defers the continuance and perpetuation of preposterous rituals.

Language is very powerful. It makes and unmakes us. Language helps us to have an identity and at the same time it can cause us to lose an identity. Language offers us meaning which is more than meaning as it makes us do/perform certain things: "If a word …might be said to 'do' a thing, then it appears that the word not only signifies a thing, but that this signification will also be an enactment of the thing. It seems here that the meaning of a performative act is to be found in this apparent coincidence of signifying and enacting" (Butler 198). Jaja absents from the communion as "The wafer gives him bad breath (8) and "the priest keeps touching his mouth and it nauseates him" (8). Jaja's reaction to rituals and his reference to the nauseous smell emitting from the body of the priest express his utter dislike of religious rituals. Eugene replies with an anger- swollen face that the "waifer" must be called "host" as it has a sacredness attached to it and the priest is the body of the Lord. If Jaja does not receive it, he will be doomed. Jaja welcomes his doom and Eugene "picked up the missal and flung it across the room, toward Jaja" (8). Insistence on calling "waifer" "host" because "waifer" is not a religious word and insistence on calling the foul-smelling body of the priest as the body of the Lord bear testimony to his underlying hypocrisy and the fact that he is a religious psycho. Throwing the missal at Jaja smacks of his aggression towards those who disobey the religion he believes in and, moreover, those who disobey him. It proves how eager he is to maintain authority and his authority feels challenged and threatened by Jaja's disobedience.

When Jaja challenges Papa Eugene's authority, he also challenges and disrupts the other authorities—personal, familial, ecclesiastical, national, and colonial as well which start crumbling down as Eugene according to Aunty Ifeoma is "a colonial product". This disruption began much earlier at Nsukka and the contravention is desperately needed for the convenient sprouting of "hibiscuses". The chapter is a prelude to what is to come and prepares the ground for the farewell of the "winter" of changelessness to the "spring" of change and newness.

In an interview with Eve Daniels, Adichie says that taking shots at religion and politics in the novel through the character of Kambili Achike, the 15-year-old narrator has made the treatment less convoluted, and the narrative is not encumbered with too many controversies and disputations:

> It is always challenging to write about politics and religion while telling an interesting story that will hold your reader. I think a younger narrator made me more careful not to over-burden my fiction with polemics, or with my own politics. It is also more believable to see the complexities and absurdities of religion through the eyes of a younger person who is not cynical or jaded.
> (Daniels 1)

In her speech for the Faith and Culture Lecture Series, Adichie makes it clear that religion and religious ideologies hinder women and deny equality to women. Religion is an institution which is not conducive to women as it is used as a means of the subjection of women, and so, it is not congenial for feminism either:

Not just Catholicism, but the religions I am mostly familiar with, in the mainstream way they are practiced are not the most women-friendly institutions….Feminism is just that simple idea that women are fully equal and there's a sense in which religion has been used to justify oppressions based upon the idea that women are not fully equal human beings" (Subramaniam & Roberts 32)

Like Kambili, Adichie also grows up as a Catholic in the Catholic ambiance in Nigeria. While her experience as a Catholic is happy, she does not like a certain aspect of it: "Part of my quarrel with the Catholic Church is how often there is an elevation of the institution over the person" (Subramaniam & Roberts 2017).

Papa's deference and observance of rituals are laid bare to us through the keen-edged gaze of Kambili. Through the tongue-in-cheek gaze of Kambili, her ironically jesting and joking observations, Adichie reveals Papa Eugene's observance of merry-go-round ecclesiastical rituals with shallow and hollow devotion minus any genuine piety:

> Papa always sat in the front pew for Mass, at the end beside the middle aisle, with Mama, Jaja, and me sitting next to him. He was the first to receive communion. Most people did not kneel to receive communion at the marble altar, with the blond lifesize Virgin Mary mounted nearby, but Papa did. He would hold his eyes shut so hard that his face tightened into a grimace, and then he would stick his tongue out as far as it could go. (*PH* 6)

While Jaja's response to his father's imposition of rules is bluntly direct and point-blank; he has simply refused to obey, Kambili's response is nuanced, subtle, and shaded, mixed with witty jibes and tinged with a spicy sneer. To her, the statue of Mary is "blond" and the gesture of her Papa towards it is not genuine but a manufactured one, as her delving and digging gaze discovers that Papa's face does not betray reverence but "grimace".

Papa is like the Daddy in Sylvia Plath's "Daddy" under whose clout she is like a black shoe. Under his influence, Path has lived like a foot, hardly able to breathe. That Papa is an eager zealot is apparent from the "first row" he sits in and he "knelt at" "blond" Virgin Mary with a nonsensical and ludicrously farcical posture, putting on in his face "grimace" instead of grace. In the "Palm Sunday," everything is presented in a ritualized manner – the observance of religious rituals and its travesty.

Eugene leads a life which is grounded on and marked by rigorous religious rites and superabundant emphasis on piety. He has to follow drawn-out and tedious prayers before dinner, super de rigueur participation in the masses, "rosary recitations", and all of these are reinforced by the orthodox and obstinate principles of the religion.

Eugene is small-minded and has a tilted understanding of religion. He is specifically illiberal to other religious practices than the one he practices, reprobating frenziedly both Pentecostalism and the ancestral and rooted African religion. This latter prejudice leads to estrangement from his own father.

In Eugene's version of Christianity, he comes before Jesus. Eugene is the Jesus of his family and the parish as well. Father Benedict "used Papa [Eugene] to illustrate the gospels" (*PH* 6). Father Benedict posits Eugene immediately after Pope because Eugene is an influential person and he has contributed a lot to the Church's welfare. "During his sermons, Father Benedict usually referred to the pope, Papa, and Jesus —in that order" (*PH* 6). Eugene is too powerful to be placed after Jesus. This hierarchical disorder explains the kind of disordered nature of their religious practice.

Eugene's hardened extremism comes out when Aunty Ifeoma breaks the news of their father's death and the only response is: "Ifeoma, did you call a priest?" (140). Aunty Ifeoma who has looked after their father all along gets exasperated at her brother's cold-blooded and careless adherence to the credo: "Is that all you can say, eh, Eugene? Have you nothing else to say, gbo? Our father has died! Has your head turned upside down? Will you not help me bury our father?" (*PH*140). The callous and inhuman fanatic replies: "I cannot participate in a pagan funeral, but we can discuss with the parish priest and arrange a Catholic funeral" (*PH* 140).

The death of Papa-Nnukwu is very significant as it allegorises the defeat of the indigenous culture and religion, fading away of the native way of life, and the hegemony of the New religion, the religion of the colonisers, and the growth of life modelled after the West. In the familial space, Kambili's understanding of religion heightens. Whenever Eugene makes a prayer for his father, he ardently urges his God to save his father from hell. Kambili says: "When Papa prayed for Papa-Nnukwu, he asked only that God convert him and save him from the raging fires of hell" (*PH* 112).

Eugene's prayer is grim, gloomy, forbidding, and full of hopelessness. Through his prayer, he manipulates the fear by frequently referring to "eternal damnation". But Aunty Ifeoma's prayer for her father, though traditional, is minus the negative impact of Eugene. Her prayer for

Papa-Nnukwu is brimmed and blessed with filial love and hope, the cardinal aspect of Christianity: "She asked God to stretch a healing hand over him as he had stretched over the apostle Peter's mother-in-law. She asked the Blessed Virgin to pray for him. She asked the angels to take charge of him" (*PH* 112). Kambili's "Amen" to the prayer of Ifeoma's prayer is a "little delayed: and a little surprising because she is new to this kind of prayer and is used to the "harrowing hell" lecture of her father.

Eugene is a Christian Satan who blandly disregards his own native practices and culture. At the death of his father, he insists on a "Catholic funeral" because he cannot take part in a "pagan funeral". Aunty Ifeoma protests vehemently:

> Aunty Ifeoma got up and started to shout. Her voice was unsteady. "I will put my dead husband's grave up for sale, Eugene, before I give our father a Catholic funeral. Do you hear me? I said I will sell Ifediora's grave first! Was our father a Catholic? I ask you, Eugene, was he a Catholic? *Uchu gba gi!*" Aunty Ifeoma snapped her fingers at Papa; she was throwing a curse at him. Tears rolled down her cheeks. (*PH* 140)

Eugene is indeed an apparatus of the colonisers and a blind propagandist, a man carrying the "white man's burden" to put into effect their religion. The death of Papa-Nnukwu "tolls the death knell" of nativism and the triumph of colonialism. But all of this comes to an end with the murder of Eugene by his wife at the end of the novel, signalling the fall of Patriarchy, the exit of colonialism, the defeat of religious extremity, and the blooming of liberalism intervened by women.

Eugene is a crooked and cockeyed religious pervert and we witness testimonial evidence of his freak religious degeneration when he punishes Kambili for living with his heathen father at Aunty Ifeoma's. Kambili ought to inform him of the presence of the heathen but Kambili has not done so, which means she has sinned knowingly, and hence, she must be purged of her sin:

> You should not see sin and walk right into it." He lowered the kettle into the tub, tilted it toward my feet. He poured the hot water on my feet, slowly, as if he were conducting an experiment and wanted to see what would happen. He was crying now, tears streaming down his face. I saw the moist steam before I saw the water. I watched the water leave the kettle, flowing almost in slow motion in an arc to my feet. The pain of contact was so pure, so scalding, I felt nothing for a second. And then I screamed. (*PH* 144)

This is what Edgar F. Nabutanyi calls "a form of ritualized violence"; it is violence perpetrated through the enactment of the religion's utmost travesty. Eugene is not at all concerned with the spiritual wellbeing of his family "but rather in the performance of publicly visible religious uprightness" (Nabutanyi 78).

Besides Kambili, her mother is also a victim of Eugene's freakish religious practices. No sooner does she return home after the miscarriage, she starts taking care of the "etagere" and the "figurines" in the house. The figurine is, as if, her surrogate baby that she has lost in the "accident", an impassive aide onto whom she can shift all her strong, suppressed resentments and other emotions. The figurines are a reflection of and a witness to her silence, her resigned and mumbling acceptance of Eugene's command. The figurines also symbolise the fragile and brittle world of the imposed authority and religious intimidation represented by Eugene and the dismantlement of this authority in the end is no doubt proleptic of the futility of religious dogmatism. While cleansing the figurines, she also cleanses her bad emotions. This hyperactivity of Mama helps to relieve her stress and express her unspoken defiance and oppose her husband's ways.

Eugene brings or particularly drags God into every subject under the sun and to everywhere–from business to bedroom. When Kambili comes second, he brings God; when his wife has a miscarriage, he brings God; when there is a national crisis, he brings God. He takes God and Catholicism so personally and politically that he becomes a demigod and overplays the role. For Eugene, anything and anyone contrary to his belief and ideology is evil–it may be his biological father, his very own culture and way of life. His father Papa-Nnukwu is heathen to him, and so, he allows his children to visit him for fifteen minutes a year during Christmas. The Aro festival at Abagana and the "mmuo" at the festival are the "remnants of ungodly traditions" for Eugene.

Eugene considers himself to be a crusader, but is a pseudo one. One day, Kambili has period cramps and she has to take Panadol; but her stomach is empty and so she, at the suggestion of Jaja, takes cereal and when Papa discovers that Kambili has eaten 10 minutes before Mass, he pounds on Jaja, Mama, and Kambili with his belt.

Eugene unleashes physical and psycho-religious offense on his family members. Even people who are traditionalists know how mean he is and one of the elders in his native village castigates him using animal imagery: "You are like a fly blindly following a corpse into the grave" (53).

Bothered by his mania and zealotry, his sister tries to make him remember the inaptness of his interference in the matters of God and religion. He is reminded by his sister that he "has to stop doing God's job. God is big enough to do his own job. If God will judge our father for choosing to follow the way of our ancestors, then let God do the judging" (*PH* 71). But Eugene continues his extremism which prevents the light of reason from entering into his enterprise, and he is far from being rational in his pursuance.

Religion becomes an inescapable force in the hands of persons like Eugene and Father Benedict–controlling, imposing, limiting, and shaping the lives of others. Though the title is secular, there is a religious overtone in the Chapters' headings. The novel begins with "Palm Sunday" and gradually takes us back to the days before "Palm Sunday" when Papa is at the steering wheel of the family.

The fear of God is needed, it is "good" fear, fear for the evil as an antidote to the moral and existential crisis, but this fear of God should not be manipulated and exploited and turned into a medium of gender oppression. In *Purple Hibiscus*, religion becomes synonymous with the oppression of colonialism and patriarchy.

Eugene has falsely understood religion as the "serious personal convictions as to morals or the nature of the universe" (Russell 21), denying the social importance integrally attached to it. People like Eugene to whom renovation of the church is more important than the gospel have not understood Christianity at all. They do not make effort to understand the essence of Christianity and rather than following the teachings of Jesus, they adamantly stick to the buildings, rules which are nothing but the façade of Christianity. The essence of being a Christian is aptly illustrated by Bertrand Russell in WHY I AM NOT A CHRISTIAN:

> Churches may owe their origin to teachers with strong individual convictions, but these teachers have seldom had much influence upon the Churches that they founded, whereas Churches have had enormous influence upon the communities in which they flourished. To take the case that is of most interest to members of Western civilization: the teaching of Christ, as it appears in the Gospels, has had extraordinarily little to do with the ethics of Christians. The most important thing about Christianity, from a social and historical point of view, is not Christ but the Church, and if we are to judge of Christianity as a social force we must not go to the Gospels for our material. Christ taught that you should give your goods to the poor that you should not fight, that you should not go to church, and that you should not punish adultery. Neither Catholics nor Protestants have shown any strong desire to follow His teaching in any of these respects. (Russell 21)

In *Purple Hibiscus*, Religion becomes "a disease born of fear and as a source of untold misery" (Russell 20). The central argument of Anthony Chennells in "Inculturated Catholicisms in Chimamanda Adichie's *Purple Hibiscus*" is that the novel is an attack on the imposed hegemony of old-fashioned Catholicism on African people. Chennell writes:

Adichie's *Purple Hibiscus* belongs to a new generation of novels that take for granted Christianity as part of contemporary African culture and although the novel criticises the Eurocentric and exclusive Catholicism of previous generations, and demands respect for Igbo spirituality, no attempt is made to recover traditional religion in everyday life or to inculturate Catholicism in religious practices that are no longer central to the majority of the people (15).

But what does not align with the novel is Chennells' claim that the novel does not attempt to salvage the religion rooted in Igbo culture that is lost in the hegemony of Christianity or the novel reveals the complete lack of the application of Catholicism in the day-to-day- life. The novel juxtaposes the hegemony of Christianity, Catholicism with the native Igbo. The former is concentrated and concretized in Eugene and the latter in Papa-Nnukwu and the exercise of religion in the true sense of the term is manifested in Aunty Ifeoma.

It is people like Eugene who turn back on beliefs, religious practices which are their own. He utterly dislikes them who hold on to the native culture. Eugene, the self-declared Christian hates his father who, according to him, is a heathen whereas Papa-Nnukwu who has firmly stuck to idol worship, the traditional African/Igbo religion, has always prayed for the welfare of his son: "Chineke! I have killed no one, I have taken no one's land, and I have not committed adultery...Chineke! Bless my son, Eugene. Let the sun not set on his prosperity" (*PH* 125).

"Women in literature were still what men, or the men-women, wished they were" (Lessing 62). Towards the beginning of the novel things have happened according to the will of Eugene. Beatrice and Kambili obey him, follow his nonsense and cruel rules unquestioningly. But as the novel progresses into further depths, things start taking place according to the will of Aunty Ifeoma, Kambili and her mother Beatrice which reaches climax in the end of the novel with the death of Eugene by poisoning.

In a pejorative sense a "mestizo" is a marginal being. The novel begins with Kambili as a "mestizo" in the derogatory sense as she has a marginal position in the household dictated by her father Eugene Achike . In his household, Eugene is the proud oppressor, the "comprador intelligentsia" and the others— his wife Beatrice Achike, his daughter Kambili Achike, and his son Chukwuka Achike (Jaja) are the oppressed. For Eugene, those who are Christian are godly and those who are not Christian are ungodly and heathen, even if that person is his own biological father.

In the conflicting domestic zone, and amid the binary of oppressor /oppressed; Christian/non-Christian; godly/ungodly, Kambili dismantles the unequal power relation that is the very source of oppression, and makes a "critical mobility through which [she] might gain a new mestiza consciousness" (Delgadillo 17). And the key reinforcement for Kambili's mobility towards a new consciousness is Aunty Ifeoma, the married sister of Eugene Achike.

Like the ultimate redeemer during Christmas, the savior Aunty Ifeoma steps into Eugene's world with her talismanic and hypnotizing influence, with her playful, soft, kind, floating smile and daring appearance. She comes and pulls Kambili's breast saying, "Look how fast these are growing" (54), and in front of her, even the relentless Eugene relents. Kambili is surprised and is proud:

When she barged into the dining room upstairs, I imagined a proud ancient forebear, walking miles to fetch water in homemade clay pots, nursing babies until they walked and talked, fighting wars with machetes sharpened on sun-warmed stone. She filled a room. (*PH* 60)

The polar opposite to Eugene's house of iron curtain is the house of Aunty Ifeoma. In Eugene's house no one has free will. Everyone is subject to the will of the Church and God the Father. Aunty Ifeoma's house is exactly the opposite. In her house no one is hostile to free will. It is free from the dead set of religious rules, unrelenting and intransigent order of day-to-day activities, a fertile and free space where things and people flourish, blossom, and sprout. There are thus two worlds in the novel – the world of Papa Eugene and the world of Aunty Ifeoma. Kambili's blooming starts in the second world.

Aunty Ifeoma is "tall, exuberant, fearless, loud, and larger than life" (71). She criticizes Eugene for being a bigot and for being indignantly disregarding and indiscreet to his own father who is sick and dying. Eugene does it in the name of religion and God: "Eugene has to stop doing God's job. God is big enough to do his own job. If God will judge our father for choosing to follow the way of our ancestors, then let God do the judging, not Eugene" (71).

Aunty Ifeoma's words have a "teasing lilt"; her voice has a "steeliness in her tone" which pierces even Eugene. There is a marked dialectic of faith in a verbal exchange in which she undermines Eugene's obsession with the Church and his tendency to take whatever the church says for granted. Ifeoma and her children wanted to visit Akope village where the appearance of The Blessed Virgin is said to have taken place; but Eugene objects as the Church is yet to certify the truthfulness of such apparitions. Ifeoma's usual rejoinder hits Eugene that he is not above god and he should stop helping the cause of God as God is self-sufficient, and he does not need narrow-minded people like Eugene to serve him.

Aunty Ifeoma has introduced Kambili and Jaja to the mores of their own culture which is to Papa "devilish folklore". The Aunty Ifeoma Effect is felt by Kambili: "That night, I dreamed that I was laughing, but it did not sound like my laughter, although I was not sure what my laughter sounded like. It was cackling and throaty and enthusiastic, like Aunty Ifeomas" (*PH* 66).

Ifeoma refers to following one's own faith rather than the imposed and interpellated faith advocated by the Church. Eugene institutionalizes faith. He believes what the Church makes him believe. The church is the foundation of his faith, while Ifeoma talks about individual faith and faith to a humane religion, not to the machine.

While critiquing the oppression of women under Christian fundamentalism, Adichie also critiques the position of women in the Igbo tradition. Igbo culture is not at all favorable to women and most of that unfavorability is expressed through the characters of the grandfather, Papa-Nnukwu. During his conversation with his daughter Ifeoma, Papa-Nnukwu says that it was a mistake on his part to send his son Eugene to a missionary school. But he did not send Ifeoma to a missionary school because she was the girl child. Papa-Nnukwu even refuses to take Ifeoma into confidence: "you are a woman. You do not count" (63). That women are very pliant and biddable become clear when at *mmuo* festival Papa-Nnukwu says: "This is a woman spirit, and the women *mmuo* are harmless" (64). Again, when Jaja makes an enquiry about the traditional Igbo festival, Papa-Nnukwu flares at him: "Don't speak like a woman!" (65).

And some women accept and imbibe this unfavorable and discriminatory attitude to them. Beatrice to a great extent reveals this. She feels esteemed as her husband has not married another woman. She seems to represent the traditional viewpoint of Igbo women: "A husband crowns a woman's life, Ifeoma. It is what they want" (57). But women want their husbands to be the crowns of their lives to a certain extent. The load of torture becomes impossible for her to tolerate and towards the end, she decides to poison her husband.

Ifeoma is also religious but her religion is not dictated by ecclesiastical institutions, but tempered with common sense and practicality. It is not bound by hard and fast rules, but is strengthened by choice and free will. In the midst of the Rosary Prayer, Kambili's cousin Amaka starts singing while Ifeoma and others except Kambili and Jaja join the singing. But such a freakish behaviour on their part would have been preposterous and unacceptable in Eugene's house. In Ifeoma's house, Obiora and Amaka can fearlessly converse on the apparition of the Virgin Mary. Obiora even distrusts in the apparition: "People are making this whole apparition thing up"... "What is she now, the Political Virgin?". Here in this household "Morning and night prayers were always peppered with songs, Igbo praise songs" (*PH* 103).

Aunty Ifeoma comes with a balanced and rational worldview and provides Kambili with an alternative look into things which are different from Eugene's. She tells Kambili: "Your Papa-Nnukwu is not a pagan, he is a traditionalist". Through Aunty Ifeoma's agency, Eugene's version of religion is questioned. While Eugene prays for and longs for the conversion of his father into Catholicism, his father laments his son's conversion and accuses Christianity and Christian Missionaries of misleading his son. Papa-Nnukwu ironically recounts how the missionaries came to their region with an apparently true story, a facade of religiosity, and encroached into the region with that falsified mist of religiosity and how Eugene got blindly initiated to that, forsaking his own tradition his own kind:

> I remember the first one that came to Abba, the one they called Fada John...they say our type of sun does not shine in the white man's land.... In the afternoon they gathered the children under the ukwa tree in the mission and taught them their religion.... One day I said to them, Where is this god you worship? They said he was like *Chukuwu, that* he was in the sky. I asked then, Who is the person that was killed, the person that hangs on the wood outside the mission? They said he was the son, but that the son and the father are equal. It was then that I knew that the white man was mad. The father and the son are equal?... That is why Eugene can disregard me, because he thinks we are equal. (*PH* 63)

Papa-Nnukwu witnesses the intrusion of the Missionaries into the Igboland, their proselytizing, and winning the native people with the Bible. He laughs at the version of Christianity his son Eugene imbibes and tries to enforce in his typical fashion. He sarcastically points out that Eugene's violation of the filial bond sanctioned by, justified in, and stemming from his baptism leads to his mindless jump into a new religion. Papa-Nnukwu offers a critique of the version of Christianity Eugene and his kind practise.

Orthodox Christianity becomes a ridiculous absurdity when it is practised by fanatics like Eugene. This kind of jibe points at the huge gap between what Christianity is and what it becomes.

Ifeoma's attitude and her way of taking care of things are dynamic, round and rotund and are typical of West African women. She has "mestiza consciousness". In her, the diverging ways of Eugene and Papa-Nnukwu merge and this is metaphorically conveyed to us when we are told about the full blooming of the unusual and rare purple hibiscuses in her garden, "with a deep shade of purple that was almost blue" (96). Kambili is taken by surprise and educated in the new, flowered world of Aunty Ifeoma: "I didn't know there were purple hibiscuses" (96). She is unlike Eugene who cannot treat everyone and everything in a proportionate, nonpartisan commensurate manner.

Adichie is not against religion or Christianity, but against such religious practices as Eugene's which cause gendered oppression. She is for the religion as practiced by Aunty Ifeoma:

> From a viewpoint that is at once traditional, religious, African, and reformist, Adichie reveals deep scepticism towards absolutism, patriarchy, infallibility and a hierarchical relationship between the deity and believers, and between men and women. Instead she offers a hybrid, creative and freshly dialogic view of religion, the body, and Nigerian society seen within a global framework (Stobie 433).

The title embodies Kambili's journey from a bud to a flower: "The purple hibiscus becomes a metaphor for freedom and independence. While a flower may seem delicate in constitution, purple is historically associated with royalty and the divine. The purple flower then comes to signify Kambili's urge to bloom, her natural instinct to look for the light" (McElhatton 1).

The flower in the title encapsulates and symbolizes an alternative viewpoint' that is representational of the "mestiza consciousness". It is at Aunty Ifeoma's that Jaja and Kambili's eyes are opened to the world. It is here Jaja comes to know that his name reminds of the headstrong King, Jaja of Opobo who displayed courage and conviction in defying the British in the past. Jaja learns this lesson of judicious defiance from Ifeoma: "Being defiant can be a good thing sometimes...Defiance is like marijuana- it is not a bad thing when it is used right" (*PH* 108).

In a similar vein, Kambili overcomes her demureness and stuttering diffidence while staying with Aunty Ifeoma. When her cousin Amaka jibes at her for her ignorance regarding Orah leaves, Kambili remains silent and looking at her silence, Aunty Ifeoma says: "Kambili, have you no mouth? Talk back to her" (126). With her inspiring words, Kambili blurts out calmly: "You don't have to shout, Amaka... I don't know how to do the orah leaves, but you can show me" (*PH* 126). "The bubbles of air" (133) symbolising her fear and hesitation no longer prevent her from expressing herself. Ifeoma is thus instrumental in dispelling the fear inculcated in Kambili's mind.

Apart from the hibiscus flowers, Kambili's mobility, empathy, self-reliance and the gradual unfolding of her new inclusive consciousness is foreshadowed in the image of the "enterprising snail" which Kambili sees in the company of the Nsukka woman Mama Joe and which starts "crawling out, being thrown back in, and then crawling out again.

Determined. [Kambili] wanted to buy the whole basket and set that one snail free" (PH 175). Like the snail Kambili silently comes out of the shell of timidity and moves to heal the crack.

Besides Ifeoma, Father Amadi has a great deal of influence on Kambili. Unlike Eugene and Father Benedict, Father Amadi is not at all interested in power. He is primarily concerned with the people. He is not prepossessed to either the Igbo culture/religion or the Christian religion. He has been able to integrate propitiously both the religion, language, and culture of the colonisers and the natives. His songs and prayers are delivered not only in English but also in Igbo. Initially, Kambili faces a problem in intimating with Father Amadi and is confused with his ways as she is raised in a different setting under her father Eugene where Igbo is considered to be inferior to English. Kambili says, "I did not fully comprehend his English-laced Igbo sentences at dinner because my ears followed the sound and not the sense of his speech" (*PH* 101). Kambili takes her time. But the moment she understands the sense of his speech, she identifies with him completely. Father Amadi helps Kambili unlearn the narrow learning and indoctrination she has received from her Father. The following sensitive response of Kambili shows the deep impact Amdi has on her: "Father Amadi was like blue wind.... He had a singer's voice, a voice that had the same effect on my ears that Mama working Pears baby oil into my hair had on my scalp" (*PH* 101).

Kambili's intellectual and religious growth comes to full circle through her enlightening engagements with her mother, with Aunty Ifeoma and through her symbolic encounter with the apparition of the Virgin Mary. They become the Holy Trinity for her existence:

Kambili's mother and aunt function as physical models for Kambili. Her mother, Beatrice, is the battered woman who turns into a husband-murderer because she is unable to protect the fruit of her womb, born or unborn. Her polar opposite is her sister-in-law, Ifeoma, who is comfortable in physicality as a woman, and who does not fear speaking truth to power. Observing female suffering, rebellion and power acts as a spur to Kambili's development, as does her engagement with the apparition at Aokpe. Providing a luminous representation of the Virgin Mary as pure spirit does not deny the place of the body within the text, but emphasises that the spiritual realm can be occupied by a being conceived as feminine, allowing for imaginative entry into this dimension by women... (Stobie 432).

Flowering under their collective influences—which of course are clear backlashes at Papa Eugene and his fundamentalist indoctrinations—Kambili starts to emulate these influences and undergoes a vegetative growth in her intellectual and religious persona. She grows into a "mestiza". She reconciliates and knits religion to life and her own culture. She starts opening and healing the "bruises" and "burns" she has received in Eugene's house the moment she comes in contact with Ifeoma and Father Amadi. She does not dismiss Christianity altogether, but nativizes Christianity, uses it to understand, to embrace the men and the manners of her own Igbo culture:

> We stood underneath a huge flame-of-the-forest tree. It was in bloom, its flowers

fanning out on wide branches and the ground underneath covered with petals the color of fire. When the young girl was led out, the flame-of-the-forest swayed and flowers rained down. The girl was slight and solemn, dressed in white, and strong-looking men stood around her so she would not be trampled. She had hardly passed us when other trees nearby started to quiver with a frightening vigor, as if someone were shaking them. The ribbons that cordoned off the apparition area shook, too. Yet there was no wind. The sun turned white, the color and shape of the host. And then I saw her, the Blessed Virgin: an image in the pale sun, a red glow on the back of my hand, a smile on the face of the rosary bedecked man whose arm rubbed against mine. She was everywhere. (*PH* 199)

These quoted lines recap her symbolic encounter with Virgin Mary at Aokpe. Here Virgin Mary does not have her Western, patriarchal, or hierarchal tincture. The depiction of the apparition combines "intersecting discourses of race, gender, power and belief, and shows a particular female agency resulting from the vision itself, the gender of the visionary and the gender of the focaliser of the drama, Kambili" (Stobie 431-432).

Can silence be a means of resisting oppression? Though in the first half of the novel it seems so, in the second half the hitherto silent and inarticulate women start articulating and asserting themselves. Impressed and influenced by Aunt Ifeoma and Father Amadi, and exposed to their religious liberalism coupled with humanitarian values and concerns, Kambili comes out with a pronounced voice. Even her mother 'speaks' through her action. Eugene's oppression is put to an end by his wife Beatrice who murders him by slow-poisoning. Beatrice breaks her silence finally and reacts fatally to Eugene's years of torture of her and of her children. Murder is a heinous crime in itself but here the cold-blooded murder of Eugene by his wife is the emancipatory murder.

Here murder becomes a necessary evil. When Kambili remarks "God works in mysterious ways", Jaja replies "Of course God does. Look what He did to his faithful servant Job, even to His own son. But have you ever wondered why? Why did He have to murder his own son so we would be saved?" (*PH* 181). Jaja defends his father's murder and justifies it by sanctifying it. Though his father was a religious man, only loyal to God, the murder is, as if, the design of God executed through human agency. The imperative murder is committed to saving them. So, when police comes, Jaja saved his mother and "told them he had used rat poison, that he put it in Papa's tea" (*PH* 211). He takes the responsibility on himself and goes to jail. In their familial space, the dictator cum father is no more.

But quite interestingly neither the mother nor the daughter/son feels the need to recall the father. He is forgotten for good. Rather, the focus is on Jaja's well-being and his release, the deliverer. Indeed, he becomes "the mythical stubborn and defiant King, Jaja of Opobo" (107), as referred to by Aunty Ifeoma in the past. The king "did not sell his soul for a bit of gunpowder like the other kings", and so does Jaja in the novel who follows Aunty Ifeoma's advice: Defiance is …is not a bad thing when it is used right" (107). The different kind of silence referred to in the ending of the novel is not the silence borne out of fear but the silence of peace, of emancipation and of suppressed sorrow. The end signals the promise for the end of the tyrant Father's oppressive rule. "Things fall apart" for a cause.

In the end, Kambili manages to come out of the haul of the binaries, rejecting the extreme end of everything:

> But we are not rivals, God and I, we are simply sharing. I no longer wonder if I have a right to love Father Amadi; I simply go ahead and love him. I no longer wonder if the checks I have been writing to the Missionary Fathers of the Blessed Way are bribes to God; I just go ahead and write them. I no longer wonder if I chose St. Andrew's church in Enugu as my new church because the priest there is a Blessed Way Missionary Father as Father Amadi is; I just go. (*PH* 188)

The novel ends with this new, non-binary and non-partisan understanding of religion which resolves all conflicts and generates hope. Jaja comes out of prison. Mama, Kambili, and Jaja are together at last with the positive absence of Papa: "Above, clouds like dyed cotton wool hang low, so low I feel I can reach out and squeeze the moisture from them. The new rains will come down soon" (*PH* 189).

Fundamentalism is a "universal phenomenon" and Sohail and Eugene are eager fundamentalists. Of course, they bmight have been forced by their immediate circumstances: Sohail is traumatised by the Liberation War and by personal loss and Eugene tries hard to fit in the shoes of the colonisers. But they chose to be fundamentalists, vanguards of Islam and Roman Catholicism respectively. They may "operate under different religious slogans, but [they use] God to justify injustices and discrimination" (Saadawi 12).

Sohail and Papa Eugene's religious extremism along with their ultraconservative and dyed-in-the-wool stances get dissipated, mellowed and sponged in the new mestiza consciousness of Maya and Kambili. Maya forgives and Kambili forgets. Both of them let things go. They go beyond Sohail and Papa Eugene's surface understanding of religion by feeling with and feeling into life and discover the Hopkinsian "inscape" (the "simple and beautiful oneness") and "instress" (the ecstasy of the experience of inscape). And in doing so, they come out of their liminality and carve out new spaces for themselves and pioneer "mestiza consciousness" in these novels.

Conclusion

Thus, women subjectivities in the novels of Tahmima Anam and Chimamanda Ngozi Adichie proscribe divisive thinking and illustrate a symbiotic and sustainable outlook on life. Whatever women do, wherever they look – up, down, or around, they see things as they are; they see a fellow human being, not an enemy. As long as humans exist, there shall be divisions; there shall be wars; there shall be racism and there shall be religious extremism. Difference will definitely be there. But we have to understand that the difference is nothing but "ordinary" and "normal". To understand and respect the difference is what makes us human. It helps us see the reality of the world, and make peace and sustain ourselves in a diversified world (Adichie 34). In course of time, division, war, racism, have become essential human conditions. These are necessary evils. But through our way of looking at things, "little acts of kindness", small attitudinal and behavioural changes, we can make a habit of looking at things not in parts but in whole so that we continue to exist harmoniously. In the present feats of women in the fictional universe of Anam and Adichie, are embedded wise life lessons and a vision of the future. And "that is what [writers] are supposed to do when [they] are at [their] best—make it all up—but make it up so truly that later it will happen that way" (Hemingway and Baker 2003).

The subjectivities and the identities of women is to a great extent occasioned, necessitated and formed not so much by the prevailing discourses as much by their direct engagement with the immediate critical points of their lives and the critical periods in their social habitat. The novelists have not claimed that the consciousness of their characters is the "be-all and end-all". Their novels are "evidence of feminist consciousness raising, all evidence that women can bond across race to establish forms of solidarity that enable us all to have greater access to lives of optimal well-being" (Hooks 40). The subjectivity of women is pregnant with a discourse of their own.

Anam and Adichie deessentialise gender by portraying multidimensionality of women. Women belonging to different nationalities respond to series of events. We see an extension of their agency. We see "bifocality or reciprocity of perspectives (that is, seeing others against a background of ourselves and ourselves against a background of others), juxtapositioning of multiple realities" (Harrison 235). They disengage with "Western feminist eyes" or discourse. Theirs is an inclusive and participatory discourse, the discourse of active engagement and intervention. The call is to participate, to include, to empathise, and not to divide. Their fiction is "holistic fiction that reflects [their] vision of a pluralistic yet human-centred set of interlocking experience" (Harrison 241).

The development of the consciousness of the protagonists of Anam and Adichie that opens out and includes is connected to the crisis and is consequent to the search and exploration of their selves that have faced and undergone at the beginning. When *A Golden Age* begins, Rehana goes through familial crisis and she needs to prove herself so that she can overcome her crisis. Olanna in *Half of a Yellow Sun* is at a loss to tackle things when war breaks out. Kambili has to deal with ritual maniac father. The adopted, "amphibian" identity of Zubaida haunts her from the beginning. Female protagonist like Imemelu in *Americanah* and Maya in *The Good Muslim* begin their exploration through posture of refusal of the persons or ideas they represent of the prevailing situation who and which are "not just walled against outer destructive nature and the void, but walled against itself by inner barriers of judgmental rejection that prevent communion and destroy it from within" (Fand 112). Ifemelu refuses to accept the racist atmosphere in the U.S. and Maya cannot not digest her brother's fundamentalist ways.

  The growth and development of an inclusive, non-binary consciousness or in Anzaldúan term, "mestiza consciousness" in the women characters is the "post-traumatic growth"—a term derived from Richard Tedeschi and Lawrence Calhoun in the 1990s. One who goes through and survives trauma emerges as "a person with more compassion for [her/him and others] who could accept limitations without being limited by them" (Tedeschi *Growth After Trauma*). Rehana, Olanna, Ifemelu, Zubaida, Maya, and Kambili suffer psychological trauma. Rehana has experienced the loss of her husband, temporary loss of her children, loss of Liberation war; the Biafran War has shattered the private world of Olanna. Ifemelu is terribly upset by the practice of othering in the USA. Zubaida is disturbed by her identity crisis. The quake of the Liberation War turned the familiar world of Maya into a strange one. She is shocked at the U turn her brother takes. In the case of Kambili, her father with the help of his sheer misunderstanding of religion as a bunch of idiotic rules to be followed rigorously has turned her life into hell on earth. These psychological bruises develop among them a coping mechanism because those who get through trauma "develop new understandings of themselves, the world they live in, how to relate to other people, the kind of future they might have and a better understanding of how to live life" (Collier 48).

We are not provided with any solution. It is upto us the readers to determine whether the subsumption of the polarities in unifying consciousness solves the problems or not. Women in these novels usher in a new vision, a new opening with a unique perspective, welcoming us to clear out the rust, the blockages that keep us confined in conventional out-dated paradigms. The consciousness gets embodied in the women characters of their novels who evolve from linear, one-dimensional to multi-dimensional spaces and makes transitionfrom singular to plural, from only us to all of us.

The novels of Tahmima Anam and Chimamanda Adichie seriously question stereotypes about the literary representation of war, racism and religion, and women's position in these narratives. We should come out of the dead habit of taking things granted: "We must not vitiate our ... minds with the superstition, that business is business and war is war, politics is politics" (Tagore 86). Like Tagore, Anam and Adichie urge us to get ourselves out of habituating ourselves into the status quo. War, racism, and religious extremism do not take place on their own. It is nothing per se until the human hand and brain sets it on and fuels it. Since the human hand and brain roll it on, it is a human heart with empathy and humaneness and humane enterprise that should prevent these necessary evils from spreading further infection.

Anam and Adichie's texts are "littérature engage" or, "engaged literature" i.e "literature of commitment". For them, art is not for its sake, neither is it self-reflexive. They are not so much obsessed with their craft as with their luvvies. Like the post-WW-II French existentialists, they have exemplified through their characters that "a person defines [herself] by consciously engaging in willed action" (The Editors of Encyclopaedia Britannica).

Anam and Adichie are master storytellers and master thinkers, and their narratives are master narratives of local concern. They have a very local concerns making the hidden and the unknown self-evident. The appeal is not only immediate but lasting. They have not quarantined time and space, but have dwelled on them in a given time or space and have integrated the readers into a given time and space so that they meet with the narrative and start to get hold of it and hang on to the narrative.

That both Anam and Adichie's are little or mini-narratives become manifest in their focus on the individual and on the family, an intimate group to reflect larger issues. This zeroing in on home to zoom out at the world underscores the unearthing of the subjective nature of things. The dialogisation of self, of home and the world illuminate the dynamics of women's agency in the war in multiple and conflicting ways and gestures the discourse of personal narratives having unvoiced dimensions. Anam has presented the other side of war and the other side of women during the war to the readers. Amy Finnerty in "An Interview with Tahmima Anam" observes: "Anam places readers in her characters' parlours and kitchens, bedrooms and residential enclaves - and inside their heads: the aroma of food steaming on the stove; the heavy premonition of rain; a breeze that finds its way into the folds of a sari." (Finnerty 43). Staying attuned to varied everyday experiences, through the telling of women's stories…is central to feminist's resistance to abstraction (Wibben 2).

Tahmima Anam and Adichie have shown alertness to the "dangers of single stories". "Single stories" are stories that are one dimensional, one-sided, are biased, under-represented, and most importantly dangerous for more than one reason. "Single stories" "show a people as one thing, as only one thing, over and over again, and that is what they become" (Adichie 31). The manner of telling a story, the narratorial position, the narrative stance, the time of telling the story determine who the story empowers: "It is impossible to talk about the single story without talking about power….How they are told, who tells them, when they're told, how many stories are told, are dependent on power" (Adichie 34). The story of either the Bangladesh Liberation War or the Biafran war told from a male narrative stance, focusing only on the battlefield, the casualties etc. would have given prerogative to the participation, contribution of the male combatants, would have upheld their stories and presented them as heroes, saviours and champions, and would have empowered them. This is the first and foremost danger of a single story. The second danger of "single stories" is that they "create stereotypes, and the problem with stereotypes is not that they are untrue, but that they are incomplete. They make one story become the only story" (Adichie 37). Anam and Adichie stretch the horizon of their vision by not fictionalising "single stories which rob people of their dignity and which make recognition of equal humanity difficult, which ignores the human harmony, others and focuses on difference rather than binding thread" (Adichie 47).

Anam and Adichie's fiction does not "dispossess or malign...[but] empower and humanize". Rather than "breaking the dignity of women, their novels repair that broken dignity" (Adichie 43). They have written truly and uncompromisingly. They have seen and listened what they have fictionalized. "I am" or "we are" is neither erased nor struck out. They have not let it be. Instead, we see exertion and full flowering of the subjectivity of women under threat and impendence.

According to Adichie, the feminist response in divisive and discriminatory context is not leaving the ground or protesting against it exorbitantly and furiously. But staying, standing fast and firm, accepting, and understanding "can also be a feminist choice" (Adichie 6). Women in Adichie's novels and in the novels of Anam have chosen to do the latter.

Anam and Adichie have presented women as distinct individuals, as "full persons". Their feminism is not in Adichie's words, "Feminism Lite" i.e "conditional female equality" (Adichie 13). Women have not done something because they are allowed to do so. Though at the beginning of their novels, women's agency is conditional, their agency gradually becomes discretional and unbidden. By rejecting the male-female, superior-inferior binary, by freeing women from patriarchal consent for making their choices, they have rejected "feminism lite".

Indeed, most of the time women do not say much but they do much. And silence does not become expressive of their helplessness, but a sort of agency that sometimes becomes eloquently powerful. It may be that their characters are not likable because they have desisted to make them appear likable. Rather, they have made their characters "to be their full selves, selves that are honest and aware of the equal humanity of other people" (Adichie 6).

Both Anam and Adichie are saviours. They are, in the words of Walter Benjamin, "angels of history" (257). In *A Golden Age* and in *Half of a Yellow Sun*, they have revived the crumbled parts of history that hitherto remained unknown under the yoke of the dominant ideology. The revival of the human remnants of history makes fragmented history complete. Their novels move with "stylistic grace"; without going under the weight of personal and national losses. Rather, the "tight narrative vertebrae move through the [catastrophe] in prose of a beautiful sparsity...choosing what to salvage from the flotsam and jetsam of history, ...conjuring the emotive connection between people with poetic precision" (Sethi 25). We experience how "from the wreckage and destruction grow voice[s] of real eloquence" (Sethi 25).

Anam and Adichie's novels present them as feminists. They are feminists and in their fictional worlds, and we not only find an illustration of their worldview, but also a "philosophy of action and engagement that is emancipatory in its premise" (Chaudhuri & Mukherji 1). They have "replace[d]the authoritative male subject at the centre of traditional historiography with a powerful female subject who would rewrite history and repossess the authority of the self" (Chaudhuri & Mukherji 1). Their feminist praxis is not virulent and toxic, but it wholesomely oozes out of the life experiences of their characters. They believe that being a feminist does not mean complete denial of one's femininity. None of their characters deny their femininity. Neither do the novelists. They remain firmly anchored to the cause of their motherlands and of women.

They have given women a "sense of identity", have taken "pride in their own history", and have shown that women matter and they "matter equally" (Adichie 6). In *We should All be Feminists*, Adichie says, "My own definition is a feminist is a man or a woman who says, yes, there's a problem with gender as it is today and we must fix it, we must do better. All of us, women and men and do better" (17). Indeed, they have shown us how to do better even in the midst of worse. They are not merely feminists. They are humanists.

To conclude, women characters in the discussed novels of Tahmima Anam and Chimamanda Adichie make, in the words of Gloria Anzaldua, "a new culture with [their] own lumber, [their] own bricks and mortar and [their] own feminist architecture" (qtd. in Delgadillo 18).

Borrowing the words of the Nigerian critic Chikwenye Okonjo Ogunyemi, Anam and Adichie can be called "Griottes" i.e. "women writers who are transformation agents—in that they cause imperceptible shifts in established discourses" (qtd. in Oshindoro 3). They invite us to emend and emulate "the paradigms by which we live". In their novels, they have foregrounded a "space outside of the centre and assert it as the space from which new cultures and identities emerge" (Delgadillo 17).

Works Cited

Achebe, Christie. "Igbo Women in the Nigerian-Biafran War 1967-1970." *Journal of Black Studies*, vol. 40, no. 5, 2010, pp. 785–811., doi:10.1177/0021934709351546.

Adichie, Chimamanda Ngozi . Half Of *A Yellow Sun*. Harper Perennial, 2007.

---. *Americanah*. 4th Estate, 2013.

---. *Purple Hibiscus*. Fourth Estate, 2017.

---. "The Danger of a Single Story." *TED*, July 2009, www.ted.com/talks/chimamanda_ngozi_adichie_the_danger_of_a_single_story?utm_campaign=tedspread.

---. *Dear Ijeawele, or, A Feminist Manifesto in Fifteen Suggestions*. 4th Estate, 2018.

Adichie, Chimamanda Ngozi, et al. *Americanah*. Literatura Random House, 2017.

Adichie, Chimamanda Ngozi. *We Should All Be Feminists*. Fourth Estate, 2014.

Adkins, Brent. *Deleuze and Guattari's A Thousand Plateaus: a Critical Introduction and Guide*. Edinburgh University Press, 2015.

Afrin, Natasha. *The Bones of Grace: Rewriting History*. 3 Aug. 2018, www.thedailystar.net/book-reviews/the-bones-grace-rewriting-history-1615573.

Aigner-Varoz, Erika. "Metaphors of a Mestiza

Consciousness: Anzaldúa's Borderlands/La Frontera." *MELUS*, vol. 25, no. 2, 2000, pp. 47–62., doi:https://doi.org/10.2307/468218.

Akbar, Arifa. Review of *The Good Muslim* by Tahmima Anam. *The Independent*, Independent Digital News and Media, 23 Oct. 2011, www.independent.co.uk/arts-entertainment/books/reviews/the-good-muslim-by-tahmima-anam-2286451.html

Akbar, Arifa. "Americanah, By Chimamanda Ngozi Adichie." *The Independent*, Independent Digital News and Media, 11 Apr. 2013, www.independent.co.uk/arts-entertainment/books/reviews/americanah-by-chimamanda-ngozi-adichie-8568626.html.

Akhter, Farzana. "Negotiating the Politics of Power: Tahmima Anam's The Good Muslim and Women's Role in War and Nation-Building." *Asiatic*, vol. 12, no. 1, June 2018, pp. 93–107.

Akingbe, Niyi, et al. "'Reconfiguring *Others*': Negotiating Identity in Chimamanda Ngozi Adichie's *Americanah*. *Rupkatha Journal on Interdisciplinary Studies in Humanities*, vol. IX, No. 4, 2017, pp. 37-55. doi: https://dx.doi.org/10.21659/rupkatha.v9n4.05.

Allardice, Lisa. "Chimamanda Ngozi Adichie: 'This Could Be the Beginning of a Revolution'." *The Guardian*, Guardian News and Media, 28 Apr. 2018, https://www.theguardian.com/books/2018/apr/28/chimamanda-ngozi-adichie-feminism-racism-sexism-gender-metoo

'Americanah' Author Explains 'Learning' To Be Black In The U.S. 27 June 2013, www.npr.org/2013/06/27/195598496/americanah-author-explains-learning-to-be-black-in-the-u-s.

Amin, Aasha Mehreen. "The Women in Our Liberation

War." *The Daily Star*, 20 Dec. 2016, www.thedailystar. net/supplements/victory-day-2016-special/the-women-our-liberation-war-1330396

Amonyeze, Chinenye. "Writing a New Reputation: Liminality and Bicultural Identity in Chimamanda Adichie'SAmericanah." *SAGE Open*, vol. 7, no. 2, 2017, p. 215824401771277., doi:10.1177/2158244017712773.

Amuta, Chidi. "The Nigerian Civil War and the Evolution of NigerianLiterature." Hal Wylie et al., eds. *Contemporary African Literature.* Washington: Three Continents P, 1981.

Anam,Tahmima. *A Golden Age.* Harper Collins, 2007.

---. *The Good Muslim.* Harper, 2012.

---. *The Bones of Grace.* Penguin Books, 2017.

---. *Rabindranath Tagore's Legacy Lies in the Freedom-Seeking Women of His.* 23 Oct. 2011, www.independent.co.uk/ arts-entertainment/books/features/rabindranath-tagores-legacy-lies-in-the-freedom-seeking-women-of-his-fiction-2279473.html.

Anam, Tahmima. *THE BONES OF GRACE.* 28 June 2016, www.kirkusreviews.com/book-reviews/tahmima-anam/the-bones-of-grace/?page=71.

Anderson, Benedict. *Imagined Communities: Reflections on the Origin and Spread of Nationalism.* Verso, 2006.

Androne, Mary Jane. "Adichie's *Americanah*: A Migrant Bildungsroman." *A Companion to Chimamanda Ngozi Adichie*, by Emenyonu Ernest, James Currey, an Imprint of Boydell & Brewer Ltd, 2020.

Ballard, Chris, et al. "The Ship as Symbol in the Prehistory of Scandinavia and Southeast Asia." *World Archaeology*, vol. 35, no. 3, 2004, pp. 385–403., doi:10.1080/0043824 042000185784.

Basu, Shrabani, and Tahmima Anam. "'I Looked at the

Past through Rose-Tinted Glasses'." *Telegraph India,* Telegraph India, 29 Aug. 2018, www.telegraphindia.com/7-days/i-looked-at-the-past-through-rose-tinted-glasses/cid/1535145.

Benjamin , Walter. *Illuminations.* SCHOCKEN BOOKS, 1969.

Besant, Walter, and Henry James. *The Art of Fiction.* Literary Licensing, LLC, 2014.

Bhabha, Homi K. *The Location of Culture.* Routledge Classics, 2004.

Biswas, Sanjib Kr, et al. "Relocating Women's Role in War: Rereading Tahmima Anam's *A Golden Age*". *The Criterion,* vol. 8, issue 1, February 2017, pp. 522-528.

Blackburn, Simon. "Preface to the Routledge Classics Edition". *WHY I AM NOT A CHRISTIAN and Other Essays on Religion and Related Subjects* by B. Russell . Routledge, 2017. pp.vi-xv.

Bolotnikova, Marina N. *A Postmodern Youth.* 16 June 2017, harvardmagazine.com/2017/07/a-postmodern-youth.

Bonilla-Silva, Eduardo. *Racism without Racists: Color-Blind Racism and the Persistence of Racial Inequality in America.* Rowman & Littlefield, 2018.

Borum, Michael. "Q & A With the Author." CHIMAMANDA NGOZI ADICHIE - HALF OF A YELLOW SUN, a Novel, www.halfofayellowsun.com/content.php?page=tsbtb&n=5&f=2.

Brah, Avtar. "Non-Binarized Identities of Similarity and Difference." *Identity, Ethnic Diversity and Community Cohesion* by Margaret Wetherell et al, SAGE Publications., pp. 136–145.

Brockes, Emma. "Confessions of an 'Americanah'." *Books – Gulf News,* Gulf News, 29 Oct. 2018, gulfnews.com/entertainment/books/confessions-of-an-

americanah-1.1320656.
Brownmiller, Susan. *Against Our Will: Men, Women and Rape*. Fawcett,1993.
Bryce, Jane. "Conflict and Contradiction in Women's Writing on the Nigerian Civil War." *African Languages and Cultures*, vol. 4, no. 1, 1991, pp. 29–42., doi:10.1080/09544169108717725.
---. "'Half and Half Children': Third-Generation Women Writers and the New Nigerian Novel." *Research in African Literatures*, vol. 39, no. 2, 2008, pp. 49–67., doi:10.2979/ral.2008.39.2.49.
Burton-Hill, Clemency. "Review: A Golden Age by Tahmima Anam." *The Guardian*, Guardian News and Media, 21 Apr. 2007, https://www.theguardian.com/books/2007/apr/22/fiction.features.
Butler, Judith. "Burning Acts–Injurious Speech." In *Performativity and Performance*, by Andrew Parker and Eve Kosofsky Sedgwick, Routledge, 1995.
CAPO-CHICHI, Laure Clémence ZANOU, and Fifamè BODJRENOU. "Women's Roles during Biafran War in Half of a Yellow Sun Adichie (200." *Revue Du CAMES Littérature, Langues Et Linguistique*, vol. 4, 2016, pp. 151–166.
Carter, Ronald, and John McRae. *The Routledge History of Literature in English: Britain and Ireland*. Routledge, an Imprint of the Taylor & Francis Group, 2016.
Chakraborty, Samhita. *Tahmima Anam Completes Her 'Bangladesh Trilogy' with The Bones Of Grace*. 24 Aug. 2018, www.telegraphindia.com/entertainment/tahmima-anam-completes-her-lsquo-bangladesh-trilogy-rsquo-with-the-bones-of-grace/cid/1408047.
Chaudhuri, Maria. *Beloved Strangers: a Memoir*. Bloomsbury Circus, 2014.

Chaudhuri, Supriya, and Sajni Mukherji. "Introduction ." *Literature and Gender: Essays for Jasodhara Bagchi*, Orient Longman, 2002.

Chhachhi, Amrita. Extract from "The State, Religious Fundamentalism and Women Trends in South Asia". *Women Against Fundamentalism*, vol. 1, Nov. 1990, p. 14.

Chaves, Alexandra. "'My New Book Is a Rom-Com': Tahmima Anam on Her next Novel 'The Startup Wife'." *The National*, The National, 27 Feb. 2020, www.thenational.ae/arts-culture/books/my-new-book-is-a-rom-com-tahmima-anam-on-her-next-novel-the-startup-wife-1.985189.

Chennells, Anthony. "Inculturated Catholicisms in Chimamanda Adichie'sPurple Hibiscus." *English Academy Review*, vol. 26, no. 1, 2009, pp. 15–26., doi:10.1080/10131750902768374.

Coetzee, Carli. "Afropolitanism as Critical Consciousness: Chimamanda Ngozi Adichie's and Teju Cole's Internet Presence." *Afropolitanism: Reboot* , Routledge, 2017.

Coker, Oluwole. "The Paradox of Vulnerability: The Child Voice in *Purple Hibiscus*." *A Companion to Chimamanda Ngozi Adichie*, by Emenyonu Ernest, James Currey, an Imprint of Boydell & Brewer Ltd, 2020.

Collier, Lorna. "Growth after Trauma." *Monitor on Psychology*, vol. 47, no. 10, Nov. 2016, p. 48.

Crenshaw, Kimberle. "Mapping the Margins: Intersectionality, Identity Politics, and Violence against Women of Color." Stanford Law Review, vol. 43, no. 6, 1991, pp. 1241-1299., doi:10.2307/1229039.

Cruz-Gutierrez, Christina. "'Hairitage Matters': 'Hair', 'Imitation' & *Americanah*." *A Companion to Chimamanda*

Ngozi Adichie, Boydell & Brewer, 2017, pp. 245–261.
Cummins, Angela. "Taslima Nasreen and the Fight against Fundamentalism" *Women Against Fundamentalism*, vol. 6, Feb. 1995, p. 53-57.
Cummins, Anthony. "*The Bones of Grace* by Tahmima Anam – Review." *The Guardian*, Guardian News and Media, 29 May 2016, www.theguardian.com/books/2016/may/29/tahmima-anam-bones-grace-novel-review-canongate-bangladesh.
Dale, Scott. "The Power Of The Quill: Epistolary Technique In Richardson's Pamela." *Revista Letras*, vol. 53, 2000, pp. 53–64., doi:10.5380/rel.v53i0.18862.
Daniels, Eve. "MPR: A Q&A with Chimamanda Adichie." *Minnesota Public Radio*, 21 Aug. 2003, news.minnesota.publicradio.org/features/2003/08/21_newsroom_adichie/.
Das, Chaity. *In the Land of Buried Tongues: Testimonies and Literary Narratives of the War of Liberation of Bangladesh*. Oxford University Press, 2017.
Das, Veena, and Stanley Cavell. Life and Words: Violence and the Descent into the Ordinary. Univ. of California Press, 2008.
Dasi, Eleanor Anneh. "The Intersection of Race, Beauty and Identity: The Migrant Experience in Chimamanda Ngozi Adichie's Americanah." *Studies in Linguistics and Literature*, vol. 3, no. 2, 2019, p. 140., doi:10.22158/sll.v3n2p140.
Delgadillo, Theresa. "Religion and Latina Literature: An Excerpt from Spiritual Mestizaje: Religion, Gender, Race, and Nation in Contemporary Chicana Narrative." *Diálogo*, vol. 16, no. 2, 2013, pp. 17–18., doi:10.1353/dlg.2013.0041.
Det Kgl. "Chimamanda Ngozi Adichie – "Americanah" -

International Authors' Stage." *YouTube*. YouTube, Bibliotek. Retrieved 15 September. 2018.

DiAngelo, Robin. *White Fragility: Why Its so Hard for White People to Talk about Racism*. Beacon Press, 2018.

DiAngelo, Robin. *What Does It Mean to Be White? Developing White Racial Literacy*. Peter Lang Publishing Inc. New York, 2016.

Donne, John. *Devotions upon Emergent Occasions*. Kessinger Publishing, 2004.

Du Bois, W. E. B. *The Souls of Black Folk*. OUP, 2007.

Elkin, Lauren. "A Tribute to Female Flâneurs: the Women Who Reclaimed Our City Streets." *The Guardian*, Guardian News and Media, 29 July 2016, www.theguardian.com/cities/2016/jul/29/female-flaneur-women-reclaim-streets.

Emenyonu, Ernest N. "Introduction ." *A Companion To Chimamanda Ngozi Adichie*, James Currey an Imprint of Boydell & Brewer Ltd., 2017, pp. 1–13.

Ernest Emenyonu. *A Companion to Chimamanda Ngozi Adichie*, James Currey, an Imprint of Boydell & Brewer Ltd, 2020.

Emerson, Ralph Waldo. "War." Mar. 1838, Boston , pp. 1–8.

Evans, Diana. "Americanah by Chimamanda Ngozi Adichie." *The Times*, The Times, 5 Apr. 2013, www.thetimes.co.uk/article/americanah-by-chimamanda-ngozi-adichie-3g07r5t5x3l.

Falola, Toyin, and Ogechukwu Ezekwem. *Writing the Nigeria-Biafra War*. James Currey, 2016.

Fand, Roxanne J. *The Dialogic Self: Reconstructing Subjectivity in Woolf, Lessing, and Atwood*. Susquehanna University Press, 1999.

Felluga, Dino Franco. *Critical Theory: the Key Concepts*. Routledge, 2015.

Finnerty, Amy. "An Interview with Tahmima Anam." *Wasafiri*, vol. 30, no. 4, 2015, pp. 43–46., doi:10.1080/02690055.2015.1068995.

Forster, E. M. (Edward Morgan). *Aspects of the Novel*. Rossetta Books, 2002.

Gaertner, Samuel L., et al. "Aversive Racism: Bias without Intention." *Handbook of Employment Discrimination Research: Rights and Realities*, by Laura Beth. Nielsen and Robert L. Nelson, Springer, 2011, pp. 377–393.

Guarracino, Serena. "Writing «so raw and true»: Blogging in Chimamanda Ngozi Adichie's *Americanah*" *Between*, vol. IV, no. 8, November 2014, pp.1–27.

Guarracino, Serena. "Tales of War for the 'Third Generation': Chimamanda Ngozi Adichie's Half of a Yellow Sun." *Le Simplegadi*, no. 15, 2016, pp. 55–64., doi:10.17456/simple-27.

Haque, Mahmudul, and Shabnam Nadiya. "Jibon Amar Bon." *Translation Review*, vol. 80, no. 1, 2010, pp. 134–135., doi:10.1080/07374836.2010.10524033.

Harrison, Faye V."Writing Against the Grain ." *Women Writing Culture*, by Ruth Behar and Deborah A. Gordon, University of California Press, Berkeley, CA, 1996.

Hartley, George. "'Matriz Sin Tumba': The Trash Goddess and the Healing Matrix of Gloria Anzaldúa's Reclaimed Womb." *MELUS: Multi-Ethnic Literature of the U.S.*, vol. 35, no. 3, 2010, pp. 41–61., doi:10.1353/mel.2010.0007.

Hawley, J. C., (2008), "Biafra as Heritage and Symbol: Adichie, Mbachu, and Iweala." *In Research in African Literatures*, Volume 39, Number 2, Summer 2008, pp. 15-26.

Hayman, Robert L. "In the Nature of Things: Myths of Race

and Racism." *The Smart Culture: Society, Intelligence, and Law*. New York Univ. Pres, 1998.

Heaney, Seamus. "Digging." *Death of a Naturalist*, Faber and Faber Ltd, 2016.

Hemingway, Ernest, and Carlos Baker. *Ernest Hemingway: Selected Letters, 1917-1961*. Scribner Classics, 2003.

Hernandez, Amanda D. "Developing a Mestiza Consciousness Theoretical Framework." *Sociological Spectrum*, vol. 40, no. 5, 2020, pp. 303–313., doi:10.108 0/02732173.2020.1790446.

Hewett, Heather. Review of *Finding Her Voice*, Review of *Purple Hibiscus by Chimamanda Ngozi Adichie The Women's Review of Books*, vol. 21, no. 10/11, July 2004, pp. 9–10.

Hodges, Hugh. "Writing Biafra: Adichie, Emecheta and the Dilemmas of Biafran War Fiction."*Postcolonial Text* 5:1 (2009).1-13.

Hong, Terry. "An Interview with Tahmima Anam." *Bookslut*, 2011, http://www.bookslut.com/features/2011_07_017958.php.

Hooks, Bell. *Writing beyond Race: Living Theory and Practice*. Routledge, 2013.

Hooks, Bell. *Feminist Theory: from Margin to Center*. Routledge, 2015.

Hossain, Tazrin. "*One is Not Born, But Rather Becomes, A Woman*": Becoming Woman in Tahmima Anam's Works. 2007. East West University, M.A. dissertation.

Hussein, Aamer. "*The Good Muslim* by Tahmima Anam – Review." *The Guardian*, Guardian News and Media, 29 May 2011, www.theguardian.com/books/2011/may/29/good-muslim-tahmima-anam-review.

Ikediugwu, Ogechukwu A. "FEMINIST INCLINATIONS IN CHIMAMANDA NGOZI ADICHIE'S HALF OF

A YELLOW SUN AND *PURPLE HIBISCUS.*" *New Academia*, Volume: II, no. Issue: IV, Oct. 2013, pp. 1–15.
Irigaray, Luce. *Luce Irigaray: Key Writings*. Continuum, 2004.
Islam, Khademul. *The Definitive 1971 Novel*. 9 Aug. 2008, www.newageislam.com/books-and-documents/ the-definitive-1971-novel/d/books-and-documents/ khademul-islam/the-definitive-1971-novel/d/476.
Iwuchukwu, Onyeka F. "Racism and Identity in Onwuemes Riot in Heaven." CLCWeb: Comparative Literature and Culture, vol. 15, no. 1, Jan. 2013, doi:10.7771/1481-4374.2177.
James, Paul. "The Social Imaginary in Theory and Practice." *Revisiting the Global Imaginary: Theories, Ideologies, Subjectivities: Essays in Honour of Manfred Steger*, by Chris Hudson et al., Palgrave Macmillan, 2019, pp. 33–47.
Kapoor, Mini. "Completing a Graceful Arc." *The Hindu*, The Hindu, 12 Sept. 2016, www.thehindu.com/books/ literary-review/mini-kapoor-reviews-the-bones-of-grace/article8629524.ece.
Kelley, Robin D.G. "A Poetics of Anticolonialism." *Monthly Review*, 13 Oct. 2015, monthlyreview.org/1999/11/01/ a-poetics-of-anticolonialism/.
Kimber, Charlie. "Interview: Chimamanda Ngozi Adichie." *Socialist Review*, 1 Jan. 1993, socialistreview.org. uk/310/interview-chimamanda-ngozi-adichie.
Kurg, Regina-Nino. "Edmund Husserl's Theory of Image Consciousness, Aesthetic Consciousness, and Art." *The University of Fribourg*, 2014.
Kuruvilla, Elizabeth. *Novel Writing Is a Political Act: Tahmima Anam*. 20 May 2016, www.livemint.com/Leisure/ pU62v3rM2KBrGLOLWgROvO/Novel-writing-is-a-

political-act-Tahmima-Anam.html.
Lal, Saumya. "Silence and the Ethics of Partial Empathy in Tahmima Anam's *The Good Muslim.*" *The Journal of Commonwealth Literature*, 2019, p. 002198941989065., doi:10.1177/0021989419890658.
Lauret-Taft, Sabine. "'You'Re Just a Housewife. What on Earth Could You Possibly Do?': The History of the Bangladesh War of Independence Told by Women in Tahmima Anam's A Golden Age." *Commonwealth Essays and Studies*, vol. 43, no. 1, 2020, doi:10.4000/ces.4107.
Lessing, Doris. *A Proper Marriage*. Flamingo, 2007.
Lewis, Jone Johnson. "Subjectivity in Women's History and Gender Studies." ThoughtCo, Aug. 26, 2020, thoughtco.com/subjectivity-in-womens-history-3530472.
Lieshout, Veerle H. van. "A Different Story of War: Women Writers Countering Stereotypes and Writing Agency into the Story of Conflict." *Utrecht University*, 2017.
Lissa, Christopher. "Tahmima Anam." *Sydney Morning Herald*, 4 June 2011, https://search.proquest.com/docview/869913346?accountid=175698.
Loomba, Ania, and Ritty A. Lukose. *South Asian Feminisms Contemporary Interventions*. Duke University Press, 2012.
"Lupita Nyong'o: Colourism Is the Daughter of Racism." *BBC News*, BBC, 8 Oct. 2019, www.bbc.com/news/entertainment-arts-49976837.
Neary, Lynn. *At Home, at War: Tahmima Anam's 'Golden Age'*. 11 Jan. 2008, www.npr.org/templates/story/story.php?storyId=18004188.
Majid, Amrah Abdul, and Dinnur Qayyimah Ahmad Jalaluddin. "The Conflicts between the Secular and

the Religious in Tahmima Anam's *The Good Muslim.*" *GEMA Online® Journal of Language Studies*, vol. 18, no. 4, 2018, pp. 26–41., doi:10.17576/gema-2018-1804-03.

McElhatton, Heather. "MPR: Themes and Threads in Chimamanda Adichie's 'Purple Hibiscus.'" *Minnesota Public Radio*, 21 Oct. 2003, news.minnesota.publicradio.org/features/2003/10/21_newsroom_purplehibiscus/.

McGuire, Matt. "When the War Is Over, Literature Can Help us Make Sense of It All". *The Conversation,* The Conversation, 30 Nov.2018, theconversation.com/when-the-war-is-over-literature-can-help-us-make-sense-of-it-all-32424.

Moore, John H. *Encyclopedia of Race and Racism.* Macmillan Reference USA, 2008.

Nabutanyi, Edgar Fred. "Ritualized Abuse in *Purple Hibiscus* ." *A Companion to Chimamanda Ngozi Adichie,* James Currey, 2017, pp. 73–85.

Nast, Condé. Review of *The Good Muslim* by Tahmima Anam. *The New Yorker*, The New Yorker, 19 June 2017, www.newyorker.com/magazine/2011/08/08/the-good-muslim.

Ndula, Janet. "Deconstructing Binary Oppositions of Gender in *Purple Hibiscus:* A Review of Religious/Traditional Superiority & Silence." *A Companion to Chimamanda Ngozi Adichie,* by Emenyonu Ernest, James Currey, an Imprint of Boydell & Brewer Ltd, 2020.

Njoku , Carol Ijeoma. "Contrasting Gender Roles in Male-Crafted Fiction with Half of a Yellow Sun." *A Companion to Chimamanda Ngozi Adichie,* by Emenyonu Ernest, James Currey, an Imprint of Boydell & Brewer Ltd, 2020.

Nwokocha, Sandra. "Subversive Responses to Oppression in Chimamanda Ngozi Adichie's Purple Hibiscus." *The Journal of Commonwealth Literature*, vol. 54, no. 3, 2017, pp. 367–383., doi:10.1177/0021989417720817.

Oniwe, Bernard Ayo. ProQuest LLC, 2018, pp. 69–106.

Oshindoro, Michael Eniola. "Solidarity Between Women in Chimamanda Adichie's *Purple Hibiscus*" *Africana Studies Student Research Conference*.

Owen, Wilfred. "Strange Meeting ." *Poems*, Penguin Classics, 2017, pp. 81–82.

Parashar, Swati. (2013). What wars and 'war bodies' know about international relations. Cambridge Review of International Affairs. 26. 10.1080/09557571.2013.837429.

Perry, Richard John. *"Race" and Racism the Development of Modern Racism in America*. Palgrave Macmillan, 2007.

Porter, Lavelle. "Dear Sister Outsider by Lavelle Porter." *Poetry Foundation*, Poetry Foundation, www.poetryfoundation.org/articles/89445/dear-sister-outsider.

Pyle, Christine. "Symbolism in *A Golden Age*: Rehana as Bangladesh". English 3080. Feb. 26, 2010. Web.25 Aug.2015.

Rackley, Lauren. "Gender Performance, Trauma, and Orality in Adichie's Half of a Yellow Sun and Purple Hibiscus." *The University of Mississippi*, 2015.

Raboteau, Emily. "Book Review: 'Americanah' by Chimamanda Ngozi Adichie." *The Washington Post*, WP Company, 10 June 2013, www.washingtonpost.com/entertainment/books/book-review-americanah-by-chimamanda-ngozi-adichie/2013/06/10/a9e5a522-d1de-11e2-9f1a-1a7cdee20287_story.html.

Raghavan, Srinath. *1971: A Global History of the Creation of*

Bangladesh. Harvard University Press, 2013.
Rahman, Farhat. "Female Sexuality and Islam". *Women Against Fundamentalism*, vol. 1, Nov. 1990, p. 10.
Rahman, Mahmud. *In Bangladesh, Writing Fiction about the Liberation War May Well Become Impossible*. 22 June 2016, scroll.in/article/810215/in-bangladesh-writing-fiction-about-the-liberation-war-may-well-become-impossible.
Ramaswamy, Chitra. *Chimamanda Ngozie Adichie on Writing about Race*. 27 Apr. 2013, www.scotsman.com/arts-and-culture/chimamanda-ngozie-adichie-writing-about-race-2478218.
Ranasinha, Ruvani. *Contemporary Diasporic South Asian Women's Fiction: Gender, Narration and Globalisation*. Palgrave Macmillan, 2016.
---. "War, Violence and Memory: Gendered National Imaginaries in Tahmima Anam, Sorayya Khan and Contemporary Sri Lankan Women Writers." *Contemporary Diasporic South Asian Womens Fiction: Gender, Narration and Globalisation*, Palgrave Macmillan, 2016
Reese, Hope. *Chimamanda Ngozi Adichie: I Became Black in America* ... 29 Aug. 2018, https://daily.jstor.org/chimamanda-ngozi-adichie-i-became-black-in-america/.
"Revolution And The Question of *The Good Muslim*." *NPR*, NPR, 31 July 2011, www.npr.org/transcripts/138829973.
Richardson, Samuel. "Preface." *Clarissa, Volume 1* (of 9). Project Gutenberg eBook, 2005.
Rifbjerg Synne. "Chimamanda Ngozi Adichie–*Americanah*". International Authors' Stage, Copenhagen, 19 May 2014.*YouTube*, Uploaded by Det Kongelige Bibliotek,

20 May 2014, www.youtube.com/watch?v=b8r-dP9NqX8.

Robinson, Andrew. "In Theory Bakhtin: Dialogism, Polyphony and Heteroglossia." *Ceasefire Magazine*, 11 Jan. 2012, ceasefiremagazine.co.uk/in-theory-bakhtin-1/.

Rosefeldt, Paul Nagim, "The Absent Father in Modern Drama." . *LSU Historical Dissertations and Theses*. 5592, 1993. https://digitalcommons.lsu.edu/gradschool_disstheses/5592

Roy, Amit. "Dealing with the Past Is Important." Eastern Eye, 3 June 2011, pp. 14–15, http://www.easterneye.eu/.

Roy, Nilanjana S. *Speaking Volumes: Tahmima Anam's The Good Muslim*. 2 June 2011, nilanjanaroy.com/2011/06/02/speaking-volumes-tahmima-anams-the-good-muslim/.

Rushdie, Salman. *Shame: a Novel*. Picador USA, 1983.

Russell, Bertrand. *WHY I AM NOT A CHRISTIAN and Other Essays on Religion and Related Subjects*. Routledge, 2017.

Saadawi, Nawal El. "Fundamentalism- A Universal Phenomenon". *Women Against Fundamentalism*, vol. 1, Nov. 1990, pp. 12-13.

Sackeyfio, Rose. A. "Double Consciousness & the Self in *Americanah*". *A Companion to Chimamanda Ngozi Adichie*, edited by Ernest N. Emenyonu. James Currey, 2017, pp.213-227.

Sackeyfio, Rose A. "Revisiting Double Consciousness & Relocating the Self in *Americanah*." *A Companion to Chimamanda Ngozi Adichie*, by Emenyonu Ernest, James Currey, an Imprint of Boydell & Brewer Ltd, 2020.

Sadique, Mahfuz. "Daughter of a Golden Age." *Slate*. February, 20 June 2010. http://www.newagebd.com/slate/2007/feb/03.html

Saikia, Yasmin. Women, War, and the Making of Bangladesh: Remembering 1971. Oxford University Press, 2011.

Salma, Umme. "Representations of Transculturation and Agency in Bangladeshi Diaspora Novels in English." *The University of Queensland*, 2020.

Sen, Mandira. Review of *A Golden Age* by Tahmima Anam. *Women's Review of Books*, January/February 2008, pp. 5-6.

Sen, Mandira. *The Pure and the Impure*, Review of *The Good Muslim* by Tahmima Anam. *Women's Review of Books*, vol. 29, no. 05, Sept. /October 2012, pp. 30–31.

Sethi, Anita. "Interview with Author Tahmima Anam." The National, The National, 15 June 2011, www.thenational.ae/arts-culture/books/interview-with-author-tahmima-anam-1.376840.

---. "The birth of a nation in grief and grace; *A Golden Age* by Tahmima Anam", *The Independent*, 16 Mar. 2007.

Shaikh, Farhana. "Tahmima Anam's Golden Age Starts Here?" *The Asian Writer*, 17 July 2008, http://theasianwriter.co.uk/2008/07/17/tahmima-anams-golden-age-starts-here/.

---.*On Meeting Tahmima Anam*. 17 Nov. 2009, theasianwriter.co.uk/2008/11/12/on-meeting-tahmima-anam/.

Shampoe, Kelsey Virginia. "Americanah: Ifemelu and Her Blog." *Https://Sites.psu.edu/Shampoercl/2014/09/04/Americanah-Ifemelu-and-Her-Blog/*, RCL, 4 Sept. 2014, sites.psu.edu/shampoercl/2014/09/04/americanah-ifemelu-and-her-blog/.

Shamsie, Kamila. "Review: A Golden Age by Tahmima Anam." *The Guardian*, Guardian News and Media, 17

Mar. 2007, https://www.theguardian.com/books/2007/mar/17/featuresreviews.guardianreview21.

Sheikh, Farooq Ahmad. "Subjectivity, Desire and Theory: Reading Lacan." *Cogent Arts & Humanities*, vol. 4, no. 1, 31 Mar. 2017, pp. 1–12., doi: https://doi.org/10.1080/23311983.2017.1299565.

Sholder, Hannah. "Yasmin Saikia, Women, War, and the Making of Bangladesh: Remembering 1971." Review of *Women, War, and the Making of Bangladesh: Remembering 1971*. *South Asia Multidisciplinary Academic Journal*, 15 May 2012, pp. 1–4, journals.openedition.org/samaj/3393.

Sjoberg, Laura. *Gendering Global Conflict: toward a Feminist Theory of War*. Columbia University Press, 2013.

Smith, Wendy. Review of *The Good Muslim* by Tahmima Anam. *The Washington Post*, WP Company, 12 Aug. 2011, www.washingtonpost.com/entertainment/books/book-review-the-good-muslim-by-tahmima-anam/2011/07/06/gIQA5Ph4BJ_story.html.

"Sociology of Race." *Sociology*, sociology.iresearchnet.com/sociology-of-race/.

Solutions, Tribune Content. "Forgotten History: The Role of Women in War Times." *Chicagotribune.com*, 1 Nov. 2017, www.chicagotribune.com/suburbs/advertising/primetime/ct-ss-pt-forgotten-history-the-role-of-women-in-war-times-20171101dto-story.html.

Spleth, Janice. "The Biafran War & the Evolution of Domestic Space in *Half of a Yellow Sun*." *A Companion to Chimamanda Ngozi Adichie*, by Emenyonu Ernest, James Currey, an Imprint of Boydell & Brewer Ltd, 2020.

Staff, NPR. "Revolution And The Question Of *The Good Muslim*." *NPR*, NPR, 31 July 2011, www.npr.

org/2011/07/31/138829973/revolution-and-the-question-of-the-good-muslim.

Stobie, Cheryl. "Dethroning The Infallible Father: Religion, Patriarchy and Politics In Chimamanda Ngozi Adichie's Purple Hibiscus." *Literature and Theology*, vol. 24, no. 04, 9 Nov. 2010, pp. 421–435.

Subramaniam, Tara, and Sherman Roberts. "Feminist Values Compatible With Religion, Author Adichie Argues." *The Hoya*, 18 Mar. 2017, thehoya.com/feminist-values-compatible-with-religion-author-adichie-argues/.

Sullivan, Shannon. *Good White People: the Problem with Middle-Class White Anti-Racism.* SUNY Press, 2014.

Sylvester, Christine. *War as Experience: Contributions from International Relations and Feminist Analysis.* Routledge, 2013.

Tagore, Rabindranath. *Nationalism.* Macmillan & Co, 1918.

Taylor, Jenny. "What Is the Tablighi Jamaat?." *The Guardian*, Guardian News and Media, 8 Sept. 2009, www.theguardian.com/commentisfree/belief/2009/sep/08/religion-islam-tablighi-jamaat.

Tedeschi, Richard G. *Growth After Trauma.* 16 June 2020, hbr.org/2020/07/growth-after-trauma.

Tedeschi, Richard G. "Richard G. Tedeschi, PhD." *Psychiatric Times*, 1 Apr. 2004, http://www.psychiatrictimes.com/authors/richard-g-tedeschi-phd-0

Temple, Emily. *Chimamanda Ngozi Adichie on How to Write and How to Read.* 9 Apr. 2019, lithub.com/chimamanda-ngozi-adichie-on-how-to-write-and-how-to-read/.

The New Yorker Festival: "Chimamanda Ngozi Adichie on Facing Racism in America." *The New Yorker Videos*, The New Yorker, 9 Oct. 2017, https://video.newyorker.com/watch/the-new-yorker-festival-chimamanda-ngozi-adichie.

The Editors of Encyclopaedia Britannica. "Littérature Engagée." *Encyclopædia Britannica*, Encyclopædia Britannica, Inc., 20 July 1998, https://www.britannica.com/art/litterature-engagee.

Torres, Hector A. "Mestiza Consciousness and Dialect(Ic)s: Gloria Anzaldúa's Borderlands/La Frontera: the New Mestiza." *UNM Digital Repository*, digitalrepository.unm.edu/engl_fsp/6/.

Tunca, Daria. *Conversations with Chimamanda Ngozi Adichie*. University Press of Mississippi, 2020

Uko, Iniobong I. "Reconstructing Motherhood: A Mutative Reality in *Purple Hibiscus*." *A Companion to Chimamanda Ngozi Adichie*, by Emenyonu Ernest, James Currey, an Imprint of Boydell & Brewer Ltd, 2020.

Vitolo, Daniela. "History, Border, and Identity: Dealing with Silenced Memories of 1971." *The Routledge Companion to Pakistani Anglophone Writing*, by Aroosa Kanwal and Saiyma Aslam, Routledge, 2019, pp. 35–45.

Vuletic, Snezana. "From Colonial Disruption to Diasporic Entanglements: Narratives of Igbo Identities in the Novels of Chinua Achebe, Chimamanda Ngozi Adichie and Chris Abani." *Stockholm University* , 2018.

Wagner, Vit. "Love, Death and the Romance of War; Author, to Talk Tonight, Puts a Family through Bangladesh's Bloody Fight in A Golden Age." *Toronto Star*, 29 Jan. 2008, search.proquest.com/docview/439363636/E3BB3A5B2A164618PQ/3?accountid=175698.

Walker, Alice. In Search of Our Mothers Gardens: Womanist Prose. Open Road Integrated Media, 2011.

Walker, Alice. "If the Present Looks Like the Past, What Does the Future Look like?" *In Search of Our Mothers' Gardens: Womanist Prose*, Open Road Integrated Media,

"War." *Merriam-Webster.com Dictionary*, Merriam-Webster, https://www.merriam-webster.com/dictionary/war. Accessed 21 Oct. 2020.2011, p. 257.

Warnke, Georgia. *After Identity Rethinking Race, Sex, and Gender*. Cambridge University Press, 2007.

Welland, Julia. "Joy and War: Reading Pleasure in Wartime Experiences." *CORE*, Cambridge University Press, 1 Jan.1970, core.ac.uk/display/157620196.

Wenske, Ruth S. "Adichie in Dialogue with Achebe: Balancing Dualities in *Half of a Yellow Sun*." *Research in African Literatures*, vol. 47, no. 3, 2016, pp. 70–87., doi:10.2979/reseafrilite.47.3.05.

Wibben, Annick T. R. *Feminist Security Studies: a Narrative Approach*. Routledge, 2011.

Wilden, Anthony. *Jacques Lacan: Speech and Language in Psychoanalysis*. Johns Hopkins UP, 1968.

Winter-Levy, Nikita Lalwani and Sam, et al. "A Daughter of Bangladeshi Revolutionaries Makes Sense of Life After War." *The New Yorker*, www.newyorker.com/books/page-turner/tahmima-anam-trilogy-of-life-after-war-in-bangladesh.

Wolfreys, Julian, et al. *Key Concepts in Literary Theory*. Edinburgh Univ. Press, 2011.

Yeats, William Butler, and Richard J. Finneran. *The Collected Poems of W.B. Yeats*. Palgrave Macmillan UK, 1989.

Yerima, Dina. "Regimentation or Hybridity? Western Beauty Practices by Black Women in Adichie's Americanah." *Journal of Black Studies*, vol. 48, no. 7, 2017, pp. 639–650., doi:10.1177/0021934717712711.

Yuval-Davis, Nira, and Gita Sahgal . "Refusing Holy Orders ." *Women Against Fundamentalism* , vol. 1, Nov. 1990, pp. 3–5.

Zanten, Susan Van. "A Conversation with Chimamanda

Ngozi Adichie." *Image Journal*, Issue 65 imagejournal.org/article/conversation-chimamanda-ngozi-adichie/.

Ziwira, Elliot. "Religion, Oppression in 'Purple Hibiscus'." *The Herald*, The Herald, 2 Nov. 2014, www.herald.co.zw/religion-oppression-in-purple-hibiscus/.

Zug, George R, and William E Duellman. *Amphibian*. 4 Feb. 2020, www.britannica.com/animal/amphibian.

Black Eagle Books

www.blackeaglebooks.org
info@blackeaglebooks.org

Black Eagle Books, an independent publisher, was founded as a nonprofit organization in April, 2019. It is our mission to connect and engage the Indian diaspora and the world at large with the best of works of world literature published on a collaborative platform, with special emphasis on foregrounding Contemporary Classics and New Writing.

www.ingramcontent.com/pod-product-compliance
Lightning Source LLC
Chambersburg PA
CBHW020522080526
44583CB00013B/699